Politics and Culture
in Contemporary Iran

Politics

Politics and Culture

in Contemporary

Iran

Challenging the Status Quo

edited by
Abbas Milani
Larry Diamond

LYNNE
RIENNER
PUBLISHERS

BOULDER
LONDON

Published in the United States of America in 2015 by
Lynne Rienner Publishers, Inc.
1800 30th Street, Boulder, Colorado 80301
www.rienner.com

and in the United Kingdom by
Lynne Rienner Publishers, Inc.
3 Henrietta Street, Covent Garden, London WC2E 8LU

Library of Congress Cataloging-in-Publication Data
A Cataloging-in-Publication record for this book
is available from the Library of Congress.

ISBN 978-1-62637-146-0 (hc : alk. paper)
ISBN 978-1-62637-147-7 (pb : alk. paper)

British Cataloguing in Publication Data
A Cataloguing in Publication record for this book
is available from the British Library.

Printed and bound in the United States of America

 The paper used in this publication meets the requirements
of the American National Standard for Permanence of
Paper for Printed Library Materials Z39.48-1992.

5 4 3 2 1

Contents

Preface

This book has been three years in the making. It began when we received a grant from the Smith Richardson Foundation to invite scholars and activists to visit the Stanford campus and present what eventually became the core of the book. Later, in May 2012, we convened a workshop, this time with the help of a small grant from the Flora Family Fund and matching funds from members of the Iranian diaspora. During that workshop, our contributors exchanged views and ideas about each other's draft chapters. (The only contributor who could not participate was Simin Behbahani, whose passport had been confiscated by the Iranian regime.) Subsequently, a process of further review and revision resulted in the pages that you have before you.

We are grateful for the financial support of the Smith Richardson Foundation, the Flora Family Fund, and the Hoover Institution. Together, they made possible the recruitment of authors, the presentation of draft chapters, and the research, editing, and production of our manuscript.

We are grateful as well to a number of individuals who made completion of the book possible. Our special gratitude goes to Shervin Emami, who helped to prepare the manuscript for the publisher and who also translated (with Philip Grant) Mohsen Namjoo's chapter from Persian to English. We are also grateful to Skye Picker for helping us to answer some of the publisher's queries. Pasang Sherpa and Alice Carter helped to manage the many logistical details of our contributors' visits to our campus and of the workshops, and Shannon Schweitzer helped us with final preparations. We also express our sincere gratitude to Lynne Rienner for her excellent suggestions on the structuring and title of the book.

We thank our contributors for their patience and responsiveness, and especially our Iranian contributors, who have taken significant risks and made substantial personal sacrifices in order to maintain their intellectual and artistic integrity and their commitment to the values of democracy and freedom of expression.

We dedicate this book to the Iranian people, who have suffered so much and persisted so tenaciously in their aspirations for freedom. The publication of the book is only the beginning of a dialogue that we believe is indispensable if the world is to understand the vibrant society that thrives beneath the dour appearance of the current Islamic theocracy.

—Abbas Milani and Larry Diamond

Politics and Culture
in Contemporary Iran

Introduction

Abbas Milani and Larry Diamond

In his annual State of the Nation message, delivered the day after the Persian New Year (Nowrooz) in 2014, Supreme Leader Ayatollah Ali Hosseini Khamenei lamented at some length over what he said was the country's cultural malaise. A few weeks later, he told a meeting of the eighty-six-man Assembly of Experts (also known as the Council of Experts)—constitutionally responsible for choosing and overseeing the work of the supreme leader—that what keeps him awake at night is the culture war and the fact that the country is drifting away from what he considers the safe and sanguine ethos of Islamic values. Since then, hardly a week has gone by when some high-ranking official, close to Khamenei's coterie of power, has not voiced anxiety about the country's cultural drift.

A hint of the sources of his anxiety could be seen in the 2014 annual Fajr Festival—a film festival organized each year in Tehran around the time of the Islamic Revolution's victory in 1979. Iranian cinema has been much acclaimed internationally, but domestically eight years of the Mahmoud Ahmadinejad presidency produced stagnation and a proliferation of "Islamic" movies. These were invariably a poor imitation of old Hollywood, Bollywood, or even crassly commercial movies of prerevolutionary Iran, laundered with a superficial dose of piety and repackaging the cardboard heroes of previous blockbusters as martyrs of Islam or of the eight-year war with Iraq (1980–1988). In 2014 something unusual and telling happened at the festival. Every movie that had a whiff of "official" or "Islamic" ideology was booed and interrupted with incessant clapping. Of course, clapping itself is a taboo according to the official ideology; singing the praise of Allah and his Prophet or the supreme leader is Islamic, while clapping is dismissed and derided as a relic of Western influence.

Iran today is undergoing a profound, even historic sociocultural transition. Much of the media, however, and many scholars have ignored this transition to focus instead on either the nuclear issue or the political and economic aspects of the country's turmoil. Sometimes, the issue of sanctions and the falling value of the Iranian currency and other times Ahmadinejad and his denial of the Holocaust have been the focus of attention. Occasionally, the increasing role of the Islamic Revolutionary Guard Corps (IRGC) in every facet of Iranian society and its growing economic dominance has caught the attention of Western media and scholars. For a while, the functions and rising power of the IRGC's elite unit—the Qods Brigade—and its commander, General Qassem Suleimani, took center stage. At times, commentators have contemplated the relative power of Ayatollah Khamenei and the IRGC. Iran's command economy and the endemic corruption in a system partially dominated by *bonyads* (foundations) and directly controlled by Ayatollah Khamenei himself have not failed to attract some attention. Ayatollah Khamenei's possible sickness, his penchant for anti-Americanism, and the already raging battle to shape the process of choosing his successor have been a favorite topic of commentators and journalists. During Ahmadinejad's last two years as president, his cantankerous relations with Khamenei, as well as Khamenei's increasingly tense relations with his friend of fifty years, Ali Akbar Hashemi Rafsanjani, have been hard to ignore. Other analyses have focused on the rift between the heads of Iran's three ostensibly independent branches of government. Of course, there has also been much attention devoted to the crisis over Iran's nuclear programs and the prospects for a broader rapprochement between Iran and the United States. But other elements of Iran's dynamic society have received less than adequate attention. In particular, the ongoing struggle for freedom and its often subtle but persistent efforts to defy the regime's procrustean prescriptions, not just on politics but on every facet of daily life and culture, has received less attention than it deserves.

When the tumults of Iran have appeared in the form of a mass-mobilized movement for democracy and against electoral rigging—as they did in June 2009, when by some estimates 3 million people came out in the capital city of Tehran alone to peacefully protest against what they thought was a rigged election—the world certainly paid attention. But the media coverage was short-lived. The role of social media, even Twitter, was the subject of some attention. Iran was declared, maybe prematurely, to have attempted the first Twitter Revolution. The prominent role played by women in both the education system and in political protests also caught the eye of some journalists, photographers, and scholars. The shocking images of Neda Aghasoltan, a young woman killed by a bullet while she was peacefully protesting in the aftermath of the 2009 election, became iconic of the Green Movement: a peaceful social movement that came to support the presidential candidacy of Mir-Hossein Mousavi, and eventually to protest what people believed were rigged results.

Neda and the Green Movement, no less than the nuclear negotiations, have figured prominently in English-language reporting and analysis. However, when the struggle for democracy or individual freedoms has taken more subtle or subaltern forms, when acts of dissent and even defiance of regime authority have become more politically metaphorical and less literal, media attention and scholarly scrutiny have been scant. In the language of literature, as Jorge Luis Borges reminded us, censorship is the mother of metaphors; in the language of social action, too, oppression and censorship, brutality and limits on freedom, and finally clumsy attempts at cultural engineering—all hallmarks of the Islamic Republic's behavior in most of its thirty-four-year tenure—beget social metaphors, and more specifically, attempts to resist and dissent in symbolic domains. Unless we listen to these voices and deconstruct the political meaning of their acts, we will, in our view, fail to grasp the real complexities of Iran today—and thus we will fail to anticipate its future.

For far too long, the motto that if it can't be measured then it does not exist (or is of no significance) has blinded many scholars to the immeasurable shifts in Iranian cultural values and social practices. In the long run, these deep transformations of culture and social relations taking place in Iran today may prove to have a bigger impact on its democratic prospects than the overt cleavages and conflicts in the current political system.

A veritable renaissance and reformation are under way in virtually every aspect of the cultural, social, aesthetic, sexual, and even religious canvas of Iran. Many of these developments are being forged (often at great risk) from within Iran's borders, and in different discursive forms. Thus, only those intimately familiar with the nuances of these cultural, aesthetic, and social theoretical domains can document the dimensions of these changes. The Iranian diaspora—some 5 to 6 million exiles—is even more reflective of this change. Their increasing financial, managerial, scholarly, and political power has allowed them to become an important agent of transformation. Because of the possibilities of the information age and social media, the diaspora is now a virtual part of

Iranian civil society—the cauldron of transformation with which we are most concerned in this book. Unless we understand these changes, we cannot effectively appraise the prospects for a democratic transition in Iran. Nor can we realistically assess the fragility of the regime's cultural and social hegemony, despite its seemingly stable political domination. What makes the erosion of the regime's cultural hegemony even more perilous is that, according to some economists inside Iran (not a few sympathetic to or working with the regime), it is accompanied by a serious economic crisis.

Arguably the most alarming report on the economy coming from within the country was delivered by Mohsen Ranani in March 2014 at a think tank led by Iran's past reformist president Mohammad Khatami. Not just the ex-president himself, but many top policymakers were in attendance. Many websites inside and outside the country published the text of the talk.[1] Ranani said that the Iranian economy had entered a stage of what he calls "singularity"—in effect, a point of no return. Both the national economy and the morphology of the city of Tehran—the economic and political epicenter of the country, with about 20 percent of Iran's population—had, in his words, become "black holes." The regime has for years tried to reduce the population of Tehran with all manner of inducements; it has even passed laws to move the capital, but so far only about six thousand people (out of some 14 million in metropolitan Tehran) have been convinced to leave the city. In the same period, thousands more have arrived. In such moments of singularity, Ranani believes, economic black holes can only be changed by major outside forces. As structures move to singularity they become less controllable and less predictable. What would happen in Tehran, he asks, if there were a serious water shortage or an earthquake (Tehran is on a major fault line)? No one, according to Ranani, knows.

In a healthy economy, a 1 or 2 percent reduction in currency value usually brings an increase in exports. A decrease in interest rates begets more investment. Not in Iran. An almost eighty percent reduction in the value of the currency over the last year of the Ahmadinejad presidency did nothing to increase exports;[2] it simply depleted people's net worth. Corruption has, according to Ranani, become so systemic that any effort to correct it will fail or crash the system. In fact, Transparency International ranks Iran 144th out of 177 countries in its 2013 Corruption Perceptions Index, tied with such stellar exemplars of good governance as Nigeria, Cameroon, and the Central African Republic.[3]

It is no secret that the broad bulk of Iranian society is clearly frustrated and dissatisfied with the current situation. On June 14, 2013, they gave a first-round victory to presidential candidate Hassan Rouhani, identified (however moderately) with the language and agenda of reform. Rouhani's decisive victory was, in Ranani's view, what system theory would call an anomaly. As people experienced the impending crisis, they could have reacted in one of two ways: revolted in anger or bet on the possibility of a way out through Rouhani. They chose the latter alternative, but this period of tentative hope wouldn't last long. People have already entered the phase of watching. The next phase will be reaction: if promises are not fulfilled they will react, and how they will react is unpredictable.

Ranani's argument fits with the underlying assumption of our volume: it is as facile to posit a structurally stable Islamic regime in Iran as it is to overlook the regime's continuing ability to maneuver and act to contain, co-opt, or suppress potentially perilous forces of dissent. The regime has shown that it can avert catastrophic crisis, yet it has proved still unable to structurally reform itself and find a way out of the impasse. Tactical political elasticity is at best a sign of the Machiavellian guile of a fragile regime. The structural elasticity of a rational system responding to grievances and adapting to change are signs of strategic stability. As the chapters of this book show from a variety of perspectives, the Iranian people clearly demand strategic stability, which requires genuine reform to reestablish the bases of regime legitimacy. To date, however, the clerical conservatives have only shown a willingness to make tactical concessions.

As Ranani makes clear in his economic analysis, the tactical retreat by conservatives in accepting President Rouhani's election victory does not mean that the economic crisis has ended. As an example of the economic perils that continue to threaten stability, Ranani refers to the issue of the liquidity crisis: Iran's currency saw a 650 percent increase in liquidity during Ahmadinejad's tenure. With stagnant production and an average increase in commodity prices of 420 percent, Ranani concludes that inflation has grown 230 percent less than liquidity. The large sums of money represented by that overblown liquidity are still out there in society, not in productive circulation but in limbo. Those who control this capital are waiting to see what the markets and the regime will do. If they lose hope in political stability and economic development, they will search for a profitable solution—in buying foreign currency, for example, or investing in gold—once again decreasing the currency's value and fueling inflation.

Today Iran suffers from the most serious stagflation in its history. For forty consecutive years, with the possible exception of one, Iran has experienced double-digit inflation. It is, according to Ranani, the only country in the world with such a record. In other words, the Rouhani government finds itself virtually checkmated when it comes to its economic policies. It can't limit liquidity, it can't get investors interested in investing because of ambiguities and insecurities, and it is facing a massive fiscal deficit while lacking the political courage or capital to end debilitating cash subsidies. Its effort to convince rich and middle-class Iranians to voluntarily give up the cash subsidies each Iranian now receives—around thirty dollars per person per month—was an embarrassing failure. The Rouhani government's decision to continue to pay cash subsidies and try to balance the budget by increasing fuel prices will have unpredictable economic and political consequences. The fact that factions in the regime are already gunning for Rouhani will only add to the perils that he and ultimately the regime might face in solving the economic crisis.

Adding complexity to the difficulties of finding the right strategy to ameliorate the economic malaise is a threefold ambiguity. First, some in the regime (including many in the IRGC and maybe even Ayatollah Khamenei) have not yet decided whether Rouhani is a threat or an opportunity. Second, Rouhani himself has not made it clear where he stands. Is he willing to challenge the status quo, particularly the economic interests of the IRGC? His threat to release the names of all who have large outstanding debts to the virtually bankrupt Iranian banks has created considerable consternation, with some commanders of the IRGC using surprisingly threatening language. Moreover, though Rouhani is more used to dealing in back rooms, increasing threats from conservatives led him to threaten to invite people back onto the streets if the conservatives continue their war of attrition. One critical consequence of these ambiguities and tensions has been that markets have remained unsure. The dangerous economic slide of Ahmadinejad's final months as president has slowed down, but stability still eludes the regime.

The third source of continuous ambiguity and instability in the system, according to Ranani, is the mood of the people themselves. If they lose hope that Rouhani can solve the impasse, then they might become unpredictable. The liquidity crisis will then rear its head again and prices will skyrocket even more. Only political stability and wise policy can help the regime out of its perilous singularity phase, and neither appears to be on the horizon.

Indeed, the prognosis of economists like Ranani, elements of which are often repeated by members of the Rouhani government, only confirms our view of the regime's vulnerability. Because of the oppressive nature of the government; the general public's frustration with what they judge to be its utter corruption, hypocrisy, and incompetence; and the regime's often abrasive attempt to dominate and reshape virtually every element of people's daily lives—from sartorial and sexual demeanor to preferences for rituals and names of newborn babies—dissent has by necessity or design often found alternative sites of resistance. In these spaces, ordinary Iranians seek to replace regime values with alternative—often democratic, sometimes defiant, occasionally reckless—substitutes. In today's Iran, these domains of culture are critical sites of quotidian resistance and more often than not an indomitable force in rejecting theocratic soul-craft. Tehran and many other Iranian cities, big and small, today can be compared to Prague before the fall of communism, where a small jazz club was no less a vibrant site of resistance to ruling dogmas than the writings of lapsed Stalinists searching for a "socialism with a human face." In spite of the regime's bravura and brutality, we see Iranian society today as a seething volcano waiting for a democratic refashioning of politics, culture, aesthetics, and even the economy.

In our view, then, it is essential to look beneath the surface of high politics to grasp the deeper layers of action, innovation, struggle, and rebirth in culture, society, and politics. The purpose of this volume is to attempt to fill part of the lacuna in the analytical literature about Iran.

* * *

Ayatollahs Ruhollah Khomeini and Ali Khamenei, the two supreme leaders of the clerical regime since 1979, have often declared that the primary purpose of the Revolution was to move the Iranian people onto a pious and Islamic path. Their model fits squarely with what Sheldon Wolin, in his classic study of political philosophy, calls "soul-craft"—a remolding of a society's values and ways—rather than the "statecraft" that merely attempts to create the best workable political system.[4] Understanding this link, we can see how far the social, cultural, and moral reality in today's Iran is different from the stated goals of the regime. In fact, the regime has utterly failed to achieve what it set out as its primary strategic goal. But this failure of the regime's social engineering is not just the result of the anachronism of the model or incompetence in its execution. It is even more the product of a relentless process of resistance and defiance, a process predicated on society's clear aversion to violent change and its desire to negotiate the least costly path of transition out of the current singularity.

An old adage of politics is that when a society's ways and values—the norms, expectations, beliefs, and behavior of civil society—become incongruent with the structure of power in that society, change can't be far away. Cultural dissonance in society, no less than cognitive dissonance in individuals, can't endure indefinitely. Our goal here is to lay bare the nature of the incongruence that defines contemporary Iran; at the same time we hope to shed some light on the burgeoning new cultural, aesthetic, and political discourse. In charting the complexities of this landscape, we have not only selected some often ignored areas of scrutiny but also solicited chapters from contributors who are, in their scholarship, writing about their own lives. We have tried to follow as much as possible the notion of "thick description" offered by Clifford Geertz—namely, instead of speaking for a movement or a culture, allow members of that culture to speak for themselves.[5]

Forty years ago, scholarly works on Iran were no more than a handful. The politics of oil, Iran's strategic posture, its alliance with the West against Soviet Union, and occasionally its pre-Islamic era were the primary focus of the meager attention the country received from the academic community. Even among scholars of Islam, scant attention was paid to Twelver Shiism (Esna A'shari), the brand of Islam dominant in Iran for at least the last five centuries. Islam was upon the death of the Prophet split into two enduring factions. In fact, in "covering" Islam, as Clifford Geertz and Marshall Hodgson have argued, imagining one Islam, instead of many Islams, was the most common misperception of Western views of the Islamic world.[6]

The 1979 Revolution that toppled the shah not only shifted the region's tectonic political plates but led to a virtual new cottage industry of Iranian and Shiite studies. A plethora of memoirs and magazine articles combined facts and fiction to unravel the mysteries of the Revolution in Iran. These memoirs were often self-serving, and sometimes the inevitable consequence of the ravages of time on fallible memory. Nearly all of the Western journalists who wrote in the aftermath of the Revolution spoke no Persian and were at the mercy of their translators. Polish journalist Ryzyard Kapuscinski's much-acclaimed *Shah of Shahs*, considered something of a classic, and Michael Foucault's interjections on the Revolution in Iran are arguably the most egregious examples of this genre. Both writers spent a few weeks in Iran and then wrote books on not just the roots of the Revolution but also the character and life of the shah, the traits of the Iranian nation, and the "refreshing" paradigmatic changes brought about by Ayatollah Khomeini. Recent scholarly books on these ill-informed but much-hyped interventions have underscored the dangers of such overly ambitious projects.[7]

If popular books suffered from too many questionable generalizations, academic books and articles on Iran invariably focused, often deeply and rigorously, on a specific aspect of the Revolution. Like the academy itself, scholarly work often reflected Balkanized knowledge of Iran. Valuable as each and every one of these studies are to the scholarly study of aspects of Iranian society, they invariably shine light on a tree but forget the forest.

Societies and political and cultural movements are a complicated web of interlaced, dynamically and organically interdependent factors—from the economic and aesthetic to the sociological and sexual. They never partition themselves neatly into the strict disciplines academia has demarcated for itself—and by extension for the subject matters of their studies. To understand Iran in all of its interrelated complexity, we must thus transcend the disciplinary boundaries that beget partial, albeit informed, slices of an imagined compartmentalized reality. Music and poetry; the intricate web of the IRGC and its foot soldiers, the Basij; the contours of Ayatollah Khomeini's changing theory of power; the power and presence of social networks; and the role of women in all of these spheres are all in our view indispensible to understanding Iran and its quest for democracy and modernity. In attempting to address these many facets in one volume, we hope that we have taken a necessary step in this much-needed approach.

Another distinctive feature of our collection is that, instead of bringing together only the work of scholars, we have included authors who are not just acute observers of their subjects but who embody the very changes about which they write. Instead of having others write about the movement, we have allowed actors in the movement to offer their own thick description of their reality. The result is a remarkable group of activists, poets, scholars, and artists coming together under the common roof of a single book to offer a glimpse into the vibrancy of Iranian society, and the obstacles to cultural, political, and social efforts to create a democratic Iran.

* * *

Following this introductory chapter, our book begins with a discussion of some of the critical aspects of the political domain. The foundational political idea underpinning the existing political structure in Islamic

Iran is the notion of *velayat-e faqih*. Arash Naraghi, one of the most erudite observers of Iran's political scene and himself an influential voice in shaping a kind of revisionism in the ranks of religious forces in Iran, offers a brilliant answer to the question of identifying the theory of governance in Iran. Although Iran's religious revisionists are now widely divided among different strains and levels of rethinking, debunking, or revising old ideas and beliefs, they are nevertheless an important force, particularly inside Iran and today even within the Rouhani government. In a way the election of Rouhani as president—made at least partially possible by the alliance he formed with the reformists—has both shown the continued relevance of this force and strengthened their voice in Iran. Naraghi, then, is one of the most refreshing voices to emerge from among the onetime supporters of the regime, and an important agent in shaping the reformist theological and political discourse of Shiite Islam.

Moving on from the contested philosophical foundations of the regime's political theory of power, Hossein Bashiriyeh in Chapter 2 discusses the cleavages in current Iranian politics and demonstrates the fallacy of assuming that a political monolith dominates the undemocratic landscape. Bashiriyeh is often referred to by conservative forces inside Iran as one of the key political theorists for the reformist and democratic movement in the country. Through his analytical books and essays—most of them in Persian—and through his effort to translate into Persian some of the seminal texts in political development theory, he has played an important role in shaping today's democratic discourse inside Iran. For many years he taught at Tehran University's Faculty of Law and Political Science, where many of the future leaders of Iran's reform and democratic movements were his students. In the aftermath of mass demonstrations in 2009, as attacks against him and other independent scholars and professors increased, he felt he had no choice but to leave Iran, and he now lives in forced exile. His intimate knowledge of the dynamics of decisionmaking in Iran, and of the nature of its factions, richly informs his chapter, in which he argues that today's obvious political cleavages are the embryos of tomorrow's political parties and the gradual institutionalization of democracy in Iran.

The fate of the democratic movement and discourse after the suppression of the Green Movement is the subject of Mehrangiz Kar in Chapter 3. Kar, one of Iran's leading lawyers and human rights activists, was forced into exile after her participation in a human rights conference in Berlin. In her chapter she explores from an insider's perspective the dynamics of Iranian politics after the contested presidential elections of 2009 and argues that, despite the successful repression of the Green

Movement protests, the regime has suffered a substantial loss of legitimacy. Through an analysis of the emergence of the Principalists (Osulgarayan) hard-liners in reaction to the Reformist (Eslahgaran) efforts of Khatami's time, she also shows that the postelection protests provoked serious divisions among the supporters of the regime.

For the conservatives, one of the main tools for controlling, containing, and suppressing the democratic movement has been the judiciary, whose head is appointed by Khamenei. The Guardian Council—a twelve-man body of jurists whose job was initially to ensure that all laws passed in the country conform with sharia, but which has now taken up the role of vetting all candidates for elective offices in the country—has been another critical tool of containment and control. In Chapter 4, Fatemeh Haghighatjoo, a onetime member of the Reformist parliament in Iran and the first representative to resign in protest when the Guardian Council arbitrarily disqualified a large number of her elected peers from running in the next parliamentary election, describes in detail and with clarity the nature of the legal system—how power is at once diffused and centralized—and the "legal" methods that ruling circles used to not only maintain power but also afford their hegemony a veneer of legality.

On occasions when this legal structure has failed in its containment strategies, conservative forces have in the last two decades increasingly relied on the brutal force of their paramilitary units. The most powerful are militia-cum-gang organizations commonly known as the Basij. Membership in the Basij holds many advantages: jobs, easy admission to the university, no-bid contracts, immunity from legal harassments, and neighborhood power. Although the number of its members has been hard to estimate, it is one of the regime's most important tools for popular control, as there are Basij units in virtually every institution of the country. Saeid Golkar's analysis of the Basij in Chapter 5 is easily the most comprehensive English-language study of this group's genealogy, ideological morphology, and social functions. The fact that much of the research for his chapter was conducted while he lived and taught in Iran affords its insights particular clarity and cogency.

One of the Basij's new chief functions is to engage in cyberjihad. According to regime officials, thousands of Basij forces are hired to monitor, shape, hack into, and influence social networks inside and outside Iran. During the Ahmadinejad presidency, not only did the regime tighten the screws on every facet of cultural censorship—from cinema and theater to poetry and painting—but in the critical field of social networks, it placed the IRGC in financial, technological, and political control of all forms of communication by allowing the IRGC and its allies to "buy" in a no-bid contract the entire company that controlled the information infrastructure. Following the 2013 presidential election, although the new president has advocated for more freedom in social media, conservatives have been fighting to tighten controls—among other things, declaring Facebook a tool of sin. The regime has created an army of what it calls cyberjihadists to control and influence social networks. Yet the democratic spirit of revolt and resistance has been burgeoning in this arena, and in Chapter 6 John Kelly and Bruce Etling map out the political, ideological, and aesthetic persuasions of those active in Iran's blogosphere. While much has been conjectured about what actually transpires in this domain, Kelly and Etling use quantitative measures and actual blogs to give the reader a veritable sense of the political geography of this online world.

One of the favorite targets of cyberjihadists is a site called Balatarin. Arguably no one has been as successful as Mehdi Yahyanejad in introducing Iran's social network to a new form of dialogue through this remarkably successful site. As reflected in Chapter 7, Yahyanejad's experience and expertise in launching the site, and his subsequent research, afford him a rare vista to discuss the role of the social media in Iran's democratic movement.

One of the other most dynamic and defiant forms of resistance in Iran has been the evolution of a new underground culture of music—one that synthesizes classical Iranian and Western modes, modern jazz and blues, hip-hop and rap styles to create a mixture that is both local and universal and consistently critical of the status quo. (Feature films including *No One Knows About Persian Cats* have been produced about this thriving underground scene.) In Chapter 8, Mohsen Namjoo—who was the first young musician of this tradition to become an international star—recounts his personal odyssey from a small town to some of the most renowned music halls in the world. He also describes how he and others have been innovating, indeed revolutionizing, traditional Iranian music, using every genre and every instrument of world music that suits their artistic needs. The government has made every effort to ban music altogether, particularly among women, but today a new kind of hybrid music is one of the most thriving aspects of the aesthetic revolution in Iran. Regardless of objections from religious conservatives, music by men and women has become a fascinating focal point of resistance and change, and a powerful reflection of the self-assertive individualism that is blossoming in Iran.

In Chapter 9 Abbas Milani places in historical and social context the Iranian people's century-plus-long struggle for democracy. Tracing the rise of the coalition of forces that first brought the idea of democracy to Iran in the 1905–1907 period, Milani notes that much the same coalition—with the exception of some elements of the clerical class that defended democracy in 1905 but became its enemies in the aftermath of the 1979 Revolution—has continued to provide the backbone of Iran's democratic movement. Milani concludes with an analysis of where the larger democratic movement might be heading in the years to come.

As a kind of postscript to this unusual collection, we have chosen a prose poem by Simin Behbahani. Behbahani has come to embody the defiant spirit of Iranian women in their indomitable struggle for their rights over the more than three decades of the Islamic Republic. In the field of poetry, too, she is regarded as a vanguard in reviving, and infusing with a new lexicon and imagery, one of the more traditional forms of Persian poetry: Ghazal. In her contribution to this volume, she uses a combination of pithy sentences and poetry—often her own but sometimes those of others—to give a sense of artists' aborted dreams of a country where they could create free from the fetters of censorship, and also a sense of how the machinery of control was gradually put into place. In the years before her death, Behbahani's output diminished due to her failing eyesight, but her stature as a poet and as a defender of freedom of expression has grown. Her prose poem, translated here with the help of Farzaneh Milani, is an apt ending to the story of a 125-year-old struggle for democracy in Iran—a land as old as civilization itself, and yet today filled with the youthful spirit of a savvy new society, trying to join the march to its own unique but unmistakably democratic modernity.

Notes

1. For example, see Ranani, "Egtesad Iran asir adam Etminan" [Iranian Economy in the Throes of Insecurity].

2. Steven Plaut, "The Collapse of Iran's Rial," Gatestone Institute, February 21, 2013, www.gatestoneinstitute.org/3597/iran-rial-collpase.

3. "Corruption Perceptions Index 2013—Results," http://cpi.transparency.org/cpi2013/results/#myAnchor1.

4. Wolin, *Politics and Vision*.

5. *Thick description* is a key methodological concept in Geertz's theory of cultural analysis. For example, see his "Thick Description: Toward an Interpretive Theory of Culture."

6. For Hodgson's magisterial three-volume history of Islam, and the many varieties of Islams, see Hodgson, *The Venture of Islam*.

7. While a Polish journalist has taken Kapuscinski to task for the many liberties he took with facts in virtually everything he ever wrote, Foucault has also had his reckoning with facts in Afary and Anderson, *Foucault and the Iranian Revolution*.

1

Ayatollah Khomeini's Theory of Government

Arash Naraghi

One might arguably claim that the 1979 Islamic Revolution in Iran, at least from the perspective of its revolutionary leaders, was an antisecularism movement. Ayatollah Ruhollah Khomeini, the leader of the Revolution, was an outspoken opponent of the idea of secularism, considering it contrary to Islamic principles.[1] Years before the Revolution, he wrote,

> Colonial powers want us to believe that religion has nothing to do with politics, and Islamic scholars [theologians and jurists] should not get involved in political and social affairs. This is what atheists claim. But was religion separated from politics in the time of our most honorable Prophet? Was it the case that in the time of the Prophet, some people were religious scholars, and some were politicians and rulers? Was politics separated from religion in the time of the caliphs (whether or not they were entitled to that position)? Was politics separated from religion in the time of Imam Ali? [Obviously not].[2]

In the same context, he continued, "It is a part of colonial propaganda that religion is separated from politics, that Islamic clergymen should not get involved in any sort of social activities, and that Islamic jurists have no duty to supervise their own destiny and the destiny of the Islamic community. Unfortunately, some people have come to believe them. As a result, you see what misfortune has happened to us. This misfortune is what colonial powers have wished for us."[3] He constantly emphasized that Islamic jurists should not confine themselves to simple matters of sharia. They must take a more important role in the realm of social and political life. He said, "Foreigners intend to cause Muslims and Muslim intellectuals (who are the young generation) to deviate from Islam, and they viciously try to convince them that Islam has nothing to offer but some simple verdicts about menstruation and parturition, and they want them to believe that Islamic clergymen must do nothing but study menstruation and parturition."[4]

One of the main goals of the Islamic Revolution, then, was to stop this so-called anti-Islamic trend and reverse the process of secularization in Iran. The doctrine of "Guardianship of the Islamic Jurist," or *velayat-e faqih*, as presented by Khomeini, was intended to serve this purpose. The primary goal of Khomeini and other Islamist revolutionaries was to implement Islamic jurisprudence and give Islamic jurists the power to supervise all social and political activities in the Islamic community, to ensure that everything is in accordance with Islamic laws.

The Doctrine of Guardianship of the Islamic Jurist: Two Versions

In 1978, just a few months before the victory of Iran's Islamic Revolution, Khomeini, while in Paris, wrote, "In Islam we have absolute freedom";[5] "Islam contains democracy, and in Islam people are free, they are free in what they think, and they are free in what they do";[6] "in an Islamic Republic, everyone enjoys freedom of opinion and expression";[7] "we want to act in accordance with the [Universal] Declaration of Human Rights, we want to be free, we want our country to be independent, we want freedom";[8] "Islam . . . can guarantee all forms of democracy";[9] "every citizen has a right to directly and publicly question the leader of the Islamic society, and the leader is obligated to provide them with a convincing response; otherwise he has acted contrary to his Islamic duties, and he automatically loses his position as the leader";[10] and "Islamic government is a democratic state in a real sense." When a French reporter asked him what he meant by "republic," he replied, "By 'republic' I mean the very same type of government you have here in your country."[11]

However, many people at the time forgot (or decided to ignore) the fact that almost a decade earlier (1970), while in exile in Najaf, Khomeini in a series of lectures had defended a completely different view of the nature of Islamic government. These lectures were all published in a book titled *Islamic Government or Velayat-e Faqih* [Guardianship of the Islamic Jurist].[12] In fact, it was the doctrine of *velayat-e faqih*, and not democracy, that became the foundation of the Islamic Republic of Iran. The doctrine was designed to guarantee the Islamic nature of the government through its supervision by Islamic jurists.

The doctrine, at least in Khomeini's understanding of it, is not deeply rooted in the history of Shii jurisprudence. The first Shii jurist to introduce the notion of *velayat-e faqih* as an independent chapter in Shii jurisprudence, and to emphasize the political role of Islamic jurists, was Mullah Ahmad Naraghi in the eighteenth century.[13] His line of thought on *velayat-e faqih* was not picked up on by Shii jurists until about 200 years later. It was Khomeini who resumed Naraghi's line of thought, developed his idea in more detail, and finally put it into practice.

However, Khomeini's understanding of the doctrine underwent evolution and transformation over the course of time. He presented two different versions of the doctrine. Here, first I briefly examine these two versions, and then I discuss some major critical reactions to Khomeini's view in the context of Iran's postrevolutionary Islamic scholarship and intellectualism.

First Version: The Governance of Islamic Jurisprudence

As mentioned above, Khomeini presented the first version of the doctrine while he was in exile in Iraq, in the holy city of Najaf. He delivered regular lectures on the nature of Islamic government in which he articulated and defended his first version of *velayat-e faqih*.

The first version is the theory of government restricted by Islamic law. According to this version, Islamic jurisprudence is complete (i.e., it can provide adequate resolution to any private or public matter or problem). Sharia is a complete system of laws and rules that covers all aspects of human life, and governs humans' personal and social life from birth to death. According to this version, "Islamic government" simply means to govern the society in accordance with the verdicts of Islamic jurisprudence. Khomeini wrote,

> Islamic Shari'a contains all the laws and rules necessary to build the whole social system. This legal system covers all human beings' needs, from how to treat your neighbors, offspring, tribe, people, fellow citizens, private life, marital life, to the rules that govern peace and war, and international relationships; from criminal laws to the commercial laws and laws for industry and agriculture. It has laws for one's obligations before marital sex, or at the moment of conception. It has commands on how to have sex, and even what to eat before sex, or before conceiving a child. It explains the parental duties towards infants, and how the child must be raised, and how men and women ought to treat each other and their children. It has rules and laws for all these stages in order to raise a virtuous perfect human being, a human being who is the embodiment of law, and automatically and voluntarily follows the laws. It is obvious that Islam pays considerable attention to the government and the political and economical relations in the society in order to provide the best condition for training purified and virtuous individuals. The holy Quran and *Sunna* contain all commands and orders necessary for humans' perfection and happiness. . . . According

to *revayaat* [the sayings of the Imams], Imam swears that beyond any doubt, the Quran and *Sunna* contain all that people need.[14]

The first version of the doctrine is based on three major premises: (1) Islamic law or sharia is complete—that is, it contains everything human beings need to achieve eternal happiness and worldly progress; (2) to implement the law of sharia, it is necessary to have control over the government; and (3) the ruler must be an expert in Islamic laws—that is, the ruler has to be an Islamic jurist.

Khomeini wrote,

> Islamic government is governance in accordance with law; therefore, the ruler is required to be knowledgeable of the laws. According to *revayaat* not only the ruler but also all others, no matter what profession or social responsibility or status they might have, are all required to know the [Islamic] laws, but of course the ruler must be the most knowledgeable of all. . . . Justice and the knowledge of the law are essential conditions [for being a ruler]. Other things are not relevant and necessary.[15]

The main goal of the first version is clearly to reverse the process of secularization. It rejects the separation of religion and state, and intends to regulate the public sphere in accordance with the laws of sharia. According to this version, the government is obliged to follow sharia regardless of the consequences. When a conflict occurs between "public reason" and a law of sharia, the latter takes priority. In other words, the main purpose of the first version is to "remystify" the public sphere, and of course it requires that Islamic jurists be in power.

Second Version: The Governance of Islamic Jurist

The second version was presented years after Khomeini officially took charge of the Iranian government, becoming supreme leader of the Islamic Republic of Iran. After several years experiencing the real difficulties of actually ruling a country, Khomeini clearly recognized that the first version of the doctrine was naïve and needed to be fundamentally revised. He openly declared, "*Ijtihad* (i.e., the exercise of independent or original analysis on legal issues), as currently understood and practiced in the [traditional Islamic] seminaries, is not adequate."[16] He wrote, "Government determines how we should actually deal with polytheism (*shirk*), blasphemy (*kufr*), and internal and foreign difficulties. But the kind of knowledge and debates that is common among the students of seminaries is too theoretical [i.e., too abstract and detached from reality], and as a result, not only it is incapable of resolving those [real] issues, but also it itself causes some irresolvable problems that force us to (at least apparently) violate the constitution."[17] At this point, Khomeini's theory of government made a drastic turn. According to the first version, government was restricted by the laws of sharia,[18] but now he claimed that government is among the "first principles" (*ahkam-e avallieh*) of Islamic sharia, and its requirements takes priority over all other "secondary principles" (*ahkam-e sanavieh*) of sharia, including prayer, fasting, and *hajj*.[19] He now considered government as a subdivision of the Prophet Muhammad's absolute and unquestionable right to rule and guardianship.[20] When the necessity of having an (Islamic) government has been established, it is natural to assume that the requirements of such government must take absolute priority. The interests of the governmental system take priority, and if those interests require the government to make some decisions or take some actions that violate other principles of Islamic law, then the government is allowed to do so. Therefore, the second version is to some extent a theory of Islamic law restricted by the government.

In this context, Khomeini reached the conclusion that Islamic government needed a new institution to determine the real interests of the governmental system, and so he issued a permission that the government can act in accordance with those interests even if doing so appears to be contrary to the verdicts of Islamic sharia. This institution was called "the Council for the Determination of the Expediency of the Islamic System," or simply the "Expediency Council."[21] When he, as the supreme leader, asked the government to establish such an institution, Khomeini wrote,

> You gentlemen must realize that the interest of the [Islamic governmental] system is a very important matter, and any negligence in this regard may lead to a failure of our precious Islam. Today the Islamic world considers the Islamic Republic of Iran as a great exemplar, and looks up to us to find the resolution to their problems. The interest of the people and the [governmental] system is very important, and we should not resist it [i.e., we should take it seriously and comply with it]. If we ignore it, then it may eventually weaken the kind of Islam that cares for the poor, and as a result, the kind of "American Islam," which is the favorite of arrogant and cruel people, by using the support of billions of dollars and the assistance of their internal and foreign allies, will win the battle.[22]

The second version has two important characteristics: (1) It subordinates all legal and political powers and authorities to one individual person who must be an Islamic jurist (he is called the supreme leader or *vali-e faqih*), and (2) it subordinates the laws of sharia to the interests of the governmental system, which human reason can detect independently. These two characteristics clearly indicate that a troubling paradox lies at the heart of the second version.

The first characteristic is a common factor in the first and the second versions. That is, both versions give the Islamic jurist as such a privileged right to govern; therefore *velayat-e faqih,* in its two versions, is a violation of the principle of separation of religion and state, and also a violation of people's right to choose. It shifts the language of legitimacy back to "the divine."

However, the main difference between the first and the second versions lies in the second characteristic. According to the first version, the primary principles of sharia have absolute priority over all other considerations. But according to the second version, the principle of "the (governmental) system's interest" (*maslahat-e nezam*) is not only considered as a legitimate ground for making new laws and policies but also takes absolute priority when a conflict occurs between that principle and other traditionally well-known primary principles of sharia. As far as the process of secularization is concerned, this change seems a forward step within the context of Shii jurisprudence. In the final analysis, what determines social and political policies is not some mysterious religious verdict that must be obeyed no matter the consequences. Rationally calculable interests (*maslahat*) determine the content of laws and social and political policies. For example, in June 2000 the Islamic Consultative Assembly approved of an amendment to item 1130 of the Civil Law, according to which women acquired the right to divorce when in some specific situations the burden of marital life was unbearable for them (for example, when their husbands were seriously addicted or their husbands abandoned them for more than six months). The Guardian Council rejected the amendment as a violation of sharia. However, two years later, the Expediency Council, although it explicitly agreed with the Guardian Council that the amendment was a violation of sharia, approved it in the name of the governmental system's interest.

Reactions to the Doctrine of
Velayat-e Faqih in the Context of Islamic Discourse

As mentioned above, the Islamic Republic of Iran is today officially based on Khomeini's second version of the doctrine—that is, the one according to which all legal and political powers and authorities are subordinated to the supreme leader, and the laws of sharia are also subordinated to the interests of the governmental system. The second version has raised some critical reactions among Iranian Islamic scholars.

Most traditional Islamic jurists welcome the first characteristic of the second version—that is to say, they believe that since all activities in a Muslim community must be in accordance with the laws of sharia, the Islamic jurists' responsibility is to supervise all aspects of the society, including the government, to make sure that sharia has been effectively implemented. However, they criticize the second characteristic of the second version; they believe that sharia must be obeyed no matter what the consequences might be. The Islamic government has the duty of implementing sharia, regardless of how it might affect the interests of the governmental system.

On the other hand, most Iranian Islamic intellectuals welcome the second characteristic of the second version, believing that, at least in the public sphere, "public interests"[23] must take priority over what is assumed to be the law of sharia. However, these intellectuals are critical of the first characteristic and instead are mostly in favor of a democratic form of government in which the government is a representative of the citizens, and in which the separation of religion and state is respected.

Reactions in the context of Islamic discourse can be classified into three major groups: traditionalist, modernist, and pragmatist.

Islamic Traditionalist Reactions

Among Islamic traditionalist jurists, at least two major reactions to the doctrine can be identified.

First, some traditionalist scholars, such as Ayatollah Lutfollah Sāfi Golpāyegani, strongly opposed the second characteristic of the second version of the doctrine.[24] He was once a member of the Guardian Council, but he resigned as a result of disagreement with Khomeini. This group of Islamic scholars believed that the supreme leader, or *vali-e faqih,* must remain confined to the realm of sharia, and under no circumstances should he overlook or discredit the rules of sharia. To them, the main purpose of Islamic government is nothing but implementing the rules of sharia, and if the Islamic government itself violates sharia, they point out, what then would be the difference between Islamic and secular governments?

The second reaction among traditional Islamic scholars was more radical and mostly in favor of a kind of democratic government. One of the best representatives of this view is Ayatollah Mehdi Hāeri-Yazdi (1923–1999). He was one of the most prestigious traditional Islamic scholars to challenge the doctrine of the Guardianship of the Islamic Jurist as presented by Khomeini. Hāeri defended a version of a representative form of government in terms of Shii traditional jurisprudence. His goal was to explain the notion of political legitimacy on the basis of the traditionally well-known concept of "ownership" (*malekiyyat*), and to justify the notion of "election" on the basis of the traditionally well-known concept of "authorized representation" (*wekālat*).

According to Hāeri, human beings share the ownership of nature prior to the existence of any contract or legal system. If a group of people inhabit a place prior to any other groups, then every individual in that group would have a specific (natural) right to that place. In other words, that place would become the shared or common property of all those citizens or inhabitants. He distinguishes between two types of "ownership." First is personal ownership of private property, where property belongs exclusively to an individual. For instance, when a person buys a car, that car is a private possession of that individual, and that person has personal ownership of that car. Second is personal ownership of common property, such as occurs when a specific property belongs to a group of people—that is, they all share the ownership of that common property.[25] Hāeri criticizes the notion of "collective ownership," in which a property belongs to an abstract entity called the "group" or "society" above and beyond its members or citizens. From Hāeri's perspective, such an entity has no ontological status beyond and above its members.[26] Therefore, for him, ownership is always "personal"; that is, a thing can be owned only by people and not by an abstract entity such as a "group" or "society." The kind of ownership that is the foundation of government, for Hāeri, is the personal ownership of common property. Here the common property is what he calls "the city," or Madina. Madina is the "common property" shared by all citizens. Madina requires a system of security to protect itself against all sorts of internal and external threats. The function of government is to provide the city with such security and protection.[27]

The owners of the city have a natural right to appoint a person or a group of people as their own authorized representative to secure the well-being and peaceful coexistence of all citizens in the city. If the citizens cannot reach a consensus on a specific person or group as their representative, then the only fair solution is for the minority to surrender to the majority's vote.[28] Therefore, a government formed based on the notion of personal ownership of the common property by all the citizens is a form of representative government.

Hāeri, following the tradition of Islamic jurists, claims that the task of Islamic jurists as such is to identify the general rules and verdicts of sharia. However, the jurist as such has no privileged knowledge or expertise to identify the specific instances of those general rules, or to apply those rules or verdicts to specific cases. And since politics is a branch of practical wisdom, requiring constant identification of specific cases and wise application and instantiation of general rules, Islamic jurists as such have no privileged right to government.[29]

Islamic Modernist Reactions

The modernist reaction is a position that has been taken by Iranian Islamic intellectuals. Islamic intellectuals are Muslim scholars who present a new understanding of Islam that is friendlier to the requirements of modernity. As far as politics and social life are concerned, these intellectuals are in favor of democracy, and they explicitly question the legitimacy of any interpretation of authentic Islamic texts that is incompatible with the content of human rights as understood in the Universal Declaration of Human Rights. In postrevolutionary Iran, Abdulkarim Soroush is the best representative of Islamic intellectualism, and his ideas have had a great impact on Iranians' understanding of religion and politics. He presented the idea of democratic government in an Islamic society as an alternative to Khomeini's doctrine of *velayat-e faqih* or Guardianship of the Islamic Jurist.

Soroush addresses the question of Islamic government in a broader context of reform in Islamic thought. His broader project may be termed the "humanization of religion." The process of the humanization of Islam occurs in four steps (this is a logical order rather than chronological): (1) humanization of revelation or prophetic experience; (2) humanization of the holy text or the Quran; (3) humanization of religious knowledge; and (4) humanization of religious practice.

1. *Humanization of revelation or prophetic experience.* From Soroush's perspective, the source of the Quran is what he calls the "prophetic experience." Prophetic experience is a kind of "perceptual" relation to the divine. Through this relationship, the Prophet immersed himself in the divine, and as a result of his self-transformation, his words became a manifestation of the divine. In this context, the doctrine of humanization is an emphasis on the fact that the structure and the content of revelation reflect the Prophet's own self. Humanness, through the Prophet's self, spills over into the content and structure of the revelation or

prophetic experience. In a sense, the Prophet as a transformed human being is the measure of revelation; the revelation is measured in accordance with the Prophet's humanness.[30]

2. *Humanization of the Quran.* If the Quran is a product of a prophetic experience, then the Prophet's humanness is inevitably reflected in the text. But humanization at this level has another meaning as well. Soroush emphasizes the historicity of the text itself. The Quran as a text consists of two different realms: the realm of what he calls "essentials" and the realm of what he terms "accidentals." According to Soroush, the Quran has a core that goes beyond the limitations of any particular culture, space, or time. He calls this core the essential component of the text. Muslims traditionally have believed that the content of the Quran is essential in this sense—that is, everything in the Quran is a manifestation of an eternal truth whose validity goes beyond any particular time and place. As a result, the historicity of the text was traditionally overlooked. Soroush, however, invites believers to recognize the historical context and dimension of the text. The Quran as a text reveals the culture of the people at the time of revelation. This aspect of the text is what he calls its "accidental" dimension. The accidentals are reflections of the people's culture at the time of revelation, and they are employed to convey the core—the real message—more effectively. Successful communication has at least two important requirements: first, the sender of the message must use a system of codes or symbols that the receiver of the message knows as well. For example, since God intended to initially communicate with people who spoke Arabic, he had to choose the Arabic language as a medium for the communication. But, more importantly, the message should also be proportionate to the culture of the receivers. For example, in our communication with people who have never been exposed to modern technology, we cannot assume the culture of the digital age. So the Quran embodies some important elements of human culture—more significantly, the culture of the people at the time of revelation—as a context for a more effective communication. In this sense, the content and the structure of the text itself reflect the humanness of the people at the time of revelation.[31]

3. *Humanization of religious knowledge.* Soroush distinguishes between the text and our understanding of the text. On one hand, we have the text as the pillar of religion itself (i.e., the *source* of knowledge and inspiration), and on the other hand, there is our understanding of the text, which might be called "religious knowledge," on the condition that it is systematic and methodical. The moment that human beings take religion into the abode of their understanding, they unavoidably acquire

an understanding of religion that is in keeping with human culture and human dispositions. Scientific knowledge, philosophical knowledge, and religious knowledge are three human encounters with nonhuman affairs. Science is a human endeavor to understand nature, metaphysics is a human endeavor to understand being, and in the same way, religious knowledge is a human endeavor to understand religion. Humanization of religious knowledge in this context simply means that human qualities spill over into the knowledge that human beings cultivate.

The immediate implication of this distinction, according to Soroush, is as follows: While the text is divine, our understanding of it is not. Religious knowledge is entirely a human product. It is a mixture of truth and falsehood. It is imperfect, subject to constant change, and evolves through time. There is nothing sacred about human understanding of the sacred text.[32]

4. *Humanization of religious practice*. Soroush mainly focuses on two aspects of religious practice: law (jurisprudence) and politics. His goal here is also to humanize the legal system, or *fiqh*, and politics, or more specifically, government.

As far as Islamic jurisprudence, or *fiqh*, is concerned, humanization has at least four different senses: First, it means that the law should not impose "duties that are unbearably onerous," and if the implementation of a law imposes such duties, the law automatically loses its legitimacy and will not be applicable anymore. Second, following Al-Ghazzali, Soroush classifies *fiqh* as an inherently nonreligious knowledge. *Fiqh* (especially verdicts on social matters) is solely concerned with worldly affairs and only indirectly serves some religious purpose. Third, *fiqh*, like other types of religious knowledge, is a human product, and therefore the jurists do not have any privileged status in this context.[33] Finally, and more importantly, all the laws of sharia must be consistent with the requirements of human rights. Commitment to human rights is a commitment to the requirements of justice, and a humane religion should not endorse and enforce laws that violate human rights and dignity. Soroush firmly defends the idea that "religion is for humans, not humans for religion."[34]

In the context of his reformist approach to Islamic thought, Soroush claims that Islam as a religion does not require any specific political theory, and even though it is not necessarily compatible with all sorts of political order and government, it can be consistent with many different forms of political order and governmental systems, including democracy. He also argues that Islamic jurists as such have no privileged right to government whatsoever. Furthermore, the laws of sharia cannot be implemented in society unless at least two conditions are satisfied. First, sharia must have the approval of the majority of citizens (which must be established through some democratic process, such as winning the majority of public votes); second, those laws should not violate the content of human rights as understood in the Universal Declaration of Human Rights. He explicitly declares democracy as the best available form of government for all, including Muslim countries.[35]

Soroush is not the only modernist Muslim who argues for democracy and human rights. Following Soroush's general approach, Mohsen Kadivar, an Iranian Islamic scholar and political activist, has also tried to develop the same idea in terms of the language of Islamic jurisprudence. He has argued for the two following claims:

1. The doctrine of the Guardianship of the Islamic Jurist has no religious credibility, and no reliable religious source supports the doctrine. According to this view, a jurist has guardianship only in those cases in which something must be done from a social perspective, but no individual is available to take responsibility, such as the guardianship of the orphans. Most jurists have accepted this idea, but not all. According to Kadivar, the extension of *velayat-e faqih* into the public domain is not recognized by most jurists. For most Shii jurists, including Kadivar himself, there is no sufficient basis in Islamic law to support the claim.[36]

2. Democracy and the doctrine of the Guardianship of the Islamic Jurist (in all its versions) are not compatible, and democracy is certainly preferable to the idea of the Guardianship of the Islamic Jurists.[37]

However, it is noteworthy that Kadivar and Ayatollah Hāeri's approaches to the idea of democracy are fundamentally different. Hāeri tries to justify the idea of democracy on the basis of traditional concepts of Islamic jurisprudence. In other words, he argues for democracy from within the framework of (more or less) traditional Shii theology and jurisprudence. He seems to believe that democracy is not religiously justified unless one can provide some affirmative evidence for the idea from religious sources. However, Kadivar's justification for democracy comes from his independent rational evaluation of the idea. To him, deciding on the form of the government is a rational matter, requiring independent rational investigation. Therefore, for Kadivar, to justify democracy from a religious perspective, it is sufficient to show that the alternative theories, religiously speaking, have no privilege, and the idea of democracy does not violate any of the principles of the Islamic religion.

Islamic Pragmatist Reactions

Some Iranian political scholars and strategists believe that the doctrine of the Guardianship of the Islamic Jurist must be dealt with in the context of realpolitik. The legal-political system, for these political strategists, is a function of more fundamental variables. If those variables change, the legal-political system will change accordingly. The main goal is to confine the power of *vali-e faqih* (the supreme leader) as much as possible, and transform him into a symbolic figure in the government. However, the most effective way to confine the power of the supreme leader is to mobilize people and organize them into social movements. Only power can confine power.

Probably the best representative of this view is Iranian political scholar and strategist Saeed Hajjarian, who played an important role in Iran's reform movement that led to the presidency of Mohammad Khatami in May 1997.

Theoretically, Hajjarian advocates democracy and respects secularization as the separation of religion and state. However, he believes that in reality the balance of power within Iranian government is not in favor of democracy. Therefore, considering the reality of the political situation in Iran, the best strategy is to defend a version of constitutionalism.

To understand Hajjarian's view, it is worth noting that within the Iranian government Khomeini's second version of the doctrine has been interpreted in two significantly different ways.

The first interpretation is known as the "theory of elective, conditional *velayat-e faqih*." According to this interpretation, all the public officials, including the supreme leader, must be elected through general elections, and their political power must be restricted to the functions and duties explicitly listed in Iran's Constitution.[38]

The second interpretation is known as the "theory of appointive, absolute *velayat-e faqih*." According to this interpretation, the legitimacy of all decisions and policies in the public sphere depends on the approval and authorization of the supreme leader. More importantly, citizens have no say in the appointment or dismissal of the supreme leader, and no authority to oversee his verdicts and decisions as *vali-e faqih*. The opinion of the supreme leader constitutes the measure of proper decisions regarding public domain. The most important religious duty of the people toward the supreme leader is to accept his verdicts, obey his edicts, and help him succeed. People have no right to reject his authority. The legitimacy of his authority is not based on election. He is appointed by God, and his power and authority are absolute and unchecked. The domain of his authority extends far beyond the Constitution.[39]

Within the framework of the Iranian government, there has been an intense competition between these two interpretations. However, it appears that, after Khomeini, the theory of appointive, absolute *velayat-e faqih* has dominated.

Hajjarian's constitutionalism starts from the first interpretation, however.[40] Considering the reality of politics in Iran, in his view, it is more effective to advocate and promote the first interpretation against the second one. According to Iran's Constitution, the supreme leader is elected by the Assembly of Experts, which is also in charge of overseeing the supreme leader and has the power to dismiss and replace him at any time. However, in reality, the Assembly of Experts has never shown any sign of supervising the supreme leader. More importantly, it is hardly expected that they could ever exercise their legal right to oversee the supreme leader, because according to the law, even though the people elect the members of the Assembly, their suitability and credibility must be approved by the Guardian Council prior to their election. On the other hand, the members of the Guardian Council are appointed directly by the supreme leader. In other words, there seems to be a vicious circle involved in electing members of the Assembly of Experts: they are supposed to appoint, oversee, and dismiss a person who has the right to appoint or dismiss them. In principle, if for any reason the supreme leader is displeased by the performance of any member of the assembly, he has the legal power to dismiss that person and prevent him from being reelected. This possibility does not allow the Assembly of Experts to fulfill properly their duty of overseeing the supreme leader.

Hajjarian claims that it is an urgent political task to break this vicious circle in favor of the people's rights to have control over all the public officials, including the supreme leader. This is an effective first step in restricting the power of the supreme leader. However, this task cannot be accomplished unless political and social activists can mobilize social forces in favor of this agenda. By relying on social forces, the people might be able to convince or coerce the government to change its behavior in favor of people's rights. He summarizes his strategy as follows: "Pressure from the bottom, negotiation from the top!"[41]

As far as the second version of the doctrine is concerned, Hajjarian approves of its second characteristic; namely, he believes that politically speaking it is a positive move to subordinate the laws of sharia to certain rationally calculable considerations such as the requirements of *maslahat* (public interest). He explicitly claims that within the framework of Shii jurisprudence, the second characteristic of the doctrine is an important step toward forming a modern state. *Vali-e faqih* has the religious authority to change or modify sharia in accordance with public interest, and since his political and legal legitimacy (according to the first interpretation of the doctrine) depends on citizens' approval, he represents national sovereignty. In other words, *vali-e faqih* as a representative of national sovereignty has absolute authority to do whatever is necessary to fulfill the national or public interest. More precisely, if the national or public interest requires the government to go beyond Islamic laws, he as a representative of national sovereignty has the authority to legitimize that so-called transgression.[42]

Conclusion

Khomeini presented the doctrine of Guardianship of the Islamic Jurist as a reaction to the process of secularization in contemporary Iran. His major goal as an Islamic jurist was to subordinate the public sphere to sharia. However, as the head of the bureaucratic hierarchy of Iran's postrevolutionary government, he had to face the vicissitudes of social and political life, and as a result he had to change his political views drastically. Many traditional Shii jurists have considered Khomeini's latest political view (i.e., the second version of the doctrine) as shocking. Ironically, in the context of Shii jurisprudence, Khomeini's second version of *velayat-e faqih*, in spite of his own intention, can be considered as a bold step toward secularization, a step that has effectively facilitated the process of secularization in Iranian society after the Islamic Revolution.

However, the future of the doctrine does not seem promising, even to the eyes of its hard-line advocates. On the one hand, there are some indications that the doctrine has significantly lost its religious and political legitimacy even among religious circles. On the other hand, the Islamic Republic of Iran is rapidly approaching a crisis of "vicegerency" after Ayatollah Khamenei, the current supreme leader of Iran. It is hard to imagine that any member of the second generation of Iran's government can individually earn the political and religious consensus necessary to succeed Khamenei's position as the supreme leader. The office of supreme leadership, if it survives, might take the form of a Council of Supreme Leadership. It is likely that Khamenei (directly or indirectly) will appoint a council of jurists as his successor to take charge of the office. Such a council, if ever established, is likely to consist of two groups: a majority of younger hard-line jurists, who closely follow Khamenei's political and ideological agenda, and a minority of older and more established conservative jurists, who would bring credibility and legitimacy to the council. However, the prospect of politics in Iran is blurry and constantly changing. Only the future can decide the accuracy of this speculation.

Notes

1. Of course, on the eve of the Revolution, most Islamic leaders were not familiar with the concept of "secularism" per se. However, as we will see, their understanding of their mission can be best understood as an "antisecularist" movement.

2. Khomeini, *Velayat-e Faqih,* p. 23.

3. Ibid., p. 195.

4. Ibid., p. 11.

5. Khomeini, *Sahifeh-ye Noor,* vol. 4, p. 199.

6. Ibid., p. 234.

7. Ibid., vol. 3, p. 178.

8. Ibid., vol. 2, p. 242.

9. Ibid., p. 222.

10. Ibid., vol. 4, p. 190.

11. Ibid., vol. 3, p. 145.

12. This book has been translated into English by Hamid Algar. See Khomeini, *Islamic Government.*

13. Naraghi, *Awayd al-ayyaam,* pp. 185–206. The chapter of this book devoted to the discussion of *velayat-e faqih* was published separately in Iran.

14. Khomeini, *Velayat-e Faqih,* p. 21.

15. Ibid., p. 37.

16. Khomeini, *Sahifeh-ye Noor,* vol. 21, p. 47.

17. Ibid., vol. 21, p. 61.

18. Ibid., vol. 20, p. 170.

19. Ibid.

20. Ibid.

21. The Expediency Discernment Council was established on February 6, 1988, upon the orders of Ayatollah Khomeini, and some of its major functions are as follows: (1) making decisions in those cases where the ratification of the Islamic Consultative Assembly are not confirmed by the Guardian Council, and where the deputies insist on the implementation of the ratification; (2) consultation in those matters referred thereto by the leader; and (3) selection of an Islamic jurist member of the Council of Guardians of the Constitution as a member of the Leadership Council.

22. Khomeini, *Sahifeh-ye Noor,* vol. 21, p. 176.

23. Of course, there is an ambiguity here: What Ayatollah Khomeini called "the interest of the governmental system" is not the same as what in modern political language is called "public interests." However, as we will see, the fact

that in Khomeini's second version of the doctrine the law of sharia, in a sense, was subordinated to certain rationally calculable considerations has been welcomed by Islamic intellectuals in Iran.

24. For Ayatollah Safi's view, see, for example, the letters he (as a member of the Guardian Council) and Ayatollah Khomeini (as supreme leader), exchanged (Sāfi, "Majma-e Tashkhis-e Maslahat va Jaygah-e Qanooni An" [The Expediency Discernment Council and Its Legal Status]). For Ayatollah Khomeini's response, see Khomeini, *Sahifeh-ye Noor,* vol. 20, p. 160.

25. Medhi Hāeri-Yazdi, *Hekmat va Hokumat,* pp. 95, 99–108. The Iranian government refused to issue the permit required for this book to be published in Iran. The book was published in London in 1995. Here is a link to the e-version of this book in Farsi: http://andischeh.com/wpfa/wp-content/ketab/ejtemaie /nazarat-sabz-haeirii.pdf, accessed July 12, 2014.

26. Ibid., pp. 95, 126, 159, 161, 165.

27. Ibid., pp. 69–71. Hāeri explained his latest view on this subject to an Iranian audience in the following interviews: Hāeri, *Nameh-e Farhang*; Hāeri, *Hamshahri Newspaper*, p. 6; Hāeri, *Kherad-nameh Sadra.*

28. Hāeri, *Kherad-nameh Sadra*, pp. 107–119.

29. Ibid., pp. 80–81.

30. Soroush, *The Expansion of Prophetic Experience,* pp. 3–23. See also "The Word of Mohammad: An Interview with Abdul Karim Soroush," in *The Expansion of Prophetic Experience*, pp. 271–275.

31. Soroush, "Essentials and Accidentals in Religion," in *The Expansion of Prophetic Experience,* pp. 63–91.

32. Soroush, *Qabz va Bast-e Te'orik-e Shari'at.* See also Naraghi, "Lubb-e Lubab-e Qabz va Bast."

33. Soroush, "Maximalist Religion, Minimalist Religion," pp. 96–101. In this chapter he also briefly reports the content of a paper he presented at Harvard University, "Is Fiqh Possible?"

34. See, for example, Soroush, "The Idea of Democratic Religious Government," pp. 128–130.

35. Ibid. See also Naraghi, "Abdulkarim Soroush va Kamal-e Proje Roshanfekri-e Dini."

36. Kadivar, "Velayat-e Faqih and Democracy." See also Kadivar's excellent books on the issue of political theories in the history of Shii jurisprudence: *Nazari-ehai-e Dolat dar Fiqh-e Shi'i, Hokumat-e Velai'i,* and *Daghdagh-hai Hokumat-e Dini.*

37. Kadivar, "Velayat-e Faqih and Democracy."

38. According to Iran's Constitution (Article 110), the duties of the supreme leader are listed as follows:

(1) Following are the duties and powers of the leadership:
  1. Delineation of the general policies of the Islamic Republic of Iran after consultation with the Expediency Council.
  2. Supervision of the proper execution of the general policies of the system.
  3. Issuing decrees for national referenda.
  4. Assuming supreme command of the Armed Forces.

5. Declaration of war and peace and the mobilization of the Armed Forces.
6. Appointment, dismissal, and accepting the resignation of:
   a. the religious men on the Guardian Council;
   b. the supreme judicial authority of the country;
   c. the head of the radio and television network of the Islamic Republic of Iran;
   d. the chief of the joint staff;
   e. the chief commander of the Islamic Revolution Guards Corps; and
   f. the supreme commanders of the Armed Forces.
7. Resolving differences between the three wings of the Armed Forces and regulation of their relations.
8. Resolving problems, which cannot be solved by conventional methods, through the Expediency Council.
9. Signing the decree formalizing the election of the President of the Republic by the people. The suitability of candidates for the Presidency of the Republic, with respect to the qualifications specified in the Constitution, must be confirmed before elections take place by the Guardian Council, and, in the case of the first term of a president, by the leadership.
10. Dismissal of the President of the Republic, with due regard for the interests of the country, after the Supreme Court holds him guilty of the violation of his constitutional duties, or after a vote of the Islamic Consultative Assembly testifying to his incompetence on the basis of Article 89.
11. Pardoning or reducing the sentences of convicts, within the framework of Islamic criteria, on a recommendation from the Head of the Judiciary.
(2) The leader may delegate part of his duties and powers to another person.

The first interpretation has been supported by the views of two great Shii scholars, Ayatollah Nematollah Salehi Najaf-abadi and Ayatollah Hossein Ali Montazeri. For Ayatollah Salehi's view, see Salehi, *Velayat-e Faqhi Hokumat-e Salehan*; and for Ayatollah Montazeri, see Montazeri, *Dirasah fi Wilayat al-Faqih wa Fiqh al-dawlat al-Islamiah*.

39. Two important advocates of this view are Ayatollah Muhammad Taghi Mesbah-Yazdi and Ayatollah Abdollah Javadi-Amoli. For Mesbah-Yazdi's view, see Mesbah-Yazdi, *Porsesh-ha va Pasokh-ha*; for Javadi-Amoli's view, see Javadi-Amoli, *Velayat-e Faqih: Velayat-e Feqh va Edalat*.

40. For Hajjarian's view on the Doctrine of Guardianship of the Islamic Jurist, see Hajjarian, "Farayand-e Orfi shodan-e feqh-e Shi'i" [The Process of Secularization in Shi'ite Jurisprudence], reprinted in Hajjarian, *Az Shahed-e Qodsi ta Shahed-e Bazari*. See also Hajjarian, "Ja'meeh Shenasi-e Feqh."

41. For Hajjarian's view on the role of the Assembly of Experts, see, for example, Hajjarian, "Nameh be yek rafiq." This letter/article is addressed to Abbas Abdi, and it is a response to Abdi's critical remarks on some of his ideas.

42. See Hajjarian, "Farayand-e Orfi shodan-e feqh-e Shi'i," pp. 77–79.

2

Cleavages in Iranian Politics Since 1979

Hossein Bashiriyeh

The concept of cleavage has been used in the discipline of political sociology in order to explain political fragmentation and conflicts as well as the institutionalization of political forces, parties, and factions in democratic as well as nondemocratic polities. The existing literature on political cleavages in stable Western democracies and in emerging Eastern European democracies is extensive for the former and expanding as far as the latter is concerned,[1] but there has been little attempt to study Middle Eastern polities from this perspective.

In this chapter, I apply cleavage theory to the case of Iranian politics since 1979. Iran's political development has not thus far been studied in terms of cleavages and cleavage patterns. Of course, a number of informative analytical and historical works have been written on political conflicts and factionalism in Iran after the Revolution,[2] but a political-scientific analysis in terms of fundamental cleavages has been missing. Thus, my aim in this chapter is to employ such a perspective in order to try to discover the main political issues and cleavages, the cleavage structure, and the cleavage pattern lying behind the political conflicts among various political groupings and factions that have emerged since the Revolution of 1979. Such a perspective is useful in that it helps us find the basic and simple cleavage issues behind the plethora of recurring events and repeating episodes, as well as basically similar but apparently different factions and cliques. Thus, we may be able to give some intellectual order to a political situation that has seemed very chaotic to all observers, outside and inside the country.

Of course, the process of cleavage crystallization as a basis for political party formation and voter alignment has proved to be very slow and difficult, as one may expect in the cases of authoritarian and totalitarian political systems in a state of transition. The general ten-

33

dency of such political systems is to obliterate, eliminate, or suppress and deactivate, as much as they can, all sorts of cleavages, from ethnic to class, from sectarian to ideological, and from cultural to geographical, in order to create a seamless totalitarian society. However, the history of authoritarian and totalitarian regimes shows that although political cleavages may be temporarily deactivated and demobilized, they can never be obliterated. Hidden and silent power struggles going on beneath the apparently solid and monolithic power structure eventually lead to cracks, rifts, and splits within the regime or ruling class, and between them and other emerging forces.

An underlying guiding assumption here is that nondemocratic, authoritarian, and totalitarian regimes usually seek to prevent the emergence of political cleavages or to eliminate or inactivate existing ones, in an attempt to create a semblance of unity, totality, and cohesion; however, to the extent that even a feeble and fluctuating cleavage pattern emerges, these regimes enter into a process of instability and transition, which may lead to the crystallization of the cleavage pattern as the basis of party formation and voter alignment (i.e., electoral democratization). From this perspective, the regime that emerged after the Revolution in Iran, as a kind of electoral theocracy, has basically tended to inactivate all cleavages in order to establish a unified, monistic, and "monotheistic" disciplinary and controlled polity. Nonetheless, in the process of power struggles among various internal factions (intra-elite rivalry), fluctuating political cleavages have been emerging that so far have led to extreme factionalism, but they might be capable of eventually producing a multiparty system.

Theory of Political Cleavages

Political cleavages have been studied in terms of their types, causes, and consequences for political stability and change. There is obviously a great deal of disagreement about the meaning of the concept of "cleavage," as is the case with many other concepts in the social sciences. I shall briefly review some of the main theories and definitions of cleavages below, but, for the purposes of this chapter, by *cleavages* I mean relatively lasting or long-term and structural conflict lines that generate opposing political attitudes and preferences and divide people over a number of important issues (cleavage issues) for a rather long period of time, as opposed to shifting and temporary confrontations over secondary issues. In addition, a political cleavage is not just a mere division between groups of people with specific characteristics but contains an element of conflict leading to heated and serious or even violent confrontation and collision; it thus involves political awareness and organization. As a result, an inactive or dormant cleavage may not be regarded as a real political cleavage. Latent social cleavages (such as class, ethnic, and sectarian-religious cleavages) become political when they generate political conflict and confrontation. From this perspective, therefore, we should not deal with structural, social cleavage lines per se unless they become politicized, leading to an alignment of political attitudes and behavior. According to one definition, "First, a cleavage is rooted in a relatively persistent social division which gives rise to 'objectively' identifiable groups within a society—according to class, religion. . . . Secondly a cleavage produces some set of values common to members of the group. . . . Thirdly a cleavage is institutionalized in some form of organization."[3]

The seminal work on the theory of cleavages has been Seymour Martin Lipset and Stein Rokkan's introduction, entitled "Cleavage Structures, Party Systems, and Voter Alignment," to the volume they edited in 1967 on Western European party systems, *Party Systems and Voter Alignment*. There they discussed the development of stable cleavage patterns and the party systems that resulted from them in Western Europe. According to Lipset and Rokkan, two critical junctures in the history of Western Europe led to the development of four main social cleavages:

1. The Reformation and the various national revolutions led to the emergence of two salient cleavages: (a) center vs. periphery and (b) church vs. state.
2. The Industrial Revolution gave rise to: (a) urban vs. rural cleavage and (b) worker vs. owner cleavage.

By inference, I argue that in the case of nondemocratic regimes in transition, cleavage patterns do not easily become stabilized or crystallized in such a way as to produce a stable party system, but usually lead to shifting factional politics as a half-way point on the road to the rise of a stable party system. In such transitional polities, party or factional competition usually revolves around one or more conflict issues that generate the salient cleavage, and party positions issue from that cleavage. As a result, a polarization emerges between pressures for a transformation toward a more open government (democratization) and efforts to retain the authoritarian power structure. Hence, the relationship between political cleavages and the process of transition to democracy is theoretically important. The possible emergence of more conflict issues and hence more cleavages further complicates the pattern of party/factional competition and conflict.

Political theorists have discerned numerous and various types of cleavages. In their classic work, *The Analysis of Political Cleavages,* Douglas McRae and Michael Taylor classified cleavages into three types: ascriptive cleavages (racial, ethnic, etc.), opinion cleavages (religious, sectarian, ideological), and behavioral cleavages (orientations toward parties, etc.).[4]

We can divide cleavages into various types based on various criteria. In terms of political impact, as already noted, cleavages can be divided into active and inactive ones, depending on whether the issue that produces them is a heated issue. An inactive cleavage may become active (and vice versa) under changing circumstances. Thus, the social mobilization or demobilization of cleavage issues and cleavages may account for the dynamics of politics in any specific case. For example, sectarian cleavages had been very active for a long time in Western societies but became inactive as a result of the process of modernization. More recently, previously inactive sectarian and religious cleavages in Eastern Europe and the Middle East have been mobilized and activated in the wake of the ideological Cold War.

In terms of origins, social cleavages may be divided into structural and historical ones. Structural cleavages are a result of structural characteristics of societies, such as the social division of labor, age distribution, and gender division, which may lead to active class, generational, and gender cleavages. By contrast, historical cleavages are contingent and accidental in origin; the rise of specific racial, ethnic, sectarian, and religious cleavages is part of the historical trajectory of every society. For example, ethnic complexity in every nation may be a result of a number of factors, such as international invasion and migration, imperial legacy, and location on intercultural borders (e.g., Slav and German, German and French, Indian and Chinese cultural zones, etc.).[5] In the case of Iran, the diversity of ethnic and cultural groups is largely a legacy of its imperial past.

In terms of combination, cleavages may be more or less crosscutting or reinforcing. According to classic literature and research, crosscutting cleavages are conducive to the fragmentation and dispersion of the political-ideological space, leading to more stability, whereas reinforcing cleavages are more likely to produce polarization and confrontation.[6]

Cleavage patterns differ from one society to another, depending on the number of cleavages, their activity or inactivity, and their combination in a crosscutting or reinforcing fashion. Thus, we may get a single-cleavage pattern, a double-crosscutting cleavage pattern, a triple-crosscutting cleavage pattern, and so on.

My main focus here is on issue cleavages—that is, cleavages produced by the heated issues of ideological politics in ideological and authoritarian polities. A major point of distinction is to treat ideological states differently from nonideological states. By ideological states (whether communist, fascist, Islamist, etc.) I mean states in which the ruling elite seeks to transform society, culture, and human identity and behavior in terms of and according to the tenets of a totalitarian ideology. Since such states seek to demobilize or even obliterate all social, class, ethnic, and structural cleavages, it usually makes no sense to explain their politics (especially during periods of stability and order) in terms of such suppressed cleavages. Instead they inevitably produce *ideological* conflicts and issues that lead to division and cleavage; in fact, factionalism is the pulsating heart of ideological states. Therefore, I concentrate on cleavage issues and issue cleavages. In addition, when it comes to the study of a political system like the Islamic Republic with its endless factionalism, it is necessary to distinguish between primary or macro and secondary or micro cleavages. Primary cleavages in this case divide the polity into two main camps; but each camp is subdivided due to internal, more micro or secondary cleavages; the latter, in fact, provide the ground for shifting and temporary coalitions across the main cleavage.

A Brief Note About the Political History of Modern Iran in Terms of Salient Cleavages

Following the Constitutional Revolution of 1906, which turned the absolutist Qajar monarchy into a constitutional one, two largely reinforcing major political cleavages emerged and divided the political spectrum:

1. The cleavage between modernist constitutionalists (mainly intellectuals) vs. Islamist traditionalists (mainly religious leaders)
2. The cleavage between conservative-moderate factions vs. social-democratic reformist politicians

The 1906–1914 period witnessed the ascendancy of modernist constitutionalist intellectuals, who laid the legal and constitutional foundations of the modern Iranian state.

Under Reza Shah (1921–1941), partisan fragmentation came to an end as the new king, relying on the modern army and bureaucracy, maintained a strong personal rule.

During the period of 1941 to 1953, following the fall of Reza Shah, the inactive and dormant cleavages were reactivated, and consequently the polity was fragmented. The salient cleavages of this period included:

1. Secularism (of modern middle-class parties and intelligentsia) vs. Islamism/religious fundamentalism (of religious leaders and bazaar-based political organizations)
2. Intellectual socialist radicalism (mobilizing working-class trade unions) vs. liberal-nationalism (advocated by liberal intellectuals)

From 1953 to 1960, the relative militarization of politics and political repression led to the deactivation of political cleavages and the suppression of almost all political forces and parties.

The secularist-modernizing vs. religionist-traditionalist cleavage was sharply reactivated as a result of the shah's White Revolution and reaction to it on the part of a segment of the religious and mercantile forces, leading to the religious rebellion of 1963. After that, the political order created by the shah did not leave any room for cleavage activation. The two-party system created from above merely accommodated factions within the ruling elite and did not represent and reflect underlying political cleavages.

Cleavages After the Revolution

The main political developments and conflicts that unfolded after the Revolution can be studied in terms of political cleavages. Based on the theoretical discussion above, it is necessary to distinguish the types of cleavages and concentrate on the salient and active ones, which, given the type of the political system that emerged after the Revolution, have been more ideological in nature than structural; I also briefly discuss the main origins of these ideological cleavages. In terms of morphology, the stabilization or crystallization of cleavages is required for the rise of a multiparty system; therefore, I discuss the main reasons for the instability of the cleavage pattern that has emerged in the last two decades. Any degree of democratization requires a degree of stabilization or crystallization of the cleavages and the cleavage pattern.

The Revolution of 1979 was the result of a transient polarization of political forces (between the grand coalition of revolutionary or antiregime parties and organizations vs. the monarchy) rather than the fragmentation of those forces on the basis of cleavages; and of course, that was one of the reasons why the Revolution succeeded in toppling the old regime. Generally speaking, revolutions succeed as a result of the polarization of political forces but soon lead to their fragmentation on the basis of reactivated as well as emerging cleavages. In the early years of the Revolution, the reemergence or rise of several cleavages led to fragmentation and divisions in political attitudes and preferences. As noted, I am mostly concerned with "issue cleavages" rising out of the political-ideological development of the Islamic regime, rather than "trait" cleavages, including ethnic, sectarian, regional, as well as class cleavages, which were not activated in their own terms within the ruling groups. I try to describe and analyze the issue dimensions or cleavage issues that have led to the main political-ideological divisions in the Islamic Republic. From this point of view, issues are sources of political cleavages. In turn, political conflict and competition among parties and factions reflect issue-oriented cleavage dimensions. My main question is as follows: What are the long-lasting issues of Iranian politics since the Revolution that have led to divisions, rifts, and cleavages? Again, I deal here with the main "internal" cleavages rising from the primary ideological issues in the Islamic Republic. These cleavages have continued to exist and form the basis of party or factional politics in the country; so they could not be easily obliterated or eliminated. But other "external" issues and cleavages, emerging before the consolidation of power by the Islamic bloc, were eliminated as a result of the suppression or elimination of parties and groups emerging on their basis. The four main external cleavages before power consolidation included the following:

1. *Islamism vs. secularism.* The first cleavage to emerge within the revolutionary coalition was between the Islamic fundamentalist/theocratic tendency and the secularist/democratic tendency (mostly represented, respectively, by the Islamic Republican Party and the Provisional Revolutionary Government, [PRG]). With the consolidation of power in the hands of the Islamist parties, liberal secularists were ousted from the power bloc; for example, members of the liberal group the Freedom Movement, who had been elected to the First Majlis, were no longer able to enter the Second Majlis in 1983.

2. *Socialism vs. Islamism.* This cleavage emerged as a sociopolitical rift in the early years, but with the suppression of leftist parties and organizations, the cleavage was politically obliterated or at least deactivated.

3. *Cultural-ethnic cleavages*. Such cleavages were reactivated after the Revolution (mainly as a result of leftist mobilization) but were politically deactivated after local or ethnically oriented parties and organizations in Kurdistan, Azerbaijan, and Turkmenistan were suppressed by the army and the Revolutionary Guards.

4. A *peasant vs. landlord cleavage* was also mobilized in some rural areas but was subsequently more or less settled or deactivated as a result of certain agrarian policies.

No doubt, one can argue that some elements of these external cleavages have been articulated in the internal ideological cleavages within the Islamist groups in power, but this articulation has not taken place on their own terms as their significance and contours have been completely transformed. However, the specific lasting impact of one of those external cleavages (i.e., the first cleavage between Islamism and secular liberalism) on the power structure of the rising Islamic regime needs explanation. The revolutionary coalition had brought together Islamist and liberal groups within the PRG, but differences emerged between the two over the nature of the new constitution to be adopted. As both sides were more or less equally influential in drafting the new constitution, their division left its impact on the document, with its dual source of legitimacy—popular vote and elected institutions on the one hand (the Assembly of Clerical Experts, the Parliament, and the office of the president) and clerical-theocratic institutions (the Office of the Supreme Jurist, the Guardian Council, and later the Expediency Council) on the other. The resulting constitution contained a potential cleavage line between the popularly elected parliament and the "theocratic" Guardian Council (and also less clearly between the Office of the Supreme Jurist and the Office of the President). This same constitutional framework would provide the institutional setting for the unfolding of the internal cleavages among the Islamist parties in power.

The Burning Ideological Issues
After the Revolution and the Resulting Cleavages

In sum, three ideological issues have emerged since 1979. Cleavages and conflicts have resulted from those heated issues.

1. *The issue of economic regulation*. This was the first heated issue leading to political realignments and a central cleavage and conflict in the first decade of the Revolution (1980–1992). The economic issue

produced a theological one in the sense of whether to readjust or not readjust the Islamic law in view of current needs and necessities. Clerical traditionalists, opposed to economic regulation, were supporting a "traditional jurisprudence," whereas those in favor of regulation were advocating a "dynamic jurisprudence."

The cleavage that was to emerge within the Islamist/theocratic camp on the basis of this issue was between the populist radicalism of Ayatollah Khomeini and some of his associates and followers in Parliament and in the cabinet (Khomeinism) and clerical traditional-conservative Islamism (mostly represented by the Guardian Council and conservative clerics in the Majlis at the time). This jurisprudential-economic policy cleavage divided the Islamist ruling elites at the time.

2. *The issue of socioeconomic and cultural modernization after Khomeini's death.* This issue led to the second major cleavage, and polarized political actors during the postwar period from 1992 to 1997. As a result, the previously united conservative-traditionalists became increasingly divided over socioeconomic and cultural policies.

3. *The issue of political liberalization and opening up the political system and civil society.* This was the burning question that led to the polarization of political forces during the 1997–2005 period. This issue was raised in the context of growing democratization in the world and the discourse of human rights promoted by the European Union and international organizations. The cleavage rising out of this new issue was to lead to some shifts in the ideological positions of parties and factions; in particular, the old Khomeinists became proponents of democratic reform, whereas the traditional Islamists insisted on absolutist and paternalistic theocracy. Later, from 2005, a fundamentalist faction arising out of that group and enjoying their support added a discourse of social justice to absolutist theocracy. This faction, which was in power from 2005 until 2013, emerged around the two previous cleavage issues, opposing economic and political liberalization.

From a larger historical perspective, all these periodic cleavages can be reduced to one central internal cleavage dividing the two camps, but cleavage issues (economic, social, political) have been changing in the sense that the parties to the cleavage have been changing their discourse. In other words, the same central cleavage has had a number of articulations. The resulting political groupings since the Revolution are shown in Figure 2.1. Generally speaking, the origins of the ideological cleavages rising after the Revolution can be identified in a number of factors. Some of the more important ones are as follows:

1. The uncertain position of Ayatollah Khomeini as the leader of the Revolution in the early years
2. Lack of a central political party or organization, especially after the dissolution of the Islamic Republican Party
3. Lack of a clerical hierarchy in Shiism and the autonomy of individual clerics regarding religious doctrines
4. Diverse social bases of the supporters of the Islamic Revolution (the higher and lower clerics, the bazaar merchants, new middle classes)

Now I briefly describe the origin and impact of the issues and cleavages in each period.

The First Issue: Economic Regulation and the Cleavage Between Conservative Traditionalism and Populist Khomeinism, 1980–1992

The process of power consolidation by the revolutionary regime may be understood as a process of "cleavage breaking" or cleavage inactivation. It took a few years for the emerging political system to politically demobilize the cleavages by suppressing parties and organizations representing them. Thus, the fragmentation produced by the Revolution was more or less eliminated. However, the inevitable and relative toleration of an internal cleavage prevented the rise of a completely totalitarian political system in the technical sense; more accurately, the regime vacillated between authoritarian and totalitarian rule, to the extent that the intra-elite cleavage was tolerated or suppressed. Khomeini himself acknowledged and allowed the rise of the rift and difference of opinion, which was an important stance in determining the future course of conflict and factional politics. The first cleavage surfaced in the Islamic Republican Party (IRP), which was supposed to become a single ruling party, leading to the defection of the Association of Militant Clergy (AMC) faction from the powerful Society of the Militant Clergy of Tehran (SMCT).

As noted, in a simple sense the cleavage issue of this period was jurisprudential-legal, relating to how Islamic law and tradition should be interpreted and applied (tradition vs. innovation), but more fundamentality and materially it had socioeconomic causes and consequences. The main issue revolved around this question: Should the Islamic law and tradition, as understood by the majority of the clerics,

Figure 2.1   Political Groupings in Iran Since the Revolution

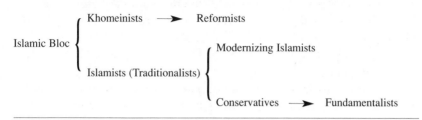

set the framework for policymaking in the country, or could policymakers go beyond those limits, as required by the exigencies of a revolutionary society?

On the one hand, traditionalist-conservative groupings and organizations, mostly representing the clergy and traditional merchant classes, advocated a sociopolitical system bound by Islamic laws and rules (especially regarding ownership of property), supported the private sector or bazaar against government interventionism, and were opposed to the expansion of the public sector, the nationalization of trade, and redistributive land reforms. On the other hand, more radical-populist groupings, representing some of the clerics and nonclerical supporters of Khomeini (the Khomeinists), advocated more egalitarian and interventionist policies in favor of the mass of the people supporting the Revolution. The jurisprudential translation of this economic policy cleavage issue was the cleavage between traditional and revisionist or innovationist jurisprudence. For the first interpretation, Islam and Islamic jurisprudence was the end; for the second interpretation, it was a means for regulating and solving the heated issues and problems of the present, especially at a time of revolution and change. The main political and religious organizations supporting the traditionalist-Islamist, noninterventionist position included the most powerful organizations of the clergy including the SMCT (the Society of the Militant Clergy of Tehran); the bazaar-based Islamic Coalition Groups (ICG); and the Society of Qum Seminary Teachers (SQST). Members of these powerful organizations occupied positions in all the important political institutions, from the Guardian Council to the Council of Clerical Experts, the Majlis, and the Islamic Republican Party.

The supporters of interventionism and economic regulation advocated a more open and innovative jurisprudence, in order to curtail the ideological power of their traditionalist clerical and mercantile opponents and to respond to the needs of the revolutionary circumstances. The Mujahedin of the Islamic Revolution (MIR) and later the AMC, which split off from the SMCT in 1988, and the IRP itself supported economic regulation. Although the IRP was a coalition of conservative and populist-statist personalities (from the MSTC and ICG), given the revolutionary circumstances and the so-called struggle against liberalism and imperialism, it initially adopted a more radical, egalitarian, and interventionist ideology, requiring a revisionist attitude toward Islamic jurisprudence. It supported the expansion of the public sector and state intervention in trade and commerce, to the detriment of the bazaar merchant class.

Some of the major issues that intensified the economic policy cleavage in this period and led to confrontation between the Parliament (mostly dominated by the interventionist groups) and the Guardian Council (dominated by the SQST and representing the traditionalist-conservative camp) included the Land Reform Bill of 1981, the Foreign Trade Nationalization Bill of 1982, and attempts at price regulation by the Ministry of Labor.[7]

The cleavage issue of 1980–1992 not only caused confrontation among main political institutions, particularly the Majlis and the Guardian Council, but also led to the disintegration of the MIR in 1986, the IRP in 1987, and the SMCT in 1988. All these splits took place with the permission of Khomeini, indicating an official support for factionalism, the end of the so-called unity, and the rise of a rudimentary two-party system rooted in the differences of the main political groupings. Thus, the cleavage ran through the whole polity, leading to polarization and the rise of two clear political camps: traditionalist-conservative Islamism on the one hand and radical-revisionist Khomeinism on the other.

Khomeini, as the supreme leader, initially sought to act as an arbiter of the unfolding disputes, but during the last two years of his life, he clearly took sides along the same main cleavage, criticizing the conservative clergy as "reactionaries" and supporting the populist groupings, by issuing a number of decrees. In particular, the famous decree of 1988 stipulating that the nature of government was a "primary rule in Islam," and thus enabling the government to go beyond Islamic law and rules when necessary, gave the government a free hand to intervene in all affairs and go beyond the so-called limits of Islamic tradition as conceived by the traditionalist clergy. This same decree eventually led to the establishment of a Council of Expediency to counterbalance the power of the Guardian Council. Khomeini's support for the antitraditionalist camp and his call to the people to vote in their favor led to the ascendancy of the populist groups in the Third Majlis.

After Khomeini's death and during the 1989–1992 period, the same cleavage issue and the same cleavage between populist-interventionism or Khomeinism and the traditional-conservative Islamist tendency continued to dominate Iranian politics, with the difference that whereas previously the Khomeinists had the upper hand, now with Khomeini out it was the traditional-conservative groups that gained ascendency in the Fourth Majlis. As a result, the Khomeinists were gradually ousted from power. Thus, the ruling groups in this period (1989–1992) reached a considerable degree of unity and unanimity, especially with regard to economic policy.

Looking at this period in more detail, a strong presidential system emerged under Ali Akbar Hashemi Rafsanjani, who adopted a policy of neoliberal economic reforms, privatization, and reconstruction, policies initially supported by the traditionalist-conservative parties. The new economic policy emphasized expertise, economic growth, the private sector, and an ethic of work, production, and consumption. Thus government restrictions imposed on the economy, such as price control and the control of foreign trade, were lifted, and instead foreign investment was encouraged and the economy was gradually opened to the world market. Private-sector investment was emphasized in order to boost domestic production and export, and on the whole, the public sector declined. All this was obviously in the interest of the bazaar-based traditionalist-conservative parties. Rafsanjani was the hero of the traditionalist-conservative groups in this period, implementing their ideal economic policies. The same old quarrels between the Khomeinists and the traditionalist-conservatives continued; the Third Majlis (1988–1992) dominated by the Khomeinists (Followers of the Line of the Imam confronting the minority faction, Followers of the Leader) and the Guardian Council engaged in their usual conflicts over economic policies. The policies of reconstruction were criticized by the main Khomeinist grouping, the AMC. However, the traditionalist-conservatives under the new president were now capable of defeating the advocates of interventionism. During the Fourth Majlis elections in 1992, the majority of Khomeinist Populist candidates (including thirty members of the Third Majlis) were vetted by the Guardian Council, based on the council's interpretation of Article 99 of the Constitution regarding its power in approving the qualifications of the candidates. Not only the Parliament, but also the Assembly of Clerical Experts came under the domination of the Guardian Council as a result of a controversial modification of the required qualifications for candidacy, granting vetting powers to the council. With their almost total elimination from the political arena, the Khomeinist forces were to find themselves in a totally new position, criticizing the monopolization of political power and authoritarianism, an issue that would become salient later. But before this, a second major issue led to a rift within the conservative camp during the 1992–1997 period.

The Second Issue: Socioeconomic and Cultural Modernization During the Reconstruction Period, 1992–1997

"Reconstruction" basically meant modernization not just in an economic but also in a cultural and social sense. The new direction included less emphasis on religious puritanism; giving priority to expertise over religious and revolutionary credentials; advocating a more tolerant, reasonable, and moderate Islam compatible with modern times; defending the importance of material and this-worldly welfare and well-being and the modern way of life; denouncing religious obscurantism, narrow-mindedness, and dogmatism; advocating a degree of autonomy for the arts and literature from religion; encouraging a new youth culture; and supporting a degree of improvement in the social conditions of women and a more positive attitude toward modern, liberal intellectuals.[8] The new turn produced a new division between the modernizing or modernist neoconservatives (the Party of Reconstruction, KP) and the traditionalist-conservatives, who were now advocating a strong absolutist theocracy and rallying around the supreme leader. In addition, as I show, the modernization program produced a new fundamentalist opposition, which emerged out of the reaction of traditionalist-conservatives to modernization.

The resulting cleavage between the "modernizers" (KP) and the antimodernization conservative-traditionalist parties more or less replaced the older cleavage at a time when the Khomeinists had been mostly driven from the political arena. The components of the modernization approach included a more open and dynamic or even revisionist interpretation of Islamic jurisprudence—required for the task of transformation and modernization, a more open and more tolerant cultural policy, economic privatization, and a more modern free-market capitalist economy. These components were combined with capitalist economic planning or government-guided capitalist economic growth (as specified in the First and Second Economic Plans), and displaying an industrial, financial, and international tendency, as well as ideological moderation in foreign policy. On the other hand, the traditionalist-conservative groups continued to advocate a traditional, mercantile bazaar capitalism free from planning and from government intervention, a strict interpretation of Islamic jurisprudence, and a culturally closed and controlled society based on absolutist theocracy. The cleavage can also be described as one between neoconservatism and traditional-conservatism. The heated issue leading to this cleavage, as we can see, was not only about economic policy and economic reform but included issues relating to social and cultural policies. The modernization tendency ("reconstruction") also included a significant component of political modernization in terms of support for party politics, pluralism, civil society, political participation, and basic human rights; the conservative-traditionalist camp continued to advocate the same Islamic-authoritarian positions as before, with increasing emphasis on absolutist and paternalist theocracy and political activism in its defense, which later produced a new fundamentalist tendency.

The reasons for the rise of the new cleavage within the conservative bloc are as follows. It began with increasing disputes between the (conservative-dominated) Fourth Majlis (1992–1996) and the Rafsanjani government over economic policies, purges of "puritan Islamists" from the government and their replacement with educated experts, hasty capitalist development, economic planning, high taxation, Western-oriented cultural policies, and charges of financial corruption. The regulatory and supervisory role of the government in planning and guiding the economy and the course of economic development, as well as high taxation in particular, were causing discontent among bazaar-based conservative groups. Obviously the free-market and import-oriented economic policies of the three preceding years had led to the rise of a chaotic mercantile economy, high inflation, and increasing accumulation of wealth in the hands of the private sector. As a result, the government found it increasingly necessary to regulate the economy, restrict imports, control prices, increase government revenues by raising taxes and tariffs, and pave the way for a more productive and industrially based economy by increasing domestic and foreign investment. All this obviously caused concern among the traditionalist-conservatives. An interventionist shift was thus taking place in economic policymaking with greater emphasis put on taxation and restriction of foreign trade. At the same time, a kind of division was emerging between traditional mercantile and modern financial-industrial capitalist tendencies. Thus the conservative-dominated Majlis opposed and modified the 1994 annual budget and cut public-sector allocations. The Second Five-Year Plan, which emphasized more government control and regulation, higher taxes and tariffs, and control of imports, caused further division and was up in the air for a year until the Majlis presented a revised version of it. The new version emphasized agriculture instead of industrial development, opposed tax holidays for state-owned companies, and criticized the decline in government subsidies; what eventually passed was, in effect, a plan for commercial development rather than industrial growth. Hence, the old war between the bazaar and government repeated itself under new circumstances.

Although the second cleavage and the dispute over an organized as opposed to a bazaar-based economy was to some extent a continuation of the older cleavage over economic regulation, it included other major issues relating to cultural and social policy. The modernizing neoconservative government and especially the Ministry of Culture under Mohammad Khatami were accused of paving the way for a Western cultural invasion by adopting a liberal policy with regard to arts, cinema, literature, and media. Eventually, in 1992, the liberal minister had to resign under pressure from the traditionalist factions and the Office of the Supreme Leader. Censorship and restrictions on cultural activities were resumed. Also, the head of the Radio-TV Organization was denounced for modernizing and westernizing TV programs and was forced to resign under pressure from the Majlis and the Office of the Supreme Leader, in spite of the president's wishes and policies. The new management was to embark on the Fight Cultural Invasion program.

In sum, the new cleavage issue was not simply over economic policy but included disputes over social, cultural, and foreign policies as well. The conservative groups in the Majlis and elsewhere were complaining not only about economic regulation, taxation, and modern banking, but also about an emphasis on expertise over religious/political allegiance, cultural liberalism, and an open-door foreign policy.

The interventionist shift antagonized the traditionalist-conservatives but proved attractive for the Khomeinists (largely ousted from power), who, modifying some of their previous socioeconomic and foreign policy positions and attitudes and accepting most of the neoconservative modernization policies, increasingly came to support the socioeconomic as well as cultural policies of the KP government. The second cleavage was thus further intensified as a result of an increasing alliance between the neoconservatives and the old Khomeinists from 1996. Both now supported some government supervision and regulation of the economy and more liberal cultural policies, and more importantly both were confronting the same foes. During the Fifth Majlis (1996–2000) elections, the two blocs coalesced and competed against the traditionalist-conservative parties and factions. The Coalition of the Imam's Line (the Khomeinists: AMC and MIR) and the neoconservative KP competed against the main traditional-Islamist parties: the SMCT, ICG, and emerging fundamentalist groups. The Guardian Council disqualified about 40 percent of the candidates, including thirty from the Khomeinist groups. Further intervention by the council, annulling election results in a number of districts, ensured supremacy for the traditionalist-Islamists in the new Majlis. (The majority traditionalist faction in the parliament was called the Society of Hizbullah; the minority, the Association of Hizbullah.)

The new alliance was in a way natural or even unavoidable, given the traditionalist parties' increasing domination of the political scene. The new allies had also moved toward a middle ground in terms of economic, social, and foreign policy perspectives. The alliance supported political pluralism and participation, government regulation of the bazaar, and a more limited or constitutional kind of theocracy, as opposed to the discourse of absolutist, paternalist theocracy then emerging among the conservatives. In a way political groupings were changing their positions at least superficially: the Khomeinists, who had supported absolutist (as opposed to traditionalist) theocracy under Khomeini (since he was sympathetic to them), were now opposed to absolute theocracy, because Khamenei, the new supreme leader, had favored the traditionalist-conservatives since his accession. On the other hand, the traditionalist-conservatives who had supported the law and tradition of Islam against political manipulation by the supreme leader under Khomeini were now advocating a notion of absolutist religious leadership even going beyond the constitution. Obviously the traditionalist-conservative groups now increasingly needed to rally around the supreme leader in opposition to the new alliance.

This alliance was to have a significant and lasting impact on the political cleavage pattern, paving the way for the third major period (1996–2005) in the ideological trajectory of the Islamic Republic, characterized by a cleavage between Islamic democratic reformism and conservative authoritarianism, or constitutional-republicanism and absolutist theocratic Islamism.

The Third Issue: Political Liberalization and the Cleavage Between Islamic Democratic Reformism and Conservative Theocratic Islamism, 1996–2005

During the 1996–2005 period, the main issue creating the salient cleavage and dividing political actors was the dispute over the priority of republicanism or Islamism in the Islamic republican political system. Although some actors on the two sides of the cleavage of the 1980–1992 period were apparently present, the cleavage itself was not a reproduction of the salient issue of the preceding period; in other words, the salient issue had changed from a merely economic one regarding economic policy to a decidedly political one over the type of regime. This was a completely new formulation; cleavage issues as well as some of the actors had changed, and new political forces had emerged and joined the dispute. An explosion of new political groupings and associations took place between 1997 and 2005. Some older groupings like the MIR and the AMC adopted new platforms; on the other hand, new political parties like the Participation Front (PF) were emerging. Cleavage issues as well as actors were changing. The new cleavage sharply divided the political spectrum during the 1997 presidential election, the 1999 parliamentary elections, and again in the 2001 presidential election.

As indicated above, the roots of the new cleavage were formed during the Fifth Majlis elections with the alliance of modernist neoconservatives and the old Khomeinists, who formed the Association of Hizbollah in Parliament against the majority traditionalist factions. As we have seen, during the postwar reconstruction period under Rafsanjani, initially the traditionalist-conservative parties had united and dominated the state and had expelled most of their rival Khomeinists from power. But as noted, from 1992 onward, a new cleavage issue over modernization led to division within the traditionalist-conservative camp itself, and the traditionalist-bazaar-based factions increasingly dominated the political scene and obtained a majority in the Fifth Majlis. As the next (1997) presidential election was approaching, the same parties were planning to capture the presidency as well. The Khomeinist-KP alliance first nominated the former premier Mir-Hossein Mousavi as their candidate for the presidency, but since he declined to accept, former minister of culture Khatami announced his candidacy in January 1997 and was supported by the alliance. On the other hand, the traditionalist-conservatives, despite a great deal of infighting, squabbling, and reservations, eventually nominated the Majlis speaker, Ali Akbar Nateq-Nuri. During his election campaign, Khatami advocated the same policies and programs of the reconstruction government, including an emphasis on the regulatory role of the state, primacy of expertise, economic development, and social freedom, but he also raised new issues such as the promotion of civil society, democracy, constitutionalism, political participation, and individual freedom, which went beyond the discourse of the previous decade and gave rise to a new cleavage: that is, between constitutional-republicanism and the absolutist-Islamic theocracy based on the cult of leadership that the traditionalist circles were producing. As mentioned earlier, the new issue was more political in nature and was concerned with the type of regime. If the reconstruction regime had tried to reconcile Islam with a version of modernity, the reformist government under Khatami tried to reconcile Islam with a version of democracy. The emphasis was now on popular consent and sovereignty, political pluralism, competition and participation, civil society, human rights, the rule of law and constitutionalism, republicanism, a limited version of theocracy as a legally bound office elected by the people (not appointed by God), and so on. On the other hand, the conservative Islamist camp, including the traditional-conservative groups and parties dominant in various state institutions, as well as the fundamentalist circles emerging in opposition to the policies of reconstruction and modernization (see below), defended the absolute rule of the jurist as appointed by God and discovered by the Clerical Experts, religious guardianship and supervision of the people as "infants," and an Islamic authoritarian political structure based on absolute obedience to the leader. All the major political, coercive, and ideological apparatuses and institutions of the state, including the Office of the Supreme Leader, the Council of Clerical Experts, the Guardian Council, the judiciary, the Revolutionary Guards, the rightist clerical parties, and their mouthpieces among the press (such as *Kayhan* and *Resalat*), supported this perspective. The cleavage eventually led to violence, intimidation of the independent press, and murder of some intellectuals instigated by the traditionalist-Islamic factions, in retaliation for the Reformists' victory in the presidential elections of 1997 and in the Sixth Majlis elections in 2000, when the reformist parties obtained a majority and embarked on a course of social and political reforms through legislation.

During the Sixth Majlis elections, although the Guardian Council disqualified some 700 candidates, the reformist parties won the majority of the seats (189), and the traditionalist-conservative parties obtained only 54 seats. Twelve conservative parties and factions had formed a coalition named the United Front of the Followers of the Imam and the

Leader. The Reformists won almost all of the 30 Tehran seats. (Independent candidates obtained 42 seats.) Only 20 percent of the incumbent members of the conservative-dominated Fifth Majlis were reelected.[9]

Fundamentalist Conservatism vs. Reformism, 2004–2013

As mentioned above, new fundamentalist factions were already emerging out of the traditionalist-conservative groups and followers of the supreme leader in response both to the capitalist modernization policies of the 1992–1997 period and the democratic reformist tendency of the 1997–2005 period. Fundamentalism, as an antiliberal, antidemocratic, and antiglobalization tendency, was basically a postwar (Iran-Iraq War) development. Its main social base included war veterans, the "mobilized" corps (the Basij militia), the Revolutionary Guards, security forces loyal to the leader, and more generally the disenchanted, marginalized, and impoverished lower urban layers not benefiting from the modernization, privatization, and democratization policies that had proved mostly beneficial to the upper and middle classes. By contrast, as we have seen, the traditional merchant classes and the bazaars were the main social base of support for the traditionalist-conservative groups, and the new urban middle classes largely supported the democratic-reformist groups and parties. In reaction to the policies and programs of modernization and reform first adopted by the KP neoconservatives, mostly in the economic arena, and then by the PF-dominated reformist government, mostly relating to democratization, the fundamentalist tendency gradually emerged from within the traditionalist Islamist bloc in the early 1990s in defense of Khomeini's legacy during a period of creeping "de-Khomeinization." If the entire Islamic Revolution had occurred as a reaction to modernization and Westernization during the Pahlavi era, similarly the fundamentalist tendency emerged as a reaction to some moderate modernization and democratization efforts after 1992. Initially it was not clearly distinguishable from the traditionalist-conservative tendency, but as it developed a larger social support base of its own, and as it clarified its own positions on socioeconomic affairs in the 1990s and 2000s, it was increasingly demarcated from the traditionalist-conservative tendency, even though it remained politically allied to the conservative camp. New fundamentalist groups had previously acted mainly as the violent arm of the traditionalist-conservative factions in their confrontation with the reformists and intellectuals. Nonetheless, some traditionalist-conservative clerics continued to act as the "think tanks" of the new fundamentalism. This tendency also increasingly revived the cult of leadership and identified itself with the supreme leader, who in his turn needed to create a base of social-political support for himself, during a period of time when modernization and democratization, as two discourses undesirable to him, had become predominant. The Office of the Supreme Leader courted the fundamentalists as the supreme leader's own followers, calling upon them to fight especially against the so-called Western cultural invasion.

These fundamentalist factions, allied to the conservatives, were to emerge as the dominant factions on the political scene mainly from the Seventh Majlis elections in 2004 onward. Their ideology may best be described more in terms of what they opposed than what they proposed. Their opposition to Western modernity, modernization, cultural liberalism, modern capitalist economics, liberal democracy and democratization, Western "cultural imperialism," republicanism as the essence of Islamic government, intellectuals and intellectualism, and sociocultural freedom define some of their major tenets. On the other hand, they favored an absolutist and centralized theocracy, political elitism, religious puritanism imposed violently, Islamic resurgence, an antiliberal cultural revolution, an emphasis on the Islamist essence of the political system as opposed to its republican aspects, populist egalitarian rhetoric similar to the positions of the populist factions of the 1980s, economic interventionism, and the fulfillment of the early socioeconomic promises of the Revolution. For them, neoliberal capitalist economic modernization as well as reformist democratization had been Western projects aimed at undermining Islam and theocracy.[10]

Some of the major factors and events leading to the rise and crystallization of the fundamentalist tendency are briefly mentioned below. One main reason may be found in the resentment produced by the extension of central government control on the part of the reconstruction regime over revolutionary institutions, committees, and Guards after 1989. In particular, the incorporation of the Revolutionary Guards into the Ministry of Defense and of the Revolutionary Committees into the regular police forces in the 1989–1990 period were not well received. However, despite institutionalization and normalization, political trends during the reconstruction and reform periods led to the rise of the fundamentalist gangs and groups as a formidable and much feared, more-or-less-clandestine opposition. As discussed earlier, this new tendency was in fact nurtured by the traditionalist-conservatives as well as the Office of the Supreme Leader in their confrontation with modernizing, secularizing, and democratizing trends. For instance, in 1992, the Fourth Majlis—dominated by the traditionalist Islamists— passed a law giving official immunity and protection to the Basij militia as assistants of the regular police forces in performing similar police tasks, particularly preventing moral offenses. This was a significant move on the part of the traditionalist Islamists in their campaign against liberal social policies. Also, as the supreme leader emerged into the limelight of politics in the 1990s and increasingly sided with the traditionalists against the modernizing and later democratizing trends, he was regarded as the hero of the fundamentalist factions. The supreme leader, despite his extensive constitutional powers, had a precarious position in terms of social support, therefore, the rise of the fundamentalist tendency filled a vacuum in this regard. Fundamentalists were to act as soldiers in the campaign against the Western cultural invasion.

The same groups began to develop a cult of personality around the supreme leader as the hero of the impoverished and revolutionary masses. Some other high-ranking clerics like Ayatollahs Ali Janati and Muhammad Taghi Mesbah-Yazdi also acted as sources of inspiration. In particular, Mesbah-Yazdi, who is described as the "theorist of violence," emerged as the ideologue and the intellectual mentor of the new fundamentalism. In fact, he has been described as one of a few ideologues of Shiite puritanism and fundamentalism in Iran today. As a literalist, he has advocated the establishment of an Islamic government or theocracy as opposed to an Islamic Republic; for him, elections and parliaments are Western institutions that should be discarded. He issued a religious edict before the 2005 election calling on his supporters to vote for the Islamic fundamentalists. His Haqqani Seminary at Qum has been an intellectual center for the new fundamentalists. A number of ministers and high officials of the fundamentalist regime came from the Haqqani circle (the ministers of intelligence, the interior, and Islamic guidance). Mesbah-Yazdi also emerged as a major exponent of the "fight against Western cultural invasion." He was elected to the clerical Assembly of Experts for the first time in 1996. He also publicly advocated the use of violence against all those who seek to reform Islam.[11]

The Organization for Enjoining the Good and Forbidding the Evil was a major political instrument in the hands of the new fundamentalists. The supreme leader has articulated and enhanced the ideology of fundamentalism. Also, the Basiji Student Associations were formed in this period to oppose the old Islamic Student Associations, which had become critical of the Islamic system. As noted earlier, the new fundamentalism, as radicalized and antagonized conservatism, had originated from within the conservative Islamist camp and maintained the same basic positions but was now acquiring a broader social base. Post-Khomeini conservative Islamism also increasingly embraced the absolutist version of theocracy; among the new fundamentalists, this tendency turned into a cult of leadership. Thus, from the beginning, traditionalist Islamism and fundamentalism overlapped and appeared as one and with the same tendency when confronting common foes, but once in power after 2004 they developed some differences of opinion and policy.

It can be argued that ultrafundamentalism in this sense had been the original project of the Islamic Revolution and Republic from the beginning, but it had not had the opportunity to predominate even under Khomeini himself due to the outbreak of the war, power struggles, and factionalism. Then, the modernizing and democratizing "deviations" of the post-Khomeini period arrived, which in themselves gave more urgency to the implementation of the original project. From a sociological perspective, there has been a "fascist persuasion" in Iranian politics all along, which has gone through various phases. From the perspective of the classic literature on fascism, Islamic fundamentalism in Iran seems very similar to fascist movements. As Hugh Trevor-Roper demonstrated, fascism has had two faces everywhere: a more traditionalist-conservative face presented and supported by the pre-capitalist upper classes, and a more activist, militant, radical-populist face represented by the declining middle and lower classes. Conservatism turns into fascism when it is wounded by modernization.[12] Thus, the new fundamentalist tendency that was articulated as a political ideology, especially after the 2004 elections, seems to be a new reformulation of the original ideology of the Islamic Revolution and should be distinguished from traditionalist-Islamist discourse of the clerical establishment of the type that dominated the political scene after 1989, even though they have mostly been political allies.

The realignment of the political forces before the Seventh Majlis elections was indicative of the rise of the new ideological tendency in opposition to modernization and reform. The newly formed fundamentalist coalition, called Abadgaran, had previously won the majority in the 2003 city council elections; it was made up mostly of former Revolutionary Guards and war veterans. During the 2004 parliamentary elections, the Guardian Council further paved the way for their victory by disqualifying some 2,400 mostly reformist candidates, including eighty incumbent members. As a result, the conservative-fundamentalist coalition (SMCT, ICG, and others) obtained 156 seats (out of 290); the moderate reformists (AMC, PF, KP, and Workers House) obtained forty seats; and Independents, thirty-four seats.[13] The Abadgaran fundamentalist coalition won all thirty seats in Tehran. About one-third of the Seventh Majlis deputies (ninety-six members) were former Revolutionary Guards (and members of the Abadgaran Coalition), a group that had mostly opposed the reform movement.[14]

A new fundamentalist political organization that was to emerge and play an increasingly decisive role as the hard core of the fundamentalist tendency was the Society of Sacrifice for the Islamic Revolution (SSIR), made up mostly of Revolutionary Guards and war veterans (prominent members included Hossein Fadaee, Mahmoud Ahmadinejad, Davoud Danesh-Jafari, and Ali Yusef-Pour). The SSIR had arisen as a reaction to "deviation" in the course of the Revolution (i.e., reformism and support for democratization and globalization). The organization had criticized the various economic, social, cultural, and foreign policies of the reformist government (1997–2005) and demanded the implementation of Khomeini's "original" ideals and principles. They had charged the reformist governments of Rafsanjani and Khatami with being responsible for the economic problems, unemployment, corruption, and increasing mass poverty, and of betraying the original project and principles of the Revolution by collaborating with Western powers in the name of democratization and globalization. The SSIR was active in the formation of the Abadgaran Conservative-Fundamentalist Coalition before the 2003 city council elections. As noted, this coalition in the 2004 parliamentary elections also won all thirty parliamentary seats for Tehran. The same party worked hard for the victory of conservatives and fundamentalists in the 2005 presidential elections. Before the elections, as noted, all the antireformist conservative forces set up a Coordination Council in order to ensure internal unity and propose a single candidate. The council was made up of the SMCT, ICG, SSIR, and other conservative-traditionalist parties and finally proposed Ali Larijani as its choice for the elections. But the SSIR did not eventually approve of the council's decision and set up a Council of Coordination No. 2 itself in order to propose its own favored candidate, M. B. Qalibaf, the chief of police. Since Qalibaf was not a member of the SSIR, rifts developed within the party over the issue of nomination, some supporting Mohsen Rezaee and some Ahmadinejad. Eventually, in the second round of the elections, the party supported Ahmadinejad.[15]

As a rule, the political involvement of the Revolutionary Guards has been a major aspect of the new ultrafundamentalist tendency. As mentioned, since 2004 the political role of the Revolutionary Guards became more pronounced; in their eyes, the defense of the Revolution against the reformists and revisionists increasingly required the intervention of the

Revolutionary Guards and Basij militia, whose function has been defined as safeguarding the Islamic regime against domestic and foreign enemies. More than one-third of the candidates in the elections for the Seventh Majlis were war veterans. A former Revolutionary Guards general, A. R. Afshar, was appointed by the supreme leader to supervise the elections. High officials publicly invited the Revolutionary Guards and the Basij militia to take an active role in the elections in order to "assist" the people in electing the friends of the Revolution and discarding its reformist enemies. The leader's deputy in the Revolutionary Guards, the commander of the Guards, and the army chief of staff all emphasized the political role of the army and the Revolutionary Guards in order to ensure the election of "competent" candidates and prevent the election of candidates "associated with foreign enemies." The conservative-fundamentalist forces were thus basically united, despite some differences of opinion and conflicts emerging between the new fundamentalist government and the Majlis (discussed below). Prior to the elections, the Revolutionary Guards and the army expressed their support for the conservative and Islamist candidates against the so-called deviant forces of reformism; they called on the people to vote for "righteous candidates." The supreme leader also explicitly supported the conservative-fundamentalist parties by calling on the people to vote for Islamist candidates.

The Revolutionary Guards also had close economic relations with the fundamentalist government. In July 2006, the Oil Ministry granted a $2 billion contract to the Guards for the development of the Southern Pars Gas-Field; the Guards also obtained a $1.3 billion contract to build a gas pipeline in the south of the country and a $1.2 billion contract for expanding the Tehran Metro. As a major political and economic interest group, the Revolutionary Guards were the backbone of the new fundamentalist factions. They had already done their best to suppress the opposition and student movements during the reform period. At the height of the student movement in support of the reformist government, the Revolutionary Guards commander had threatened the dissidents with "killing them and cutting their tongues."[16]

Main and Minor Cleavages

Here I distinguish between the primary or main cleavage dividing the conservative-fundamentalist camp and the reformist-modernist parties, and a secondary cleavage between fundamentalists and traditionalist-conservatives.

The ruling alliance following the 2005 election included the Abadgaran coalition (called the "Garrison Party" by its opponents), Ansar-e Hezbollah, SMCT, SQST, and ICG; the alliance was supported by the supreme leader, and had close links to Revolutionary Guards and the Basij militia forces. This bloc advocated absolutist theocracy, anti-Western and antiglobalization foreign and economic policies, and social-cultural control.

On the other hand, the broad reformist camp included the PF, KP, MIR, and AMC. This bloc was in favor of Islamic democracy, constitutional rule, social-cultural freedom, an open-door foreign policy, and a pro-globalization stance.

Apart from general ideological differences, the two camps had confrontations over a number of policies, elections, or issues. As noted, in the 2005 presidential election, the conservative-fundamentalist Abadgaran coalition won the elections against PF and KP. In the 2008 elections to the Eighth Majlis, the fundamentalist-conservative bloc included the ruling Abadgaran coalition, SMCT, ICG, the Development and Moderation Party, the Welfare Party, and the Islamic Engineers' Association. The reformist and democratic bloc included the AMC, MIR, PF, Labor Party, Workers House, National Solidarity Party, National Confidence Party, KP, and the Association of Followers of Imam Khomeini. The Guardian Council disqualified 1,700 mostly reformist candidates (including nineteen incumbent members); altogether some 50 percent of the reformist candidates were disqualified—including all the PF and MIR candidates and the majority of the National Confidence Party candidates. The turnout was only 52 percent (30 percent in Tehran). Arrayed against the reformists was a broad coalition of old and new conservatives, fundamentalists, the Revolutionary Guards, and the armed forces.[17]

On the other hand, a secondary cleavage emerged within the fundamentalist-conservative camp over a number of specific issues, such as economic and nuclear policy; the ruling fundamentalist faction advocated an interventionist policy, a strong public sector (the purges of banks and insurance companies were justified on such grounds), a redistributive stance (as indicated in the slogan "bring oil money to people's tables"), price intervention, increases in wages, subsidies for foodstuffs, and a reduction in interest rates, all of which were opposed by conservative factions like the ICG. A rift also emerged as a result of disagreements over foreign policy orientations and the nuclear issue. Fundamentalist factions supported a hard-line policy; some, like Mesbah, the mentor of the faction, even advocated a nuclear weapons program, or called for Iran's withdrawal from the Nuclear Non-Proliferation Treaty, whereas more conservative factions advocated a more moderate stand. The supreme leader tended to support the latter by creating the Foreign Policy Coordination Council in order to harmonize foreign policy. Some conservative MPs also voiced their dissatisfaction with some of the policies of the ruling faction on a number of occasions. At the same time, the supreme leader, despite wholehearted support for the fundamentalists, sought to keep a semblance of independence and superiority as the leader by criticizing the government's economic performance. On the other hand, he indicated his support for the conservative parties by supporting privatization policies; as a rule, he tried to keep his links with the traditionalist-conservatives. This was the main reason for the occasional precautionary notices and pronouncements that came out of the Office of the Supreme Leader, admonishing officials for some of their extremist views or slogans. Similarly, some traditionalist clerics admonished the president about his religious pretensions and his claim of direct support for his policies on the part of the Hidden Imam, as well as for his political adventurism.

Early on in this period, the 2006 elections to the Assembly of Experts were a theater of confrontation between the fundamentalists and conservative clerics. The Interior Ministry sought to have the elections supervised and controlled by the Basij militia, in favor of the Mesbah fundamentalist faction and against Rafsanjani. Only 165 candidates were approved for the eighty-six seats; the SMCT received the majority (sixty-eight) of the seats.[18]

The emerging secondary cleavage became somewhat institutionalized in the form of the two fundamentalist parliamentary factions in the Eighth Majlis: the majority United Fundamentalist Front (UFF; fundamentalist government supporters) and the minority Broad Fundamentalist Coalition (BFC), which was a more conservatively oriented opposition to the fundamentalist regime (sometimes called "pragmatic conservatives"). The BFC broke away from the UFF and emerged during the Eighth Majlis elections, protesting domination of the electoral lists by the UFF and supporting greater autonomy for the parliament from the fundamentalist government—a stance that led to increasing confrontation between the government and the Parliament. The speaker of the Eighth Majlis, Ali Larijani, was regarded as a leader of the BFC (which was also supported by the Tehran mayor, Qalibaf, and Rezaee). During the Eighth Majlis elections, the UFF and the BFC presented two separate thirty-candidate lists for Tehran, although one-third of the two lists were the same. The UFF obtained 117 seats; the BFC, fifty-three seats; the Reformists, forty-six; and Independents, sixty-nine. Some of the reasons for the division had to do with the economic and foreign policies pursued by the fundamentalist government, such as a reduction in interest rates, leading to increasing investment in housing, increasing inflation, and flight of capital; the incorporation of the Plan Organization into the government structure; irregular economic interventionism; and favoritism in government appointments. Given these issues, the old conservative and traditionalist parties found themselves in a difficult situation, wondering whether or how to support the UFF and the government. The conservative camp issued its manifesto for the elections in June 2007 and called on the government to work for more social justice, economic stability, and privatization of the economy. The greatest emphasis, however, was put on maintaining unity among the conservative-Islamist camp against the reformist parties. The House Speaker called on the various factions to forget their differences and to act together. Hence, the various factions and parties set up a number of committees and sought to propose a single list of candidates, forming the United Front of the Fundamentalist Parties, which included the older conservative United Front of the Followers of the Imam and the Leader as well as the SSIR and the government faction. As mentioned, however, some critics of the president and fundamentalist policies would not cooperate and were to form the BCF.

Cleavages in the 2009 and 2013 Elections

Going back to the main cleavage, I briefly consider here the June 2009 elections from the cleavage perspective. Two issues were salient during the elections: first, the confrontation of political reform with fundamentalist conservatism, and second, the issue of economic regulation or social justice. However, as the electoral campaign indicated, the political cleavage between the two main blocs was not very sharp. The fundamentalist-conservative factions had two candidates: the incumbent president and Mohsen Rezaee, general-secretary of the Expediency Council. The president was supported by a number of fundamentalist-conservative groupings and parties, but Rezaee stood as an independent and was not backed by those parties. The secondary or internal cleavage within the fundamentalist-conservative bloc surfaced more sharply over supporting the incumbent president as a candidate for the June elections. The main, powerful clerical organization, the SMCT, was divided and was not able to make a clear decision. Its Tabriz and Isfahan branches decided to support Mousavi, but the main Tehran organization adopted a policy of "silence." The bazaar-based ICG, as part of the United Front of the Fundamentalist Parties, supported the incumbent president and accused Rafsanjani, still an SMCT member, of preventing the society from reaching a decision. According to Hassan Rouhani, then a senior member, even after holding five meetings on the issue of the elections, the members were unable to reach the required two-thirds majority decision. Several influential members, including Rafsanjani, Rouhani, Nateq-Nuri, and Mustafa Pour-Mohammadi, sharply criticized and opposed the policies of the fundamentalist government. On the other hand, Mahdavi Kani, the secretary-general of the organization, reportedly on the basis of the supreme leader's advice, personally supported the incumbent president. The policy of silence adopted by the SMCT was sharply criticized by fundamentalist newspapers, especially *Kayhan,* and the Mesbah-Yazdi faction. Similarly, the Qum clerical society, SQST, was not able to reach a required two-thirds majority for supporting a candidate, but likewise, its secretary-general, Mohammad Yazdi, declared that the majority of the members supported the incumbent president as the candidate of the fundamentalist-conservative bloc. As a very important actor in the mobilization of electoral support for the fundamentalists, the supreme leader expressed total support for the incumbent president and on several occasions before the elections implicitly called on his supporters to vote for the fundamentalist candidate. In a sense, from the beginning the Abadgaran Coalition and the Fundamentalist Front were orchestrated from within the Office of the Supreme Leader. In line with the views of the supreme leader, the Revolutionary Guards and the Basij militia also openly supported the current president, held electoral campaign conferences before the elections, and in various publications (especially *Sobh-e Sadeq Weekly,* published by the Political Office of the Revolutionary Guards) accused the reformist candidates of deviation from the path of the Revolution.[19]

The secondary cleavage within the fundamentalist bloc clearly surfaced over the nomination issue within the Majlis; a larger section of the majority faction of government supporters, UFF, supported the incumbent president. In the UFF Majlis meeting on May 24, 2009, out of the 165 fundamentalist deputies, eighty members voted for Ahmadinejad, seventy members voted against him, and fifteen members abstained from voting. Critics of the fundamentalist government within the fundamentalist faction in the Majlis included Larijani, Mohammad Reza Bahonar, and Haddad Adel.[20]

One of the consequences of the June 2009 elections was a further intensification of the secondary cleavage between the fundamentalist and the traditionalist-conservative parties. Apart from the lack of clear support from such groupings as the SMCT and the SQST, fifty Qum Seminary teachers condemned the president for attacking some prominent clerics in his electoral debates. Thus, the secondary cleavage between traditionalist and fundamentalist Islam became more pronounced.

On the other hand, the reformist-democratic parties supported two candidates: the former premier, Mir-Hossein Mousavi, and Mehdi Karroubi, leader of the National Confidence Party. Mousavi was supported by the PF, KP, AMC, MIR, and the Line of the Imam Majlis minority faction. He was rather equivocal in his electoral pronouncements in the beginning, vacillating between supporting Islamic economics and the private sector. Given that he was the leading candidate of the reformist parties, it seems that political reformism was not as clearly articulated in 2009 as in the previous elections. In the beginning, the pale and conservative reformism of Mousavi did not strike a chord with the social base of the reformist social movement, even though on the eve of the elections he declared to be more in favor of socioeconomic and cultural freedom than state interventionism. In his political program, published in May 2009, he emphasized administrative reforms and the reinvigoration of the private sector and civil society associations as the main means for achieving justice. His meeting with the supreme leader before the elections was frowned upon by more radical reformist papers and parties. As an Azerbaijani Turk, Mousavi's nomination was expected to somewhat reactivate the ethnic division in his favor in attracting the votes of the Turkish minority, numbering about 15 million. On the other hand, it seems that Karroubi, despite his recent radical slogans attacking the Guardian Council and its vetting powers, appeared more unpredictable and unreliable to the main reformist parties. As a result he was supported by political and influential reformist personalities rather than parties. His opposition to the radical reformists during the reform period, and his acceptance of the mass disqualifications during the Seventh Majlis elections, were well remembered by the reformist parties.

Thus, it seems that out of the two main active issues during the elections (i.e., economic regulation and political reformism as against the conservative-fundamentalist tendency), the main political cleavage was not well articulated initially; in fact it seems that the economic cleavage acquired some priority over the political cleavage and became more pronounced as all the candidates concentrated more on economic policy-making, economic conditions, poverty, social injustice, and the lower classes. In a sense, "reformism" had no candidate in the 2009 elections. The more moderate National Confidence Party led by Mehdi Karroubi tacitly accused the main reformist party, PF, of extremism and bearing responsibility for the reformists' past failure. After the 2008 elections, the reformist parties had almost abandoned their focus on civil liberties, civil society, democratization, and human rights, and instead emphasized economic issues, such as unemployment and inflation. Several factors must have contributed to the decline of the authoritarian-reformist cleavage, perhaps the most important being the clerical elite's policy of mass disqualification of reformist candidates after 2004, which aimed at the total obliteration of the cleavage and the disintegration of the reformist parties. In more theoretical terms, the cleavage-breaking function of the ideological regime proved rather successful in eliminating or marginalizing the more radical reformist factions and in silencing the voice of reform.

However, later on, during the electoral campaigns, the fundamentalist/reformist cleavage intensified with the rise of a "Green Social Movement" around the reformist parties. With the unprecedented mobilization of the general public in large cities in support of reformism, the fundamentalist government, fearful of the rising tide, condemned the Green Movement as a project for a color or velvet revolution against the Islamic regime. The political office of the Revolutionary Guards therefore vowed to crush the movement. The election results announced by the Ministry of Interior on June 13 were highly contested and regarded by the reformist parties as part of an "electoral coup." According to the government, out of more than 42 million votes, Ahmadinejad obtained 24 million (64 percent); Mousavi, 13 million; and Karroubi, 33,000. According to unofficial reports from within the Ministry of the Interior, however, Mousavi had obtained 19 million; Karroubi, 13.3 million; and Ahmadinejad, 5.6 million. The dispute over the results led to widespread protests, demonstrations, arrests, and the violent and brutal suppression of the Green Movement. Hence, although initially during the electoral campaign the authoritarian-reformist cleavage was not pronounced, the conflict over the results led to the intensification of the cleavage, as demonstrators chanted against "dictatorship" and called for freedom and free elections.

A brief account of the presidential elections of June 2013 in terms of the main cleavages is now in order. As we already know, all elections in the Islamic Republic are basically planned and orchestrated by the Office of the Supreme Leader and the Guardian Council, since only a few ideologically "qualified" and eligible candidates would be allowed to stand for the elections. In such an orchestrated and planned democracy, any one of the eligible candidates would eventually suit the conductor, even though some would be regarded as more intimate and trusted than others. Thus, in the presidential elections of June 2013, eight candidates out of 680 were approved as qualified. Out of the eight, two eventually withdrew; one was a lukewarm reformist, and the other was close to the fundamentalists. They apparently withdrew in the interest of other candidates.

Out of the remaining six, Hassan Rouhani was a member of the SMCT (although it did not support him as a candidate for the elections), a confidante of the leader, a member of the Assembly of Experts, and the secretary of the National Security Council for some time; he should have been considered as a lukewarm reformist as well, as he was a member of the moderately reformist Moderation and Development Party. The other five were more or less closely supported by the fundamentalist-conservative parties (Qalibaf was supported by moderate conservative factions including the Society of Engineers and the UFF; Jalili was backed by the fundamentalist Abadgaran and the Iranian Revolutionary Resistance Front, another fundamentalist grouping; the other three were also associated with fundamentalist-conservative factions). Candidates representing or supporting the reformist parties had been disqualified; no reformist candidates were allowed to run for the elections. In particular, the rejection of Rafsanjani is noteworthy. Khatami refused to stand for election. Instead they both supported Rouhani during the campaign. Thus, given the platforms and political agenda of Rouhani, as well as his close ties with Rafsanjani, the reformist parties and the remnants of the Green Movement threw their support behind Rouhani during the last days of the campaign. As a result, a social movement similar to the Green Movement itself was mobilized by popular and reformist parties to support Rouhani. He was elected president with an absolute majority in the first round of voting (with a turnout of 72 percent: 36 million voters). He emerged as a de facto representative of the reformist parties and groups associated with Rafsanjani and Khatami. The PF, KP, and Workers' House, as well as oppositional groupings like the Freedom Movement and the National-Religious Movement, supported him.

It seems that the leader and the Guardian Council had not anticipated such vast support for Rouhani, but when it happened it was welcomed and utilized as a bridge to close the deep antagonistic rift that the elections of 2009 had caused. However, given the economic and international problems caused by the previous government, it seems that the core clerical elite was not too sure about the other fundamentalist candidates as being the best choice for the survival and legitimacy of the whole system. In this sense, the elections acted as a strategy of survival. The election results were to serve several purposes: (1) they could quiet the remnants of the Green Movement and alleviate popular anger and frustration, which had been increased after 2009; (2) they could help the system in finding a solution for the economic and foreign policy issues that were threatening the regime's viability; (3) they could demonstrate that elections in the Islamic Republic were "free and fair," despite the allegations of large-scale fraud in the 2009 elections, and thus mend the deficit of legitimacy caused by those allegations. In any case, the system could not afford rigging the elections again (if it had done so in 2009), given the magnitude of the post–June 2009 uprising and rebellion and the possibility of a repetition at a time of crisis. Given the conditions, it seems that the regime did not have a clear preference among the candidates, despite public opinion to the contrary.

Conclusion

During the past three decades, three overlapping issues became salient and led to factional and party competition and internal opposition after the Revolution. As shown here, political conflict and factionalism in the first decade (1980–1992) resulted from an economic policy issue, dividing the factions over whether to support the public or private sectors. During the second period, 1992–1997, the issue of socioeconomic modernization led to polarization between modernizing neoconservatives and traditional conservatives. In the third period, 1997–2004, the issue of political reform and liberalization produced a new cleavage. During the same period, the issues of modernization and liberalization were combined into the broader confrontation between reformist and conservative-fundamentalist discourses. Overall, therefore, out of the factionalism of the last thirty years, two lasting active cleavages, forming a double-cross-cutting-cleavage pattern, have emerged in Iranian politics: the first one (economic policy cleavage) resulted from the dispute over economic regulation, and the second one (type of regime or political cleavage) resulted from the issues of modernization and liberalization. A combination of the two has formed the political-ideological space, consisting of four ideological positions in which various factions and parties in the life of the Islamic Republic can be located. This pattern is depicted in Figure 2.2.

All the ideological trends have presented their own justifications and explanations. Traditionalist-conservatives considered the tradition of Islam as superior to the Revolution and its leadership; for them, everything came from that tradition. By contrast, Khomeinists argued that the Revolution was a novel and unique event; for them, everything came from the mass revolution, so that the tradition of Islam had to somewhat adjust itself to its requirements—whence the importance of absolutist theocracy. On the other hand, modernist neoconservatives emphasized the need to go beyond both a restricted-traditional Islam as

Figure 2.2   Issue Dimensions and Cleavages in the Islamic Republic

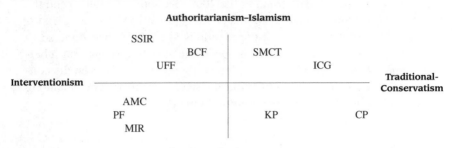

Note: AMC = Association of Militant Clergy; BCF = Broad Fundamentalist Coalition; CP = Confidence Party; ICG = Islamic Coalition Groups; KP = Party of Reconstruction; MIR = Mujahedin of the Islamic Revolution; PF = Participation Front; SMCT = Society of the Militant Clergy of Tehran; SSIR = Society of Sacrifice for the Islamic Revolution; UFF = United Fundamentalist Front.

well as the requirements of a mass revolution and to reconstruct the country as a stable, modern Islamic nation. Democratic reformism has more specifically advocated the establishment of a stable, modern Islamic democracy based on a stronger notion of popular sovereignty. Finally, new fundamentalism, as a sort of radicalized conservatism reacting to modernization and democratization, has advocated a combination of some elements of traditionalism and Khomeinism.

A final note is in order regarding the possible impact of the emerging cleavages and cleavage pattern in terms of the possible formation of a stable political party system. As we have seen, the stabilization and crystallization of cleavages is usually the basis for the formation of a party system. On the other hand, ideological regimes (despite being unable to prevent the emergence of political cleavages) have a central political tendency toward breaking or deactivating cleavages. In other words, two tendencies can be identified in ideological regimes: a totalitarian tendency to unify the polity and destroy cleavages, on the one hand, and a pluralistic tendency toward cleavage formation and fragmentation on the other. In the case of Iran since the Revolution, the two tendencies have been at work. For several reasons, cleavages have been emerging within the polity, and the central ruling groups have sought to obliterate or diminish their political impact by preventing rival parties from participation in power. As a result, political cleavages have been too unstable and fluid for the rise of a stable party system.

Notes

1. See Lipset and Rokkan, *Party Systems and Voter Alignments,* pp. 1–50; Smith, *Politics in Western Europe,* pp. 11–36; McRae and Taylor, *The Analysis of Political Cleavages;* Moreno, *Political Cleavages.*

2. See Moslem, *Factional Politics in Post-Khomeini Iran;* Behrooz, "Factionalism in Iran Under Khomeini"; Bakhtiari, *Parliamentary Politics in Revolutionary Iran;* Akhavi, "Elite Factionalism in the Islamic Republic of Iran."

3. Knutsen and Scarbrough, "Cleavage Politics," p. 495.

4. McRae and Taylor, *The Analysis of Political Cleavages,* p. 2.

5. Smith, *Politics in Western Europe,* pp. 11–36.

6. McRae and Taylor, *The Analysis of Political Cleavages,* pp. 85–105.

7. The Guardian Council vetted ninety-four acts and returned eighty-two other acts passed by the First Majlis (out of 370 acts); the corresponding figures for the Second Majlis were seventy-one and ninety-three acts (out of 316 acts); for the Third Majlis, ninety and sixty-six acts (out of 256 acts); for the Fourth Majlis, sixty-four and 105 acts (out of 342 acts).

8. See Ehteshami, *After Khomeini,* chap. 5.

9. See Sahliyeh, "The Reforming Elections in Iran: 2000–2001."

10. For an account of their emergence, see Rubin, *Into the Shadows.*

11. For more details, see Ganji, *Iranian Strategy.*

12. Trevor-Roper, "The Phenomenon of Fascism."

13. Partly due to the massive electoral purge, the nationwide turnout was about 50 percent (as compared to 67 percent in the Sixth Majlis elections); the turnout in Tehran was much lower, standing at about 33 percent.

14. Abedin, "Iran After the Elections."

15. For more details, see Samii, "The Changing Landscape of Party Politics in Iran."

16. Bjorvatn and Selvik, "Destructive Competition."

17. For more details, see Zimmt, "Iran's 2008 Parliamentary Elections."

18. See Zimmt, "Elections Results for the Assembly of Experts and Local Councils."

19. Government and revolutionary organizations have helped the fundamentalist ruling faction in its attempts to "buy votes" before the elections. Some of the actions taken by the government for this purpose include adding 100,000 to 300,000 tumans to government employees' pay in the month of May 2009; a sudden rise in the salaries of government employees and pensioners; the payment of 80,000 tumans each to 5 million farmers and villagers; distribution of 50,000-tuman travel checks to health personnel and nurses in public and private hospitals; distribution of money among 3,000 religious preachers associated with the Religious Endowments Administration; distribution of 400,000 tons of free potatoes throughout the country, and so on. *Rooz* (5 Khordad 1388); Nazila Fathi, "Support for Moderates: A Challenge to Iran's Leader," *New York Times,* May 26, 2009.

20. *Rooz* (4 Khordad 1388) [May 25, 2009].

3

Democracy After the Green Movement

Mehrangiz Kar

Iranians were not alone in the opinion that the Islamic Republic of Iran had lost its legitimacy due to the brutal repression of the Green Movement in the aftermath of the rigged 2009 presidential election. Iran's traditional and conservative political elite were aware of this fact, and the 2013 Iranian presidential election vividly demonstrated their attempts to compensate for the delegitimization caused by mismanagement of the 2009 protests.

The crisis in 2009 left Iran with a number of significant consequences that continue to affect its domestic and international affairs today. June 12, 2009, marked the beginning of a crisis inside Iran. Large protests by people opposing the election results and the subsequent reelection of President Mahmoud Ahmadinejad erupted in the streets of Tehran, as well as other cities. Eventually, this translated into a debate over the rule of the supreme leader, causing an increased influential role of the Basij and the Revolutionary Guards in Iran's domestic political arena.

Despite the government's violent repression of street protests, the demonstrations triggered political fractures inside the government and deepened tensions at the core of the Islamic Republic. Through these events, imbalances emerged, highlighting the fragility in the political machinations between the various branches of power in the Islamic Republic. As a result, the different branches of government were often tangled in internal conflict. Meanwhile, Ahmadinejad, who continuously violated the Islamic Republic's Constitution and many of the republic's founding principles, continued to dominate national debates, aiming to exert his dominance over all the key hubs of power, namely the Islamic Majlis (Parliament), the judicial system, the Expediency Council, and the Assembly of Experts (Majles-e Khobregan). This conduct led conservatives to form a coalition against him, which opened the door to his political demise.

With Ahmadinejad's term in office coming to an end, the ruling conservatives were in search of a solution that would encourage participation in the eleventh presidential election, but one that would not undermine their previous anti–Green Movement positions either. What made such efforts even more complicated was the fact that Ayatollah Ali Khamenei, Iran's supreme leader, had publicly endorsed Ahmadinejad in the early days after the disputed 2009 elections.[1] Khamenei's endorsement paved the way for the violent oppression of the protestors, along with other consequences, one of which was to encourage Ahmadinejad's megalomania.

In this chapter, I explore the reasons that led to the formation of the Green Movement, its legacy, and how it was able to influence the election of Hassan Rouhani four years later. I also investigate the limitations of Iran's civil society as one of the spheres in which the opposition could possibly prove effective. Importantly, despite Iran's political and institutional success in silencing the Green Movement, the movement was able to remain significantly relevant even after four years of constant public suppression. The Green Movement reminded people of a vital power that they held: the ability to protest. In addition, the movement led to deepened internal fractures within the conservative political camp. These fractures in turn paved the path for the presidential victory of Hassan Rouhani, a moderate conservative. In this light, the Green Movement must be considered a turning point in Iran's domestic and international development.

An Unfulfilled Demand: "Where Is My Vote?"

To this day, the famous slogan of the Green Movement, "Where is my vote?" plays an important role in the public sphere in reflecting the Iranian regime's increased loss of legitimacy. This simple question or demand is crucial in understanding the rationale behind the protests and the demand for democracy.

This question reflected the fact that the Islamic Republic could no longer govern with its pseudodemocratic façade and formality of presidential elections. The question also illustrated that the people, particularly the youth, were well aware of the difference between a legitimate democratic vote-counting system and a system where elections are used merely to legitimize and mobilize tools of the establishment.

This collective political awareness crystallized in the mass protests following the disputed June 2009 presidential election. Despite its spontaneous power and momentum, the Green Movement was not an overnight phenomenon. In reality, it was the result of thirty-four years of increasing social, political, and economic discontent, as well as disappointment in the overall trajectory of the Islamic Revolution of 1979.

The Lingering Shadow of the Reform Era

On May 23, 1997, for the first time in the nearly two decades since the inception of the Islamic Republic, an overwhelming number of people participated in the presidential election.[2] The participation rate was 79.92 percent, and the reformist candidate, Mohammad Khatami, won the election with 20,138,784 votes, which constituted 69.1 percent of the total vote.[3]

Many voters knew that Iranian elections do not conform to many of the international and democratic standards to which Westerners are accustomed. However, voters chose to participate in order to break the political stalemate and give Mohammad Khatami a chance to deliver on his promises of reform. Continuing this major political change, the tenth presidential election, on June 12, 2009, also saw an overwhelming turnout.[4] The participation rate in the 2009 election was 85.21 percent, and a former mayor of Tehran, Mahmoud Ahmadinejad, was announced the winner with 63.1 percent of the vote (24,592,793 votes).[5]

Many signs indicate manipulation or even outright fraud in the 2009 election. A comparison between the statistics of the 1997, 2005, and 2009 presidential elections can shed some light on why many observers were skeptical of the 2009 results. In this view, and taking into consideration the history of voter turnout since the inception of the Islamic Republic, the higher the participation rate, the higher chance of victory for the opposition groups, or at least those closer politically or ideologically to the opposition groups. The average participation rate in Iran's elections since 1979 has been 64.19 percent, a very high rate by global standards.[6] Voter turnout in 1997, as mentioned earlier, was 79.92 percent. Interestingly, in 2005 it dropped to 63 percent in the first round, and almost 60 percent in the final runoff.[7] However, in 2009, the voter participation rate rose again but this time to an astonishing 85 percent, the highest in two decades.[8]

As political expert Ali Alizadeh explains, it is generally perceived that an "increase in turnout" should translate into more support for "the opposition" in any country.[9] In addition, a higher turnout in Iran's elections "has always benefitted the opposition, and not the incumbent." The reason is simple, according to Alizadeh: "It is rational to assume that those who usually don't vote, i.e., the silent majority, only come out when they want to change the status quo."[10]

Different explanations exist as to why the allegations of fraud caused such massive protests in 2009. Perhaps one explanation for this outburst of frustration is the long wait that Iranians have had to endure to see political, social, and cultural reforms, while going about their lives knowing the perils of what another revolution might bring. Perhaps 2009 was not as simple as a general protest aimed at taking a stand against election fraud. Rather, the Green Movement organically came to fruition in the wake of long years of desired reforms, followed by a comeback by Iran's hardliners, which had been reaffirmed with Ahmadinejad's reelection.

It could be argued further that "Where is my vote?" was a slogan loaded with the unmet social and political demands of living within the framework of the Islamic Republic. Adding to the frustrations of many Iranians in 2009 was that the peaceful protests were brutally squashed by the government, which justified its actions by citing Article 27 of the Iranian Constitution: "Unarmed assemblies and marches may be freely organized, provided that no violation of the foundations of Islam is involved."[11] The brutality with which the protesters were confronted revealed to the world the true extent the Iranian regime was willing to go in order to make sure its clench on power would not be compromised.

In the end, Iranians used the limited legal mechanism left available for them in Iran's Constitution—voting rights—in order to voice their demands and object to the election results. In essence, this cry was for democratic change. In other words, the silent majority of Iranians, who had refused to participate in nondemocratic elections before, took part in the June 12, 2009, election and altered the course of the Islamic Republic's relatively young history.

Instead of responding to the protests and complaints in a sophisticated manner, the Iranian regime took the course of undertaking widespread human rights violations and repressing its citizens, which only added to the importance of the 2009 election. If one wishes to analyze the Islamic Republic after the 2009 election in the shortest manner possible, one could easily conclude that, after thirty years, the Islamic Republic of Iran has lost much of its legitimacy and, as a result, realized that its system of governance had to make urgent efforts to win some legitimacy back through the 2013 elections.

Violent Response to the Green Movement

Ahmadinejad's hard-line supporters, including key military institutions such as the Islamic Revolutionary Guard Corps (IRGC) and the Basij, an all-volunteer paramilitary militia and subsidiary of the IRGC, attacked unarmed protesters demonstrating peacefully back in 2009.[12] The violence in the streets was followed by unprecedented detentions and arrests.[13] In their use of street violence and subsequent detentions and torture, the Islamic Republic violated its very own Constitution and laws.

Article 38 of Iran's Constitution explicitly bars any form of torture or persecution: "Any kind of torture used to extract an admission of guilt or to obtain information is forbidden. Compelling people to give evidence, or confess or take an oath is not allowed. Such evidence or confession or oath is null and void. Any person infringing this principle is to be punished in accordance with the law."[14] However, in multiple cases, people who were arrested testified that they were tortured.[15] There were allegations of rape of the prisoners by the prison guards as well.[16] Furthermore, according to some estimates, over thirty people were killed.[17]

Nobody was held responsible for these violations. All the relevant institutions that are responsible for the rule of law within the legal structure of the Islamic Republic remained silent, abiding by the supreme leader's instructions given in his Friday Prayers' sermon, which greenlighted the violence.[18]

As a result, many civil rights activists and ordinary protestors were imprisoned and tortured. Not only were the arrested dissidents not granted fair trials, they were paraded in mass trials, widely publicized by state media, confessing to having conspired with foreign powers to form a velvet revolution in Iran.[19] In other words, the judiciary had violated Article 168 of Iran's Constitution, which orders fair and special trials for those accused of political offenses.[20] Other important but fabricated charges were that the accused were plotting regime change and acts against national security, charges severely punishable according to the Islamic Penal Code.[21]

Every human rights organization in the international community issued condemning statements emphasizing Iran's UN membership and it being a signatory to international conventions such as the International Covenant on Civil and Political Rights (ICCPR); the International Covenant on Economic, Social, and Cultural Rights (ICESCR); and the Convention on the Rights of the Child (CRC).[22] Despite such obligations, Iran's government is recognized as not respecting the norms and standards of human rights.[23]

Who Are the Principalists?

In today's Iranian political culture, principalists include a group of hard-line conservatives who have substantial disagreements with reformists and moderates. They do not tolerate the presence of reformists and moderates in the upper echelons of government. Some believe that their strong emergence was a reaction to Khatami's victory in the presidential elections and the reformists' success in 1997. Others believe that the main reason for their strong presence is the support they have always received from the highest political figure in Iran: the supreme leader.

Domestically, principalists—along with other key players who support them within Iran's political system—have come to dominate the most powerful levers of government. Moreover, they persist in implementing the further Islamization of the physical appearance of the Iranian women, as well as continuing to try to define their roles in society. Not surprisingly, the principalists have also expanded the government's restrictions in the realms of media, arts, and cultural activities. Due to the aggressive imposition of severe restrictions and censorship regulations, these hard-line policies now resemble fundamentalist principles and ideals. Internationally, their nuclear and anti-American policies gained support in various parts of the world where nations have grown accustomed to significant anti-American sentiments.

Ahmadinejad pursued a conservative-principalist approach and put his main efforts on advancing nuclear capabilities and sharpening his anti-American rhetoric. In the aftermath of the highly tense and arguably fraudulent tenth presidential elections, which kept him in office for his second term, he continued his inflexible policies against the United States and Israel. Domestically he maintained strong restrictions and oppressive policies against critics, as well as those opposing his policies in the realm of culture, politics, and economics. He and his supporters inside Iran's military and the Office of the Supreme Leader did not leave any room for prospects of even limited efforts toward democracy.

After the tenth presidential election, it was assumed that Ahmadinejad's administration would have the support of the principalists, whom he was, after all, representing. However, Ahmadinejad's second-term political conduct and public behavior, in addition to the supreme leader's miscalculation, caused a serious division among the principalists. Days after the disputed 2009 election, Ayatollah Khamenei sided with Ahmadinejad and publicly endorsed his policies; this move made it more difficult for the supreme leader to criticize Ahmadinejad later on.[24] As Ahmadinejad pursued an increasingly independent path, most principalists became critical of him. Those who remained in Ahmadinejad's circle were mostly the followers of the extreme conservative Ayatollah Muhammad Taghi Mesbah-Yazdi.[25]

Internal Fractures Within the Islamic Republic Reflected in the Judiciary

The Green Movement intensified the clashes between the people and the government as well as the internal disputes among conservative officials. Mehdi Karroubi, one of the leaders of the Green Movement, said in an interview with Netherlands Television Channel 2, "We witnessed how violently security forces beat up women, which was absolutely new to me. I wondered what they were doing. I saw many demonstrations during the shah's time, a lot of violence. I was a protester then, but I had not seen anyone beat up children and women so easily and without any psychological restraint."[26]

The late Grand Ayatollah Hossein Ali Montazeri, a critic of the Ahmadinejad administration, called the violent crackdown on protesting citizens at the hands of the security and military forces "unholy" and "illegal," admonishing that the philosophy of creating the Basij was to be in line with God and not with Satan.[27] He also criticized the behavior of various state organs, including the leader of the Islamic Republic in his capacity as the highest Shiite leader inside Iran.[28]

The late Ayatollah Montazeri was not alone in this judgment. Some jurists and clerics were on his side, but given the dominance of the conservatives, most did not have the authority necessary to turn their criticism into action and reform. Even their criticisms alone made them the targets of the principalists who regarded Ahmadinejad as their symbol in the government. Fractures developed even among this powerful and conservative group. Some of them who had grown unhappy with conservative policies over the years had become silent without completely breaking away. Even then, this silence put them at risk.

In addition, throughout the crackdown the Revolutionary Guard and Basij were illegally working as the agents of the judicial system in helping with arrests, investigations, and judicial decisionmaking. Their illegal interference in the judiciary continues in today's Iran. The judicial system, manipulated by the supreme leader, has given up its independence still further in the aftermath of the Green Movement, permitting further interference by the conservatives in all aspects of governance.

The Dual Nature of the Islamic Republic: Islamic and Republic

The Green Movement also further highlighted the Islamic Republic's dual nature. Even though this dual nature had already been widely discussed in newspapers during the reform era, the Green Movement made the undemocratic nature of this duality clearer to people. To better explain this duality, it is essential to review the relevant lines of the Constitution. Article 57 of Iran's Constitution reads, "The powers of government in the Islamic Republic are vested in the legislative, the judicial, and the executive powers, functioning under the supervision of the absolute religious leader and the leadership of the Islamic scholars or their followers, in accordance with subsequent articles of this constitution. These powers are independent of each other."[29]

This article was different in the original Constitution; it was amended as it appears in the constitutional reforms of 1989. In the previous version, the branches were separate, and the president served as their connection.[30] However, the real balance of power that separates the branches of the government has since been transferred entirely to the supreme leader.[31] The essence of the power of the president was stripped from the presidency and transferred to the supreme leader. All three branches of the government are now under the supreme leader's supervision.

Therefore, what is certain is that the powers given to the president in Article 113 and the tasks he swears to undertake in the oath of office (according to Article 121) cannot truly be undertaken without the authority he currently lacks. Thus, the Islamism that dominates the political structure is in direct conflict with any republicanism in the state, and consistently weakens it. The system of governance of the jurist (represented by the supreme leader as *vali-e faqih*) and the Islamism enshrined in the Constitution define themselves in ways that dominate the republicanism in a continuing process, the culmination of which was the events of the June 2009 election and its aftermath.

When the supreme leader ordered that the results of the election be accepted and demonstrations cease, Ayatollah Mesbah-Yazdi told a gathering of Basij militia in August 2009, from the moment that the supreme leader endorses the election of a president, it becomes necessary to support him, as the supreme leader is a placeholder for the Twelfth Imam and is viewed as his representative. Mesbah-Yazdi said, "When a president is endorsed by the *vali-e faqih*, obeying the president is like obeying God."[32]

Ayatollah Mesbah-Yazdi, whose voice was highly critical of the reform movement as well as the Green Movement, has actively promoted the supremacy of Islamism over the republicanism of the Islamic Republic. Once he even said that the vote of the people has no importance in legitimizing the ruler in the Islamic system; rather, he emphasized that the leadership belongs to the representative of the Twelfth Imam—the *vali-e faqih* or supreme leader—who is not voted for but discovered by the most expert clergy in the country (the Assembly of Experts or Majles-e Khobregan).[33]

This view was used and abused by Ahmadinejad for the exercise of power and in the hope of gaining independence from the supreme leader. Some analysts believe that Ahmadinejad, directly and indirectly, used the Twelfth Imam concept opportunistically against the supreme leader. In doing so, Ahmadinejad portrayed himself as a spiritual leader accepted by the Twelfth Imam. To this end, Iran expert Afsaneh Moqadam writes, "Ahmadinejad believes he enjoys the favor of a period of justice and truth, and Hidden Imam, as everyone knows, is closer to God than the Supreme Leader is."[34]

These attempts of Ahmadinejad, who as the president was a constitutional symbol of the Islamic Republic's republicanism, can be perceived as efforts to gain legitimacy over Islamism. These are only a few examples that demonstrate the ongoing duality of the Islamic Republic.

The supreme leader and other principalists who hold power used this very duality to weaken reformist president Khatami and his efforts to make reforms that would guarantee the promises of the third chapter of the Constitution focusing on the rights of the people. Similarly, after the Green Movement, the Islamic Republic used the Islamist aspect with an emphasis on the Twelfth Imam to attack civil society organizations, arrest civil society actors and activists, and eliminate the spaces that allow the growth of nongovernmental organizations (NGOs) working on women's rights, children's rights, and other pertinent issues.

Unconstitutional Political Behavior

Despite its undemocratic nature, Iran's Constitution does define specific limitations for each of the three branches of the political system—

namely, the executive branch, legislative branch, and judicial branch. However, the conservative executive branch under Ahmadinejad violated the Constitution so that he would be able to exert further power across the two other branches of government. In the following sections, I briefly analyze the means that conservative actors in the government pursued to project their influence beyond their constitutional bounds.

Majlis

After his falling out with the principalists who dominated the Majlis, Ahmadinejad ignored their criticisms and went on to mock the Majlis and its rights to oversight, impeachment, and questioning of government ministers. Eventually he went on to appoint Saeed Mortazavi as the head of Iran's Social Security Organization, despite serious objections from the principalists in the Majlis.[35] This incident led to an open confrontation between Ahmadinejad and Ali Larijani, the speaker of the Majlis and close confidant of Ayatollah Khamenei. In a bold move, Ahmadinejad played a recorded conversation that implicated the speaker's brother in financial corruption.[36]

Nevertheless, Ayatollah Khamenei did not take any definitive action against him at the time, and Ahmadinejad went on with his defiance. The Parliament did not take any measures to stop him either, despite threats to have him impeached and removed from office.[37] According to Deputy Majlis Speaker Mohammad Reza Bahonar, Ayatollah Khamenei wanted Ahmadinejad to finish his legal term, since "the cost of removing the president" would have been more than having him as president "for another year."[38]

In addition, the Majlis was more vocal in its opposition to many of Ahmadinejad's economic programs during his second term. Yet when Ahmadinejad delivered his incomplete annual budget to Parliament in February 2011, he provided no excuse for violating the Constitution and submitting the annual budget later than ever. Instead, he simply warned the parliamentarians to approve the budget as soon as possible and before the beginning of the Iranian New Year, March 21.[39]

Judiciary

In the aftermath of the Green Movement, government agencies—including the intelligence ministry—were able to exert influence on the judiciary and alter how trials proceeded for political prisoners. For example, the Revolutionary Guards and the Basij militia would round up people on unfounded charges of being threats to national security. Many of those who were arrested based on such charges were subsequently accused of "waging war against God" (*moharebeh*)—a crime punishable by the death penalty under the Islamic Penal Code. This involvement of the IRGC and Basij showed that the judiciary had lost what limited independence it once had.

The IRGC and Basij involvement in judicial decisions undermined due process and was used as a security tool by the government. Given the escalating economic hardships caused by Ahmadinejad's domestic economic policies and international sanctions against Iran's nuclear program, the government anticipated further protests and unrest. Therefore, it continued to encourage the unconstitutional involvement of the IRGC in the judicial process to ensure the shutdown of any indication of unrest.

The Challenges of the Opposition

The difficulties experienced by the opposition in Iran in creating a public platform and agenda challenge all experts who seek to predict democracy's future in Iran. Without an independent judicial system, opposition groups cannot state their goals and plans in public without censorship. They remain unable to publish their statements freely. This situation, understandably, worsened after the events of June 2009. President Rouhani has tried to alleviate the pressure and restriction forced on the press since he took office in 2013, but his efforts have not yet borne fruit. The prominent reformist daily *Bahar* was banned in October 2013, not long after Rouhani took office.[40] Later, in early 2014, *Aseman*, another daily paper close to the reformists, had a six-day run before it was shut down again.[41]

Beyond the press, the Islamic Republic forcefully silenced the opposition and its leading figures in the aftermath of the Green Movement. Even though many remain active clandestinely, their visibility is significantly less than before. Moreover, the opposition inside and outside of Iran is not organized. The opposition inside Iran that did not rally for any kind of regime change, but continued to promote reforms within the structure of the current system, had organized itself into two parties before the 2009 election: Mosharekat and Mojahedin-e Enghelab-e Islami. They were allowed to be only minimally active, and they were both banned in the aftermath of the 2009 election.[42]

While understanding the fractures and divisions of the opposition has always been complex due to the nature and diversity of Iran's political sphere, in the aftermath of the Green Movement this task has become even more challenging. For instance, it is difficult when drawing an image of the opposition at large to know the proportions represented by secular and democratic opposition groups. It is also hard to know to what extent the repressed segments of the opposition who were once participants in the revolution that brought about the Islamic Republic still believe in reforms within the constitutional opportunities and constraints of the Islamic Republic, or whether they privately discuss regime change options aimed at separation of religion and state. What remains clear, however, is that the increasing frustration and unhappiness of ordinary Iranian citizens who were confronted daily with social, economic, and political challenges led to Rouhani's election.

Chapter 3 of Iran's Constitution, titled "The Rights of the People," recognizes different civil liberties that presumably are guaranteed accordingly by the Islamic Republic of Iran.[43] The main articles of this chapter are as follows:

• Article 22: The dignity, life, property, rights, homes, and employment of persons are inviolable, save where laws allow.

• Article 23: Inquisition into people's opinions is not allowed, and no one can be prosecuted merely for holding an opinion.

• Article 24: The press and publications are free to publish materials unless they are harmful to Islamic principles or public rights. These are determined by law.

• Article 27: Gatherings and demonstrations, as long as arms are not carried, are allowed, provided that they do not harm the tenets of Islam and public interest and rights of others.

• Article 28: Every individual has the right to choose his/her own occupation, provided that the activity is not against Islam and public interest and the rights of others. The state is obliged to give all individuals equal opportunity to enter into various occupations in the light of societal needs for various types of employment.

• Article 30: The state is obliged to provide without charge every member of the nation with facilities to continue his/her education to the end of the intermediate level and expand higher education facilities to the extent necessitated by the needs of the country to achieve self-sufficiency.

• Article 32: No one can be arrested unless on the basis of the rules and regulations which are specified in law. Upon arrest, the accused should be informed of the charges against him/her in writing and understand them, and the case should be sent to competent legal authorities within twenty-four hours of the person being charged. The case must be heard by the court as soon as possible. Failure to comply with these provisions will result in punishment to be decided by law.

• Article 33: No person may be exiled from his/her place of residence or be prevented from residing in the location of his/her choice unless in cases specified by law.

• Article 34: Every individual has the right to have access to competent courts in order to have his/her rights defended, and all members of the nation have the right of access to such courts, and no one can be prevented from resorting to the court which the law has made available for redress.

• Article 37: Innocence is the principle and no one may legally be found guilty unless his/her guilt has been proven in a competent court.

Moreover, Iran is signatory to the International Covenant on Civil and Political Rights and the International Covenant on Economic and Social Rights, as well as the Convention for the Rights of the Minors.[44]

Those who find the Constitution limiting for constructive and democratic reforms point to the conditionality of Articles 22 to 37, which are restrictive in nature. Articles 24, 27, and 28 limit the rights envisioned in them to conform to Islamic values and not cause any "harm to Islam." Even in articles in which this condition is not explicitly stated, the basis for legality of all rights is "not being counter to Islamic values."

Despite the recognition of "the Rights of the People," many other laws found within the current legal structure of the Islamic Republic are contradictory to the principle of ensuring individual, social, political, and economic liberties. These laws are among the most important obstacles to political development and participation. The sole condition that any legislation must conform to Islamic values—particularly as these values are often not clearly defined in law and are subject to interpretation—puts this legislation at odds with human rights and democratic principles.

Definition of Islam Under the Islamic Republic's Laws

Lack of a clear definition of Islam in Iran's laws is an important obstacle to democratic legislation. It appears, therefore, that there is no hope for fundamental reform under the current conditions in Iran. For example, international human rights standards that guarantee a fair trial and the presence of an attorney throughout the trial procedure are not acceptable according to sharia; therefore, they cannot be incorporated into laws.

Religious-based discussions among jurists became much more prevalent after the legislation of more conservative laws. On the basis of such
discussions, some religious philosophers and jurists concluded that religion has become a tool in the hands of the oppressors, and that amend-
ing the laws is possible within the framework of Islam. One such philoso-
pher is Ayatollah Muhammad Mujtahid Shabistari. He believes that "not
only does the Islamic Criminal Code need to be reformed, it also has the
capacity to be reformed." He has requested fundamental restructuring
within Islamic law and has said that the punishments introduced by the
Prophet Muhammad were in fact a way of preventing the more violent
punishments prevalent at the time. According to Shabistari, Muslims now
can follow the path of the Prophet Muhammad by undertaking reform.[45]
Similar religious discussions are still ongoing. However, these Islamic
philosophers and jurists have not yet been able to influence the legislature
and the interpretation of Islam that affects the legislative process.

Islamic jurists and the religious experts in Iran whose interpretations of Islam are more democratic are continually issuing religious
opinions and interpretations that can be used as a base to inch closer to
the international standards of human rights and democracy. Such jurists
and experts have been sidelined by the governing body of Iran and hold
no significant legal authority, however. Some have even been imprisoned due to the sensitivity of the government to the religious opinions
they offered, namely Hojjatolislam Seyed Mohsen Saeidzadeh and Hojjatolislam Hassan Yousefi Eshkevari.[46]

Philosophers such as Shabistari and high-ranking ayatollahs such as
Grand Ayatollah Yousef Saanei have repeatedly expressed their opinion
regarding the opportunities Islam presents to coordinate the laws with
international human rights standards.[47] Their efforts and opinions have
been unsuccessful so far in influencing Iran's legislation.

The limited power of those clerics and philosophers who intend to
bring Islam closer to human rights is a major obstacle to passing laws
that are democratic and conform to international human rights principles. As long as the extremists play the major role in legislation and
sideline and isolate the moderates, what remains is a discriminatory
interpretation of Islam that results in nondemocratic legislation.

A Strategy of the Opposition: Civil Society

Given the complexity of and challenges posed by legal reforms, as well
as the existence of a closed society controlled by hard-line officials,

many perceive the creation of a robust civil society as the only way out of the current top-down repression in Iran. However, the principalists, the Revolutionary Guards, the judiciary, and other pertinent institutions of the Islamic Republic felt the threat of a growing civil society during the years of the reform era (1997–2005), when NGOs became visibly active in various development and rights issues.

Realizing the threat of a society in which the people begin to take control of the various aspects of their lives in organized and institutional structures, the principalists focused much of their attention on a crackdown on Iran's growing civil society. Even during Khatami's presidency, legal barriers and restrictions hindered NGOs. However, upon beginning to view NGOs as a threat, the principalists exerted more pressure than before in order to have these laws implemented, enabling their control of civil society. This crackdown further worsened in the aftermath of the Green Movement, as the regime was more alert to the fragility of its future.

Legal Barriers to NGOs

Barriers to Registration

The Interior Ministry has been given the task of registering NGOs according to Article 8 of the Parties, Societies, and Associations Act of 1981.[48] This assignment is at odds with the standard practice in many countries by which registration of these organizations is carried out simply through completing a form. Consequently, registration of an NGO in Iran follows the same procedure set for the registration of political entities, as foreseen by the 1981 act. In other words, the Article 10 Commission must approve all applications for NGO status.[49] The formalities involved in the registration of an NGO are extremely complicated; at present, even when an NGO is registered, doubts exist about its connections—or lack thereof—with the state. This situation is partly due to the fact that the process of registration through the commission means that the organization applying for NGO status is hardly likely to be approved unless it has explicit or implicit links with the authorities. Before the final decision is made, the names of those who have introduced themselves as the founders of an NGO are made available to the police. Police forces are responsible for carrying out thorough local and national background checks—including the founders' political beliefs and ideology. Therefore, founders who are critical of the state have very low chances of registering NGOs of their own.

These legal and political impediments are again rooted in the ambiguities of Article 26 of the Constitution, which makes the registration of all organizations dependent on their pursuit of "Islamic standards."[50] As a result, NGOs face the same restriction foreseen in the Parties Act, and indeed, many civil society entities, such as professional groups and minority associations, have found it difficult—even impossible—to receive registration. The fact that establishing these entities requires the endorsement of their founders' qualifications as described in Article 10 has made the interference of ideological criteria even more pronounced, rendering the establishment and growth of civil society that much more cumbersome.

Iran's Writers' Association (Kanoun-e Nevisandegan-e Iran) is one of the organizations that, despite its prominence, could never get registered. The association is an organization consisting of prominent secular Iranian authors of the old and new generations. The board and members of this organization have done all they can over the years in order to register their organization officially in the Islamic Republic of Iran but were unable to do so, even during the reform period. As the momentum for reform weakened, its members were forbidden to hold meetings and gather together. Despite all the risks and dangers, however, the members continue to illegally hold their meetings at their houses.[51]

Another example is the Defenders of Human Rights Center, founded by Shirin Ebadi, winner of the 2003 Nobel Peace Prize, which began its activity during the reform period. Even though this organization was founded by an internationally known personality, the authorities have never allowed the center to become a legally registered NGO.

Barriers to Operational Activities

Almost all those NGOs somehow connected with reformist elements have faced barriers erected by regime conservatives, who fill all of the key intelligence positions in today's Iran.

Those NGOs established during the reform movement with cultural missions have encountered many struggles and barriers to their work. For example, the Women's Cultural Center and other women's rights NGOs responsible for having established the One Million Signatures Campaign Demanding Changes to Discriminatory Laws, as well as the Stop Stoning Forever Campaign, or independent student NGOs such as Strengthening Solidarity, have been hindered from carrying out their democratic and human rights–oriented missions. Their members have been arrested, their websites filtered, their offices shut down, and their gatherings attacked by the regime. When their members have been arrested or detained, judges accuse them of acting against national security and cooperating with the West. When the bylaws and the missions of NGOs are not fully in tune with the ideologies of the Islamic Republic of Iran, it becomes extremely difficult for these organizations to operate there.

Despite barriers to operational activities, there has been success in the areas of women's health and family planning, as well as traditional charity work. Humanitarian work has a long tradition in Iran, and the Coordinating Committee of Women's NGOs was especially effective in helping victims of the Bam earthquake, for example.

Barriers to Speech and Advocacy

NGOs that want to voice their missions and work via websites and blogs encounter many security and intelligence barriers, some more repressive than others. The Office for Strengthening Unity (Daftar-e Tahkim-e Vahdat), an independent student organization, is threatened with suspension at any time for having voiced its objection to the imprisonment of the Amir Kabir students. Other examples are members of the Union for Bus Drivers and the Union for Teachers who have been arrested when defending their rights and asking for higher wages. In other cases, the regime oppresses NGO voices without resorting to detention and imprisonment. For instance, they sometimes halt the activities of NGOs simply by filtering their websites. As an example, the regime recently filtered all websites and blogs that included phrases such as "stoning," "women's rights," and "discrimination against women."

Barriers to International Contacts

Over the past couple of years, as conservatives have become stronger, barriers to international contacts have become serious threats to Iranian NGO activists. The more the West and Iran clash over nuclear weapons and ideological differences, the more dangerous it becomes for NGOs in Iran to be in touch with the West. In today's Iran, attending international conferences is a huge risk for NGO members, and upon their return home from such conferences, attendees are often questioned, detained, and accused of having cooperated with the West. Even as President Rouhani and his administration try to resolve the nuclear issue, conservatives emphasize the need for scrutiny toward NGOs.

Barriers to Resources

Two major problems that Iranian NGOs face are a lack of expertise and a lack of well-defined goals. Iran has many NGOs, but these organizations lack independence and financial resources, restricting their field of action still further. As mentioned earlier, it is very risky for NGOs to receive any kind of assistance from Western institutions. At the same time, people inside Iran are scared to cooperate—financially or otherwise—with NGOs. The number of NGO volunteers, too, is very low in Iran. They are afraid of the consequences of their contributions and try to stay away from such a challenging environment. As a result, those NGOs that have democratic or human rights–oriented missions constantly face the problem of limited resources—even if they are not shut down.

For example, the Association for the Employees of the Media in Iran, which was ultimately shut down in the years following the Green Movement, faced serious budget problems throughout its existence. This association was one of the remaining NGOs from the reform period and was resented by the conservative authorities for having assisted those journalists who either were detained or lost their jobs. Similarly, NGOs that work to control domestic violence against women also have to deal with a lack of financial and volunteer resources and are therefore not able to provide sufficient services.

Government Justifications

While the reformists planned to promote the development of civil society as their main focus, civil society itself became a battleground for reformists fighting conservative ideologues and revolutionaries. Conservatives see civil society as the main tool available to reformists for fighting their adversary and for obtaining and expanding their power. From the perspective of the conservatives, the rhetoric of expansion and development of civil society, and the promotion of new organizations, was an attempt by reformists to imitate the achievements of conservatives in creating revolutionary organizations such as the Basij.

Conservatives perceived the new civil society and its activists as the soldiers of their adversary. Taken to its extreme, a prominent view of civil society among conservatives is one that holds civil society as a modern strategy designed to overthrow the Islamic Republic. The conservatives who espouse this view continue to believe that as long as opposition groups do not have the military power necessary to overthrow the established order directly, opposition groups will instead seek to weaken the structure of the Islamist regime by means of their influence over civil society. The conservatives' fear of civil society has led to the oppression and isolation of civil society elements in today's Iran, a situation made worse as a result of the Green Movement, which was viewed as a realization of civil society's threat to regime stability.

The Rouhani administration, however, is looking for ways to promote civil society again. During his campaign, Rouhani criticized the domestic and foreign policy of the Ahmadinejad administration as confrontational and counter to Iran's national security interests. Along these lines, he promised to lift the police state that had followed the disputed 2009 election.[52]

Civil Society Strategies in Today's Iran

Given Iran's current political and social atmosphere, it is very difficult to find alternative ways of maintaining and strengthening civil society. The most important NGOs in the social movement of the past few years in Iran—such as independent students', women's, workers', and teachers' NGOs—are all accused by Iranian intelligence services to be working directly with the imperial West to sow the seeds of a velvet revolution.

Even if members of these NGOs escape, they are considered threats to the Islamic Republic of Iran, and their activities—including their private and social lives—are often restricted by the regime. The members live in fear, which often causes them to gradually lose their self-confidence as individuals and professionals. As long as the Iranian political system remains in such a state of tension, and as long as the dispute over the nuclear program remains a reason for relations with the United States to be a question of national security, there is not much hope that Iran's government will allow NGOs the freedom to act.

In my opinion, given Iran's political circumstances, it would be better to strengthen those NGOs that have as their mission providing social and health services. Since there is no possibility of strengthening cultural and human rights organizations, we should help service-oriented NGOs in achieving their missions, which will empower the Iranian people to be more active and engaged members of society. Because Iran has been suffering in recent years from numerous economic problems, such as rampant inflation, it is important to help NGOs that tackle the effects of economic problems, such as those NGOs that support street children, the poor, addicts, prisoners, and single mothers, as well as NGOs that provide education, economic, and health services to those in need. Support for environmental NGOs will also improve the quality of life for Iran's people. These organizations will allow the people of Iran to become more active and resourceful. Identifying and strategically supporting such NGOs should be a priority.

Given that Iranian civil society is at a very vulnerable and critical stage, having been under attack for years, we are responsible for doing our best in order to help the remainder of the NGOs survive and succeed in achieving their missions. Having mentioned all of these problems and obstacles, I must conclude by saying that the phenomenon of the Internet is an important force that can strengthen civil society in Iran. The Internet has opened a new window of opportunity for civil society activists to express their views and to reach out to the outside world. We in the West must pay attention to these voices before it is too late.

Conclusion

The Islamic Republic may have successfully silenced the Green Movement. However, the fact that this movement was unprecedented, energetic, and a mirror reflecting people's grievances against and demands of the regime cannot be erased from Iran's postrevolutionary history. The movement was a stage for Iranians who are no longer willing to waive their freedom and right to democracy. Hassan Rouhani's victory in the 2013 presidential election proved that people are still hoping to gain civil freedoms through democratic means. Therefore, despite their mistrust of the system of the Islamic Republic, the people once again chose the ballot box.

Moreover, the growth of civil society, or even its survival in a limited form, has become more difficult in today's repressive environment. Fearing for their political future in light of the demonstration of people power in the aftermath of the 2009 election, the conservatives have shown an uncompromising determination to eliminate any sign of an independent civil society.

Despite this pessimistic outlook and the limitations the opposition faces, the Green Movement has had fundamentally important results, one of which is the deepened internal divisions within the regime itself. To gain the upper hand in the internal power struggle, conservative factions have been airing each other's dirty economic and political linen in public. Internal distrust has rendered the foundations of the regime less secure, leading to an increase in the self-confidence of the people in challenging the government.

Meanwhile, the existence of the Internet and widespread social networking has also helped to create unofficial and virtual ways of organizing, communicating, and exchanging opinions. The Internet has also facilitated dialogue between the opposition in Iran and abroad. For instance, the letters of political prisoners not only make it outside the prison but are also widely shared across the globe among Iranians connected in cyberspace. These letters are emotional in nature and include strong political statements emphasizing human rights principles and the need to create truth and reconciliation commissions to investigate the regime's violations.

As such, even though the Islamic Republic is committed to the creation of a strong censorship regime in the cyberworld, it has not been able to stop the spread of the Internet among various socioeconomic classes. In recent months, President Rouhani has vowed to unblock social media outlets such as Facebook and Twitter. Whether he will be able to fulfill this promise remains to be seen. However, despite all restrictions, people of Iran have learned how to bypass the barriers erected by Internet filtering.

Ultimately, Hassan Rouhani's victory in the recent presidential election further proves that the Green Movement's demands are still relevant today. Whether Rouhani can fulfill his campaign promises of resolving the nuclear crisis and creating a more moderate set of domestic policies for Iran's people, however, remains to be seen.

Notes

1. McElroy, "Ayatollah Ali Khamenei Backs Mahmoud Ahmadinejad in Address at Friday Prayers."
2. Princeton University, "1997 Presidential Election."
3. Ehteshami and Molavi, *Iran and the International System*, p. 196.
4. Ibid.
5. Ibid.
6. IFES, "IFES Election Guide—Country Profile: Iran."
7. "Victory for a Religious Hardliner in Iran," *The Economist*.
8. Princeton University, "1997 Presidential Election."
9. Hashemi and Postel, *The People Reloaded,* p. 4.
10. Ibid.
11. Iran Chamber Society, "Iran Chamber Society."
12. "Iran: Violent Crackdown on Protesters Widens," Human Rights Watch.
13. Ibid.
14. Iran Chamber Society, "Iran Chamber Society."
15. Worth, "Iran Denies Allegations That Protesters Were Raped in Prison."
16. Tran, "Protesters Raped in Tehran Jail, Politician Claims."
17. Jeffery, "Iran Election Protests."
18. Fathi, "Iran's Top Leader Dashes Hopes for a Compromise."
19. "Iran's Show Trials," *Time*.
20. Iranian Constitution, Art. 168: "Political and press offenses will be tried openly and in the presence of a jury, in courts of justice. The manner of the selection of the jury, its powers, and the definition of political offenses will be determined by law in accordance with the Islamic criteria." Iran Chamber Society, "Iran Chamber Society."

21. Burke and Kamali Dehghan, "Mass Trial for Iran Protest Leaders."
22. Human Rights Watch, *Human Rights Watch World Report, 2010,* p. 499.
23. Amnesty International, "Annual Report 2012."
24. Baji, "Iran."
25. Mokri, "Basij Was Not Intended to Be in Line with the Satan."
26. Ibid.
27. Ibid.
28. Ibid.
29. Iran Chamber Society, "Iran Chamber Society."
30. Horowitz, "A Detailed Analysis of Iran's Constitution."
31. Fukuyama, "Iran, Islam and the Rule of Law."
32. Hafezi, "Iran Cleric Says Obeying Ahmadinejad Like Obeying God."
33. Mesbah-Yazdi, *Porsesh-ha va Pasokh-ha*, p, 56.
34. Moqadam, *Death to the Dictator!* p. 10.
35. "Iran Pulse—Iranian Parliamentary Corruption Scandal Implicates Notorious Figure," *Al-Monitor.*
36. Torbati, "Ahmadinejad Accuses Iran Speaker's Family of Corruption."
37. Kamali Dehghan, "Mahmoud Ahmadinejad Faces Impeachment Threat."
38. Baji, "Iran."
39. Pitchford, "Iran Parliament Passes 2011–12 Budget."
40. "Iran's Closure of Reformist Newspaper Raises Concerns About Press Freedom," *The Guardian.*
41. "A Leap Forward for Iranian Journalism Nipped in the Bud," *The Guardian.*
42. Muskus, "Iran Bans Reform Party."
43. Iran Chamber Society, "Iran Chamber Society."
44. United Nations, "United Nations Treaty Collection."
45. Shabistari, *Naqdī Bar Qirā'at-i Rasmī Az Dīn.*
46. Saeidzadeh, "About Seyed Mohsen Saeidzadeh"; Eshkevari, Yousefi eshkevari.com.
47. Website of the Office of Grand Ayatullah Saanei, www.saanei.org/index .php?lang=en, accessed March 10, 2014.
48. Pars Times, "Parties Law and Its Relevant Executive Regulations."
49. Ibid.
50. Ibid.
51. Esfandiari, "Iran's Writers Association Criticizes State Pressure."
52. "Iran Pulse—Rouhani's Biopic Surprises Iranian Voters," *Al-Monitor.*

4

Examining
Iran's Legal Structure

Fatemeh Haghighatjoo

A yatollah Khomeini, the founding leader of the Islamic Republic of
Iran (IRI), and other Islamists wanted to establish an Islamic society with rules based on sharia laws while maintaining elements of
modernity. The Constitution of the IRI reflects that very idea. As the
name suggests, the Islamic Republic of Iran is based upon the twin principles of republicanism and Islamism. The Constitution of the Islamic
Republic of Iran speaks to the relationship between these two principles
as follows:

> The Constitution of the Islamic Republic of Iran is the expression of
> the cultural, social, political, and economic institutions of Iranian soci-
> ety on the basis of Islamic values and guidelines, which is the reflec-
> tion of the deepest desires of the Islamic nation *(ummat)*. What distin-
> guishes this revolution from other movements in the history of Iran is
> its clerical and Islamic nature. The Islamic government is officially
> sanctioned on the basis of the Rule of the Jurist *(Velayat-e Faqih)* as
> the model for governance.[1]

Article 6 of the Constitution, which discusses the republican nature
of the government, states, "The Islamic Republic of Iran has to be gov-
erned according to the general beliefs and decisions of the populace as
expressed through voting: through the election of the President, Members of Parliament, and the councils and their monitors, or through referenda on topics which will be mentioned in other parts of this document."

The combination of republicanism and Islamism as the two pillars of
the Constitution was met with popular support at first, but the conflict
between the two ideas created such immense problems in its execution
that now, in the third decade of the Islamic Revolution, criticism of the
merger between religion and politics is heard all the way up to the high-

91

est religious leaders of the country. Today, the taboos on open discussion of the separation of religion and state have been broken, although the regime itself still does not tolerate any open discussion of the subject. Many have tried to show that Islam has no internal opposition to democracy, and the problems with merging the two ideas arise out of the narrow interpretation of Islam and the autocratic tendencies of the religious rulers. Nevertheless, however we look at the issue of democracy and Islam (as the official religion of Iran), we see that there is no choice but the separation of religion from the state. Islam can be one of the official religions of a country, but it cannot in any way be the precondition for running a government or negating democratic principles.

Having the experience of serving one term as a member of the Sixth Majlis (2000–2004), I attempt here to explain the workings of the regime as laid out in the Constitution; some of its shortcomings; and the necessity, possibility, and preconditions for constitutional and political reform.

The Legal Structure of the Islamic Republic of Iran

As the Constitution is established on the twin principles of republicanism and Islamism, the Constitution grants the presidency and the Parliament a republican structure, meaning that their positions are filled directly by the people through elections. Other state institutions, such as the supreme leadership and the Guardian Council of the Constitution, are based on Islamic principles. The first draft of the Islamic Republic's Constitution came out without any reference to the concept a *velayat-e faqih* (guardianship of the supreme jurist), and Ayatollah Khomeini approved it for a referendum. Sadly, however, Mehdi Bazarghan, the first postmonarchical prime minister, persisted with the formation of the constitutional assembly, which added the position of the supreme jurist and its associates and placed them at the top of the political structure. After that, the current Constitution was approved via a popular referendum in November 1979. Based on the current Constitution, all the real power rests with the supreme leader and his associates. Here I explain how the leader is chosen and what his responsibilities are, starting with the role of the Assembly of Experts.

The Assembly of Experts

The Assembly of Experts was established to guard the republican nature of the system and to prevent any potential for autocracy. The Constitution has empowered the assembly to "elect the leader," "impeach the leader," and in accordance with Article 111, "monitor the actions of the leader." However, since the elections of the Assembly of Experts are overseen by the Guardian Council, an institution directly or indirectly chosen by the supreme leader, it is clear that in reality the assembly submits to the will of the existing leader. During Ali Khamenei's occupancy of the supreme leadership, the Guardian Council has barred many otherwise qualified candidates since they are potential critics of the supreme leader.

Election of the leader. Article 107 explains the election process and grants the power to elect the supreme leader to the Assembly of Experts. According to this article,

> The experts will review and consult among themselves concerning all the religious men possessing the qualifications specified in Articles 5 and 109. In the event they find one of them better versed in Islamic regulations or in political and social issues, or possessing general popularity or special prominence for any of the qualifications mentioned in Article 109, they shall elect him as the Leader. Otherwise, in the absence of such superiority, they shall elect and declare one of them as the Leader. The Leader thus elected by the Assembly of Experts shall assume all the powers of the religious leader and all the responsibilities arising therefrom.

The conditions for eligibility are explained in Article 109:

> The following are the essential qualifications and conditions for the leader:
> a. Scholarship, as required for performing the functions of religious leader in different fields.
> b. Justice and piety, as required for the leadership of the Islamic *ummah*.
> c. Appropriate political and social perspicacity, prudence, courage, administrative facilities, and adequate capability for leadership.
> In case of a multiplicity of persons fulfilling the above qualifications and conditions, the person possessing the better jurisprudential and political perspicacity will be given preference.

Furthermore, according to Article 5, "During the occultation of the *Wali al-'Asr* (may God hasten his reappearance), the leadership of the *ummah* devolves upon the just and pious person, who is fully aware of the circumstances of his age, courageous, resourceful, and possessed of administrative ability, and who will assume the responsibilities of this office in accordance with Article 107."

Of all the responsibilities of the Assembly of Experts, the only one that has been exercised is the selection of the supreme leader, compelled by the death of Ayatollah Khomeini in 1989.

Impeachment of the leader. According to Article 111 of the Constitution, "When the Leader becomes unable to fulfill his duties or no longer fulfills all five prerequisites for leadership as laid out in Articles 5 and 109, or it is discovered that he had never fulfilled all five prerequisites, he will be removed from his position. Identifying this matter is the responsibility of the Experts as stipulated in Article 108."

According to the Constitution, the Assembly of Experts has supervisory competence over the leader and can decide to impeach him when he has neglected his responsibilities. If the Assembly of Experts does not take on this duty of supervision, then they have relinquished their constitutional power to impeach the leader. Under these conditions, not only are the original intentions of the law neglected, but the annual convention of the assembly has also become superfluous. Perhaps it was such behavior by the Assembly of Experts that led Khatami to assert that "the proceedings of the Assembly of Experts are not in the spirit of the Constitution."[2]

Supervision over the leadership. This responsibility is the most important of the assembly's duties, yet it is rarely carried out to its full extent. The following are possible reasons for undermining the assembly's responsibility:

• *Lack of conviction.* The overriding belief in the Assembly of Experts is that the position of the leader is the heir of the Twelfth Imam during his occultation, meaning that he is the representative of God on earth and the guardian of society. Questioning his authority is therefore outside the powers of the Assembly of Experts. Ayatollah Ali Meshkini, former president of the assembly, best described this situation when he asserted that "the Experts are answerable to God and the Leader."[3]

• *The process of selection for membership in the Assembly of Experts is such that the members are preselected supporters of the supreme leader.* According to Article 99 of the Constitution, supervision of the election of the Assembly of Experts is the responsibility of the Guardian Council. This point entails a conflict of interest, as the supervision of the group that is to oversee the responsibilities of the leader is in turn in the hands of a group that the leader selects. Therefore, those who are not in the orbit of the leader will not be able to pass through this filter; the generally weak actions of the Assembly of Experts prove this point. In past elections, the number of candidates running for the Assembly of Experts was the same number as the available seats, meaning that there was no real competition or campaign for the seats in the assembly.

• *According to the current procedure, each member of the Assembly of Experts was selected to be the representative of the leader in various revolutionary and official institutions, as well as in the universities.* How is it possible for those who are chosen to represent an official to objectively supervise the same official's actions? In this situation, the members of the Assembly of Experts are answerable to the leader, instead of the other way around. Accordingly, after the annual meeting of the Assembly of Experts, the members are called to present their yearly achievements to the supreme leader and to be guided by his advice.

Leadership

Article 5 of the Constitution states, "During the occultation of the *Wali al-'Asr* (may God hasten his reappearance), the leadership of the *ummah* devolves upon the just and pious person, who is fully aware of the circumstances of his age, courageous, resourceful, and possessed of administrative ability, and who will assume the responsibilities of this office in accordance with Article 107."

There are various juridical (*fiqh*) views of the *velayat-e faqih*. These opinions fall into a general pro and con divide, the analysis of which is beyond the scope of this chapter. However, since the Islamic Republic of Iran is based upon the notion of *velayat-e faqih*, I analyze here the formulation as laid out by the founder of the Islamic Republic of Iran, Ayatollah Khomeini. He believed that governing and rulership in the time of occultation belongs only to the Jurists (*faqih*s or *foqaha*). He claimed that,

> All matters dealing with governance and politics that were established for the Prophet and his Descendants (Peace Be Upon Them) are also relevant for the just *faqihs,* and it is reasonable not to distinguish between them. The *faqihs* act no differently from the Prophet and his Descendants (PBUT), and any place of importance for the needs of the Muslims, they will pass legislation of their choice that everyone must follow.
>
> The fallacy that the Prophet had a greater prerogative in governing than did Imam Ali or that Imam Ali had greater prerogatives than do the *faqihs* is void and wrong. God has given the same privileges to the *faqih*-led government in setting up armies, appointing governors, collecting taxes, and spending them in the interest of the Muslim community, as he did to the Prophet and the Righteous Imams.[4]

Thus, the leader's governing of the community (*velayat-e faqih* and *emamat-e ommat*) in effect means the ruling and oversight over all aspects of governance (executive, legislative, and judicial). According to Article 107 of the Constitution, the supreme leader chosen by the experts has all the responsibilities of the *velayat-e faqih*. There is no mechanism for the supreme leader to be held accountable for his actions. Although the Assembly of Experts is in charge of monitoring the continued qualifications of the leader, in reality it has never been able to carry out this responsibility. Khomeini said the following about the Assembly: "The Council of the founders of the government should be comprised of pious *mojtaheds* who are versed in God's laws and who are just and devoid of self-interest and worldly ambitions and whose sole desire is to carry out God's laws. They should choose a just ruler who will not abrogate God's laws."[5]

This statement can be compared to the words of Rumi, the well-known Persian poet: "I yearn for the one who will never be found."[6] It is doubtful that the number of *mojtaheds* who fit this description is more than a handful, for if they did exist, we would have heard their voices opposing the many injustices of the Islamic Republic by now. In our society today, where human rights are constantly violated, injustice reigns, and people are oppressed under the regime and their cries are heard constantly, we do not hear the voices of those *mojtaheds* voicing their discontent and asking the leader why the institutions under his control are so unjust. The only member of the Assembly of Experts who has criticized the leader is Ayatollah Seyed Ali Mohammad Dastgheyb, who has been threatened repeatedly for his criticism.

The 1979 Constitution used the terms *velayat-e faqih* and *emamat-e ommat*. However, after the enactment of the Constitution, when the regime became bogged down in bickering between its various institutions, Ayatollah Khomeini was forced to take steps to increase the authority of the supreme leader over legal and jurisprudential issues. Khomeini had clear opinions on the "absolute rule of the Jurist," and he believed that "governance is a part of the absolute rule of the Prophet of God and this is the primary pillar of Islam with priority over prayer, fasting, and *hajj*."[7] The same fatwa (an opinion given by an Islamic scholar in response to a question posed by a believer) goes on to give to the government the right to enter into people's private lives and destroy mosques in order to defend the government's own interests. Conflict between the three branches of government resulted in the institutionalization of the Absolute Rule of the Jurist during the 1988 constitutional revision. This idea has been overshadowing the country's political system ever since.

The concept of the Absolute Rule of the Jurist is now one of the sources of disagreement among the current followers of *velayat-e faqih*. Although the Constitution has defined the limits of the supreme leader's powers, some within the Guardian Council believe that Article 110 describes merely the minimum extent of his powers. During the Sixth Majlis, this question became a national debate, as the members of the Majlis tried to argue that Article 110 describes the totality and the maximum limits of the supreme leader, whereas the Guardian Council held the belief that the article is describing only a basic outline of the leader's powers. This belief became a litmus test and a basis of disqualification for the candidates running for the Seventh Majlis in 2004.

Article 110 is written as follows:

The following are the duties and powers of the leadership:

1. Delineation of the general policies of the Islamic Republic of Iran after consultation with the nation's Expediency Council.

2. Supervision of the proper execution of the general policies of the system.

3. Issuing decrees for national referenda.

4. Assuming supreme command of the armed forces.

5. Declaration of war and peace, and the mobilization of the armed forces.

6. Appointment, dismissal, and acceptance of resignation of:
   a. The *fuqaha'* (jurists) on the Guardian Council.
   b. The supreme judicial authority of the country.
   c. The head of the radio and television network of the Islamic Republic of Iran.
   d. The chief of the joint staff.
   e. The chief commander of the Islamic Revolution Guards Corps.
   f. The supreme commanders of the armed forces.

7. Resolving differences between the three wings of the armed forces and regulation of their relations.

8. Resolving the problems that cannot be solved by conventional methods through the Nation's Expediency Council.

9. Signing the decree formalizing the election of the president of the republic by the people. The suitability of candidates for the presidency of the republic, with respect to the qualifications specified in the Constitution, must be confirmed before elections take place by the Guardian Council, and, in the case of the first term [of the presidency], by the leadership.

10. Dismissal of the president of the republic, with due regard for the interests of the country, after the Supreme Court holds him guilty of the violation of his Constitutional duties, or after a vote of the Islamic Consultative Assembly testifying to his incompetence on the basis of Article 89 of the Constitution.

11. Pardoning or reducing the sentences of convicts, within the framework of Islamic criteria, on a recommendation [to that effect] from the head of judicial power. The leader may delegate part of his duties and powers to another person.

Three Branches of Power

According to the Constitution, the legislative, executive, and judicial powers are separate. Nevertheless, according to Article 57, the three powers are under the absolute supervision of the leader, which creates a contradiction in the traditional definition of the separation of powers. In reality, the definition of the supreme leader's power is such that his powers are not checked and balanced by any of the traditional institutions of power. In this way, the Islamic Republic of Iran's division of power remains seemingly incompatible with modern democracies.

The legislative branch. Although the Constitution equates the legislative branch with the Majlis, according to Article 93, "The Majlis does not have legal legitimacy without the Guardian Council." Furthermore, Ayatollah Khomeini formed an Expediency Council (EC) in order to arbitrate between the Majlis and the Guardian Council, who were in constant disagreement over the compatibility of bills with Islamic criteria, due to the lack of consistent interpretations of Islamic rules. In the 1989 constitutional amendment, the EC became an established institution of the government. Although the EC has other responsibilities, including giving advice to the supreme leader, its main duty is to make decisions about disputed bills. Thus, from my perspective, the legislative branch includes three institutions, as illustrated in Figure 4.1.

Figure 4.1   The Institutions Participating in the Legislative Process

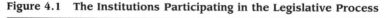

The Islamic Consultative Assembly (the Majlis). According to the Constitution, the Islamic Consultative Assembly is responsible for legislating laws that are not opposed to Islam and its principles. The Majlis also has the responsibility of monitoring all governmental agencies. In Article 20, the Constitution outlines the responsibilities of the Majlis as follows: ratifying international treaties, contracts, and agreements; minor reforms to national borders; establishing martial law; giving and receiving loans and no-interest grants; hiring foreign specialists; sharing and protecting national treasures; confirming the Cabinet; research, investigation, and public hearings; impeachment; and tending to people's demands and complaints.

The Guardian Council. The Guardian Council comprises six *faqih*s chosen by the supreme leader and six legal experts nominated by the head of the Judiciary and confirmed by the Majlis. The Constitution designates the Guardian Council as the institution that completes the legislature. Without the Guardian Council, legislation is incomplete and the legislature is without legitimacy. This council has three important responsibilities: (1) determining compatibility of the legislation passed by the Majlis with Islamic tenets and the Constitution; (2) interpreting the Constitution; and (3) supervising all elections except the city and village councils.

1. *Determining compatibility of legislation with Islamic principles and the Constitution.* The writers of the Constitution, in order to defend against the legislative power's deviation from Islamic tenets and the Constitution, established the Guardian Council. Even Iran's first constitution (1906) declared that laws should not be contrary to Islamic principles. After the Islamic Revolution, an institution was formed to guard against this. However, the past three decades have shown that many interpretations of Islamic tenets exist with regard to everyday issues, and sometimes there is no consensus among *foqaha* because each *faqih* endeavors on his own to extract legal rules from the sources of Islam. Sometimes, from a traditional perspective, the *foqaha* of the Guardian Council recognize bills that are contrary to Islamic principles. However, what the Sixth Majlis experienced was a political rejection of bills by summarily labeling them as un-Islamic. This was how, at the height of the conflict between the Majlis and the Guardian Council, the council hindered the effectiveness of the Majlis by blocking most reformist bills.

2. *Interpreting the Constitution.* According to Article 98, "The Interpretation of the Constitution is by a three-quarters vote of the Guardian Council."

3. *Supervising elections.* According to Article 99, "The Guardian Council monitors the elections of the Assembly of Experts, the presidency, Majlis, and all referenda."

The judicial branch. The judiciary is responsible for fulfilling the aspirations of the population and making security and freedom possible, two basic expectations of any society. *Security* can be defined as a guarantee of the life, property, dignity, and material rights of the people. *Freedom* can be defined as individuals' ability to achieve their potential and fulfill their desires within accepted social limits. Seyyed Mohammad Hashemi, pointing to Articles 61 and 156 of the Constitution, believes, "The judicial branch has two goals. First, it seeks to guarantee the realization of legal rights in terms of society's expectation for protection from attacks on their lives, property, dignity, and work; to take seriously the ban on spying, censorship, discrimination based on personal beliefs, and the ban on illegal arrest and punishment, all of which are continuously mentioned in the Constitution."[8] He identifies the second responsibility of the judiciary as guaranteeing the basic freedoms of expression and thought, peaceful assembly, and commerce. He believes that "according to the Constitution, no one can take away these basic rights, even though other laws and the judiciary can deal legally with whomever transgresses these rights."[9] Unfortunately, the judiciary's behavior is such that it has become the primary transgressor of these rights and is the primary threat to individuals and activists in civil society.

Executive branch. In the 1989 constitutional reform, the position of the prime minister was eliminated, and the president became responsible for choosing the cabinet and running the government. However, the president is limited in his powers.

Military and security forces. According to Article 110 of the Constitution, the military and security forces act under the commander-in-chief (supreme leader). The jurisdiction of these forces, under the control of the supreme leader, in effect creates an armed military wing in charge of repression and terrorizing the population. Although contrary to the direct instructions of the founder of the Islamic Republic, the military forces, namely the Islamic Revolutionary Guard Corps (IRGC, Sepah-e Pasdaran-e Enqelab-e Eslami), have direct influence on the political development of the country's legislative, executive, and judicial affairs. The armed forces are not only in control of the three branches of government; they also control the central pulse of the country's economic life with full immunity from the supreme leader. With their entrance into economic affairs, the private sector has been greatly weakened, while the IRGC has become the largest economic bureaucracy in the nation, with little supervision over its actions and performances.

Problems and Limitations of the Constitution

The Constitution is facing gridlocks that make it unable to guarantee freedom, independence, and social welfare, and to effectively fight injustice. It is outside my focus in this chapter to look at individual articles of the Constitution. What follows is a general critical outline.

Limitations of Republicanism in the Constitution

The Constitution has defined republicanism in sixty-six articles. The majority of these articles deal more with the Islamic nature of the regime than republicanism, and in the process limit the republicanism of the state and allow for a wide interpretation of the nature of the republic. In effect, republicanism is overshadowed by the Islamic aspect of the regime. Article 4 states, "All civil, penal, financial, economic, administrative, cultural, military, political, and other laws and regulations must be based on Islamic criteria. This principle applies absolutely and generally to all articles of the Constitution as well as to all other laws and regulations, and the wise persons of the Guardian Council are judges in this matter." Article 72 states, "The Majlis cannot enact any laws contrary to the official religion of the country or the Constitution. It is the duty of the Guardian Council to ensure this." Article 170 states, "Judges of courts are obliged to refrain from executing statutes and regulations of the government that are in conflict with the laws or the norms of Islam, or lie outside the competence of the executive power. Everyone has the right to demand the annulment of any such regulation from the Court of Administrative Justice."

Some of the principles that describe republicanism and Islamism jointly—such as Articles 3, 20, 21, 24, 26, 27, and 28—are written to allow the regulation of freedom in the name of Islam. For instance, Article 24 states, "Publications and the media are free to publish except for subjects that are contrary to Islamic tenets or public values." Article 26 makes the activities of political parties and groups conditional on their adherence to Islamic values. According to this principle, "Political parties, labor organizations, and guilds, as well as Islamic organizations or those of approved religious minorities are free to function as long as they do not abrogate the principles of independence, freedom, national unity, Islamic tenets, and the principles of the Islamic Republic." These two articles are expressions of the limitations on the press, political parties, and freedom of expression in general. The invocation of Islam has given governmental institutions the right to limit political freedoms.

If republicanism means the right of the people to decide their own future, then individuals within a society must be able to enjoy this right, regardless of ethnicity, religion, or faith. According to Article 13, Iranians from the Zoroastrian, Jewish, and Christian religions are free to participate in their own ceremonies and to conduct their personal lives according to their faith. Also, according to Article 12, other Islamic schools, such as Hanafi, Shafi'i, Maliki, Hanbali, and Zaidi, are respected. However, this law does not guarantee minority rights in any fundamental way, and in fact denies minorities their basic rights. For instance, the Constitution says that the president must be from the dominant and official sect of Shii Islam.[10] In addition, the posts of supreme leader, members in the Guardian Council, and head of the Judiciary must also be drawn from the ranks of the Shii *faqihs*, and even lower-level positions are in effect denied to religious minorities.

Of the religious minorities, the Zoroastrians, Jews, and Christians have a total of only five members in the Parliament, and they are actually denied the chairmanship of the various committees. Although these limitations are not codified, they are followed across the board. For example, in the Sixth Majlis, the Participation Front, although enjoying a majority, was not able to introduce a Sunni Kurd as a member of the presiding board of the Parliament due to clerical pressures.

Elections

According to Article 6 of the Constitution, direct popular elections are used to decide the position of president, members of the Assembly of Experts, Majlis representatives, and the local town and village councils. In Article 99, the oversight of these elections, with the exception of the town and village councils, lies with the Guardian Council; however, the council misuses its power in order to ban their rivals. In addition to meeting the basic qualifications in order to stand as a candidate, a person must actively prove his moral, political, and ideological credentials to the council before he can run for election.

A lack of transparency in the oversight of elections is one of the major problems affecting implementation of the Constitution. The drafters of the Constitution presumed that since the executive branch in charge of conducting elections is susceptible to corruption, the oversight should be given to an institution that is incorruptible. Since the supreme leader appoints the *foqaha* in the Guardian Council, this institution was presumed incorruptible and thereby given the responsibility. Nevertheless, because the Guardian Council also has authority to interpret the letter of the Constitution, it has arrogated itself an authority to oversee elections based on a broad interpretation of Article 99. The original intent of the provision was to ensure fair elections and assessment of the candidates' qualifications. Nevertheless, according to the Guardian Council's interpretation of Article 99, the members of the council have the right, not only to assess the candidates, but to formulate standards that they must fulfill in order to qualify for the position.

The Guardian Council performs the duty of election supervision by carrying out the following duties:

1. After the election administrative boards assess the candidates' qualifications, the list of candidates is referred to the Guardian Council's supervising boards. The Guardian Council, after evaluating the candidates, announces its own assessment of the individual candidates and their qualifications to stand for elections. In this phase, the qualifications are not just the general terms of the candidates' experience, age, or their ideological values, such as their dedication to Islam; candidates may be disqualified for personal and political opinions as well as for their party affiliations. These qualifications have created situations from time to time in which the supreme leader has had to intervene as a higher authority in order to allow for the requalification of certain candidates to ease tension. Thus, a major criticism of elections in Iran is that they involve an election by the state before an election by the electorate. In this process, the possibility of conducting free and fair elections is left open to question because of the intervention of the Guardian Council for personal and political reasons.

2. After the announcement of the qualified candidates, the campaigns begin, but the candidate list is still not definitive; the possibility of candidate disqualification continues—a situation that happened the night before the elections of the Sixth Majlis, when the Guardian Council disqualified a number of candidates.

3. The next duty of the Guardian Council is oversight on the day of elections, when the council appoints representatives to each ballot. Of all the steps, this phase sees the greatest amount of fraud. The Guardian Council naturally appoints monitors with similar political tendencies to its own, people who stuff the ballot boxes for their candidates or alter the results during the ballot count. In the 2005 presidential election,

when ballot monitors informed the Ministry of Interior that they had lost control of the Guardian Council representatives who were stuffing ballots in a particular polling station, the special representative of the Minister of the Interior (the political deputy of the ministry) personally arrived at the poll, only to be arrested by the Guardian Council representatives and taken in custody. It is not clear what will happen during elections under the present political conditions, in which the Minister of the Interior, the election managers, and the Guardian Council are from the same political board. Perhaps this political alignment will prevent major conflict between the institutions.

4. In the final phase of the elections, after the announcement of the results, the Guardian Council has the responsibility of declaring the elections free and fair. The Guardian Council gauges this by receiving reports from its representatives at the polls and is not accountable to any other institution. In close elections, the Guardian Council can affect the outcome of elections by disqualifying a few polls, thus changing the results in favor of its own political group. An example of this corruption occurred in the election for the Sixth Majlis in 2000. Although the strength of the reformist tendency in the elections stopped any fundamental change in the election results, the Guardian Council was able to intervene to stop a number of candidates from taking their rightful place as winners of the elections. In Tehran alone, the Guardian Council voided 700,000 votes in order to seat Haddad Adel instead of Alireza Rajai of the Nationalist-Religious (reformist) party.

Unfulfilled and Abrogated Principles of the Constitution

Iran's Constitution does include some progressive provisions, but they have yet to be realized or are distorted by the interpretation of the Guardian Council. Examples of progressive thought include Section 6 of Article 3, which aims to destroy injustice, autocracy, or tyranny. Section 7 is dedicated to securing political and social freedoms. Section 8 addresses people's right to participate in defining their own political, economic, social, and cultural future. Section 14 aims at securing the inalienable rights of individuals—men and women—with equal representation and worth before the law in an unbiased judicial process. The most important progressive provision is enacted in Article 9, which states, "Freedom, independence, unity, and territorial integrity are indivisible, and it is the role of the state and individual citizens to protect and guarantee them. No individual, group, or official has the right to harm the political, cultural, economic, and military independence or territorial integrity of the nation in the name of freedom, and no official has the right to harm the established freedoms in the name of independence and territorial integrity."

However, in opposition to such a straightforward description of freedom, no mention is made of the processes by which freedom will be protected from other hostile laws or amendments. Even in the reformist period of the Sixth Majlis, when the Parliament was debating the reform of laws that were contrary to this basic notion of freedom, the supreme leader and the Guardian Council formed an open opposition to the parliamentary deliberations. Examples of this can be seen in their opposition to reforms in the laws related to the media, the jury, prisoner treatment, and so on.

In reality, under the current tyranny, the rights of the people, which are stated in Section 3 of the Constitution, have never been realized, and the common reality remains that those with power have unchallenged access to corruption, tyranny, and oppression. While one of responsibilities of the president is guarding the Constitution, no law has been passed to describe how a president can do so. President Mohammad Khatami tried to execute this part of his responsibility by appointing several well-known lawyers to a board of the Constitution; however, the council did not last, nor was it effective.

Infringements on Parliament's Right as the Exclusive Source of Legislation

Article 71 of the Constitution identifies the legislation of new laws as the sole and inalienable responsibility of the Majlis. The supreme leadership, however, has preferred to hand out the responsibility of legislation on certain matters to institutions of its own choosing and appointment. The Expediency Council, the Supreme Council of Cultural Revolution, and the Central Council of the Military Forces are some of the nonelected institutions that have gained the right to create new regulations that supersede the laws passed by the Majlis. In practice, the representatives of the Majlis denied the right to void these laws, and the Guardian Council would strike down any bills that contradict their laws. Therefore, the Guardian Council is not only responsible for assessing the new bills in relation to the Constitution and Islamic principles, but it is also responsible for comparing the bills passed by the Majlis with the bills enacted by these other institutions, and to strike them down in cases of discrepancy. This happened on numerous occasions in the Sixth Majlis. For example, the Guardian Council struck down the bill passed by the Majlis whereby the Majlis had mandated the sale of military material and the use of the proceeds for further purchases for the armed forces. The Guardian Council found the Majlis's bill in contradiction of the internal statutes of the Central Council of the Military Forces, which had established the sale of material by the armed forces to be at the sole discretion of the Central Command of the Armed Forces.

In addition to the above-mentioned restriction of the Parliament's constitutional right, the Parliament's right to legislate and oversee has also been restricted. To illustrate, I would like to share my experience of the Sixth Majlis.

The Parliament did not have a great deal to do with economic bills, but political reform looked extremely challenging because any proposed piece of legislation has to go through the Guardian Council; thus, many proposed pieces of legislation related to political rights, such as journalism law and women's rights bills, were rejected by the Guardian Council. When that happened, the Majlis sent the bills to the Expediency Council, which, as far as many bills were concerned, ultimately ended our efforts since the Expediency Council did not take any action on them. The fundamental problem was that the Expediency Council has no deadline for reviewing any of the bills the Majlis sends to it, while at least the Guardian Council has to convey its decision within twenty-one days.

Regarding the oversight capacity of the government, the Sixth Majlis conducted investigations of many cases, but other bodies of the government refused our oversight by any and every means. In one case, we created a committee to investigate the state-run TV and radio (headed by the current speaker of the Majlis, Ali Larijani). The committee found corruption; therefore, we sent a report to the judiciary asking it to conduct a trial. Not only was there no trial against Larijani as the head of TV and radio, but the chair of the investigation committee was accused and was summoned to appear in court. A committee formed on the basis of Article 90 of the Constitution summoned judicial officials for hearings on several occasions. They refused to attend, and no constitutional law enables the Majlis to pursue those who refuse to appear.

Another tool the Majlis possesses to inform citizens and advocate for political reform agendas is public statements. In each session, a maximum of four members of Parliament can express their opinions in twenty-minute or five-minute speeches as preagenda talks, given at the beginning of each session. When members of Parliament such as myself used these opportunities to challenge the unelected bodies of our government, we ended up being prosecuted. In one of my speeches, I read my open letter to the supreme leader in which I accused him of the human rights violations committed by the judiciary, whom he supported. After that, I was arrested. Although I was put on trial, it did not stop me, nor several of my colleagues. However, you can imagine how few of us could dare—or bear—to go through that painful process. On the other hand, we needed to have consensus for such challenges. Although we had 218 reformist members out of 290 in the Majlis, we did not agree on fundamental issues such as challenging the government's unelected bodies. Some of us, a small group, wanted to make the supreme leader accountable for his actions and inactions, but we were barred from running in the next election. I do not regret any of my actions, however.

According to Article 59, legislative changes can also be enacted through a popular referendum, to be confirmed by a two-thirds majority of the Majlis and a decree of the supreme leader. We could, therefore, hold public referendums on important issues (this is common in the United States, but we never experienced it in Iran). We wanted to use that avenue for a range of topics that the Guardian Council kept rejecting. In the end, though, we realized that since we did not even have enough votes in the Parliament, it would be a mistake to go through with it, because it would only show that we were unstable on fundamental issues, hardly a position in which we wished to find ourselves. Due to the political clout of the supreme leader and the problems involved in challenging that office, there was no consensus. Even in my simple speech I wanted to make the supreme leader accountable; afterward, several of my colleagues criticized me, asking why I had opened up a direct dialogue with him and why I wanted him to be accountable. They accused me of being a radical because of that speech. They did so even though my speech was completely polite. I explained that a journalist's human rights had been violated, and said that the judiciary does indeed violate people's rights and that they are supported by the supreme leader. The judiciary thus feels protected from above and that it can behave with impunity, as unaccountable as the supreme leader himself. Criticizing the leader was taboo in Iran ten years ago.

After the Sixth Majlis, the supreme leader and the Guardian Council decided to not allow any nonloyal candidate to run in the parliamentary elections, with the result that the members of Parliament are all very loyal to the supreme leader and careful to demonstrate this every time they speak publicly. Despite this restriction, they are allowed to express their disagreement with the president and his cabinet, in order to give the impression of an existing democracy.

The only power of the Parliament that the supreme leader has been unable to erode is that concerning its dissolution. In recent years, after the experience of the Sixth Majlis which questioned the supreme leader in many ways, the leader and his allies wanted to disqualify a member of Parliament if he or she is not in line with the supreme leader. The Eighth Majlis passed a law that the Majlis as a whole can supervise its members—in fact, a tool to make sure that no one dares to challenge the leader. The law's effectiveness remains to be seen.

Infringements on
the Parliamentary Immunity of the Representatives

Articles 84 and 86 guarantee freedom of expression for the representatives of the Majlis and grant them immunity from prosecution for their parliamentary debates and deliberations. Article 84 states, "Each representative is responsible to the entire nation and has the right to express his/her opinion regarding national and international matters." In addition, Article 86 clearly states, "Members of the Assembly are completely free in expressing their views and casting their votes in the course of performing their duties as representatives, and they cannot be prosecuted or arrested for opinions expressed in the Assembly or votes cast in the course of performing their duties as representatives."

The Guardian Council and the judiciary have not only hindered these rights, but they openly disagree with this immunity and actively identify, pursue, summon, arrest, and impose heavy penalties upon representatives, with the goal of stopping them from fulfilling their duties. In the Sixth Majlis, these threats reached such heights that, at one point, the speaker of the Majlis threatened to resign from his position, physically leaving the Parliament building, and effectively preventing the arrest of Hossein Logmanian, the Hamedan representative at the time. At the same time, President Khatami sometimes complained to the judiciary about the unconstitutional abrogation of parliamentary immunity, including my own arrest. However, since neither the Guardian Council nor the judiciary saw the president as a legitimate source for identifying the constitutionality of their own actions, the Majlis representatives were not granted the protection of their freedom of expression or their parliamentary immunity. Following the January 2002 request of Ayatollah Seyed Mahmoud Shahroodi, the former head of the judiciary, the Guardian Council interpreted Article 86 of the Constitution in a strange way. It denied the immunity of members of the Parliament, an illogical interpretation that is contrary to the Constitution's original text.

The Irrelevance of the Article 90 Commission
According to Article 90, any Iranian citizen can manifest a grievance against any of the three branches of government through a written letter to the Majlis. However, the final ruling by the Majlis has no guarantee of enactment, and the process has turned into a mere ethical and political procedure. This was evident when a commission based on Article 90 was unable to summon any of the judiciary officials for their illegal actions or even gain permission to conduct fact-finding missions into the judiciary's actions. However, since—according to Article 69—the Majlis's discussions should be accessible to the public by radio, this would be a good way to expand the authority of the Majlis, by strengthening its reputation as the body that forces wrongdoers to face public scrutiny for their actions.

Constitutional Reform and Referenda

Many weaknesses exist within the Iranian legal system, and these weaknesses play a role in the lack of true democracy in Iran. Notably, the present Constitution discriminates against minorities by treating them as second-class citizens, and therefore it would need to be amended. Although the nation's legal structures are not the only impediment to the development of democracy, political freedom in Iran can be directly linked to constitutional reform. Eight years of reformist politics have demonstrated that a change in the office of the president or the individual members of Parliament will not guarantee legal access to laws that affect people's lives in a fundamental way. The basic legal structures of the Islamic Republic remain in the hands of an unaccountable individual, and the three branches of government are unable to adopt policies against that individual's wishes.

Principles to Reform the Constitution
Listed below are the essential components of Iranian constitutional reform:

- The separation of religion and the state
- Protection of democratic values
- Abiding by the Universal Declaration of Human Rights and elimination of all forms of discrimination
- Decentralization of government
- Reformulation of economic relations

• Protection of the Constitution from manipulation by the formation of a Constitutional Court

Possible Scenarios for Constitutional Reform in Iran

The elimination of the religious nature of the Iranian Constitution. The first possible scenario is eliminating the religious nature of the Iranian Constitution. In effect, this approach would mean a fundamental change in the Constitution, essentially entailing its rewriting and requiring a referendum outside of the confines of the present version. Regime opponents form an important consensus on reforming Iran's Constitution. I am in favor of this scenario, but it is not clear to what extent the regime's elites would act on this idea in order to ease a nonviolent transition to a secular, nondiscriminatory regime. To execute this referendum, we need to answer the following questions:

• Which Constitution will be put forward for a referendum?
• Who will draw up the new Constitution?
• Which institutions will conduct the referendum?
• Which institutions will monitor the referendum?
• What guarantee is there that the outcome of the referendum will be enacted?

A referendum within the confines of the current Constitution. The following two scenarios are possible within the confines of the current Constitution. Although the possibilities are limited, the current Constitution laid out the legal process for its own reform. According to Article 177, "The Islamic Nature of the Government," "Supreme Leadership," "Republicanism," "National Rule according to the Will of the People," and "the Official Religion" are fundamental ideas that cannot be reformed within the Constitution. Any constitutional reform must remove this article as well. But even within these limitations, it is still possible to reform the Constitution by upholding the republican nature of the government and guaranteeing the political liberties of the citizens by limiting the power of the supreme leader, eliminating the Guardian Council, and distributing the responsibilities among other institutions.

A possible scenario would keep the Islamic principles of the Constitution but eliminate the institutions that safeguard the regime's religious nature: the offices of the supreme leader and the Guardian Council. This approach is important to consider because it minimizes some of the active resistance that any reform is bound to garner. The clergy's influence in Iran dates back many centuries, and their influence as an institution of civil society merely increased after the Islamic Revolution of 1979. Although clerical authority as a source of religious authority has decreased significantly since the first decade of the Islamic regime, the influence of the clergy and other religious institutions is strong enough to form a powerful obstacle to any newly reformed constitution, particularly since some of the more radical religious elements embody extremist values capable of violence and fearmongering in society at large. In light of this reality, Islam remains the official religion, which is the same model as the first Iranian Constitution of 1906. Iran's people must be assured that the right to freedom of religion is guaranteed, so that the rights of all citizens, including atheists, are protected, and the Constitutional Court must punish any violators of this right. Unfortunately, the current regime discriminates against large groups of citizens, such as Sufis, Baha'is, Sunnis, and so on. Right now, it punishes women who do not conform to the dress code or people who openly eat or drink during the day during the month of Ramadan, a time of fasting.

Another possible scenario falls short of secularism; however, given the country's current status quo, finding powerful allies within the regime's elites and pursuing a nonviolent transition to a more democratic political system is more practical.

In this approach, the Islamic pillar of the Constitution and the institutions that Islamize the regime would remain in place, but their powers would be limited and reformed. According to the current Constitution, the supreme leader forms the board of the constitutional reform and the reform agenda. Thus, popular demand can make the supreme leader accept a limited tenure rather than a lifetime appointment, along with a reduction in his responsibilities and the transfer of some of his power to other political entities. This reduction may lead to some the following changes:

- The appointment of the *foqaha* of the Guardian Council becoming the responsibility of all *marjas*, the highest-ranking clerics in Iran
- The appointment of the head of the judiciary through nomination by the supreme judicial council and a vote of confidence by the Parliament
- The control of the armed forces by the president
- Appointment of the head of national radio and television by all three branches of government and allowing private radios and TVs
- The transfer of management of all economic and public-sector institutions currently under the supervision of the supreme leader to relevant institutions

• Referenda and policymaking becoming the responsibilities of
  Parliament

Under this third approach to reform, once parliament passes a law it
becomes legal and must be executed unless the Guardian Council or the
Constitutional Court object to the law within fourteen working days.
The Guardian Council would become solely responsible for overseeing
the concurrence of new laws with Islamic law, whereas the Constitutional Court would be responsible for judging the legality of laws under
the Constitution. Election monitoring would become the responsibility
of an independent institution made up of civil society groups and representatives from political parties with a two-year term limit. All of
these practices would limit the power of the supreme leader and hold
government institutions accountable for their actions. The Constitutional Court would be in charge of any complaint about violating the
Constitution to assure accountability of the institutions.

In order to bring the Iranian Constitution in line with principles of
good governance, all constitutional limits on political rights must be
eliminated—limitations such as the condition called "Adherence to
Islamic Principles." In effect, political rights must be defined and guaranteed in the Constitution. Similarly, legal obstacles to the privately
owned media must be lifted, the rights and freedoms of religious
minorities and women must be legitimized, and all discriminatory laws
must be eliminated. In order to decrease the conflict between the three
branches of government, an Expediency Council would be formed with
four representatives from the three branches of government (Parliament
and the Guardian Council, the Supreme Court, and the president and his
cabinet) and representatives of the political parties.

This method of reform within the Constitution would have many
benefits. It fits within the confines of the current Constitution and is
completely legal without seeking to overthrow the regime. In effect, it
guarantees the republican character of the state while safeguarding its
Islamic character. It seeks to create a clear and open divide between the
two without forming a threat of interference or antagonism between
them. This approach would meet the least resistance from religious con-
stituents and would leave room for all forces within Iran to find a language to participate and push for legal reforms. This third strategy,
because it allows for a direct and defined role for the highest religious
authorities (the *marjas*) in the process of reform, offers the possibility
of dividing the traditional religious establishment from the regime, and

takes away one of the regime's primary tools of propaganda as it seeks to resist reforms. This point is significant, because the forces of reform need maximum support and unity and minimum resistance from religious institutions in order to be successful. The strategy must include as many forces as possible.

There does not seem to be any possibility in the near future for constitutional reform aimed at democratization. Therefore, we must have a medium- or long-term plan for democratization. The following steps are needed:

- Strengthening civil society
- Organizing a united front for constitutional reform
- Looking at local city and village councils as an opportunity to connect with people to increase demands for constitutional reform
- Increasing internal and external pressure for the opening of political spaces and free elections
- Changing the composition of the Parliament (according to the Constitution, a referendum has to be accepted by two-thirds of the Parliament)
- Applying pressure to reduce the power of appointed and unaccountable institutions
- Continuing internal pressure and beginning negotiations with the supreme leader for the voluntary relinquishing of his power and the power of his appointed institutions
- Conducting a referendum
- Participating in an international community of scholarship and research on good governance

This process is not possible in the short term for the following three reasons:

1. The appointment of the Constitutional Amendment Council is the responsibility the supreme leader.

2. According to the Constitution, the referendum can be conducted only with the vote of two-thirds of the Parliament. This condition could not be met within the current Parliament.

3. Iran does not have a proper monitoring system that would be independent from the institutions of the Islamic Republic. A referendum would suffer from the same kind of fraud that exists in local elections. The outcome of such a vote will likely not be in favor of the people.

Conclusion

In this chapter I aimed to provide an assessment of the necessities, possibilities, and conditions for the reform of the current Constitution in Iran. There is a consensus among the regime's opponents regarding changes to the Constitution to meet the necessary requirements for a transition to democracy, which needs to be done via a referendum. However, it is less likely that the current leader of the country would agree with any referendum intended to remove his power or the Islamic character of the Constitution. Most likely, fundamental changes in the Constitution would be the outcome of fundamental changes in the nature and type of the regime, which would most likely happen only through a national uprising against it.

The Constitution has to be changed. The political structure has to be redefined in a democratic way to ensure that the will of the people is respected and that accountability and checks and balances exist for all officials. The Office of the Supreme Leader must be purged from Iran's political system. All legal discrimination against minorities must cease.

Notes

1. Constitution of the Islamic Republic of Iran, Preamble, 1998 [1377].
2. Ilna News Agency, October 21, 2006, www.ilna.ir/en/news/index.cfm, accessed July 16, 2014.
3. A. Meshkini, *Emrouz Web*, 2006 [1385], www.emruznews.com/, accessed July 16, 2014.
4. Khomeini, *Velayat-e Faqih*, p. 55.
5. Khomeini, *Kashf-ol-Asrar*.
6. Rumi, *Divan-e Shams*.
7. Khomeini, *Sahifeh-ye Noor*.
8. Hashemi, *Hoquq-e Asasi-e Jomhouri-e Islami-e Iran*.
9. Ibid.
10. Constitution of the Islamic Republic of Iran, Art. 115.

5

The Rule of the Basij in Iranian Politics

Saeid Golkar

*B*asij is a Persian word meaning mobilization. The complete name of the group, Sazaman-e Basij-e Mostazafan, means the Organization for the Mobilization of the Oppressed. Following the disputed Iranian presidential election in June 2009, it became clear that the Basij played a central role in controlling and eventually suppressing Iran's Green Movement.

The Islamic Republic has praised the members of the Basij in their suppression of the Green Movement while propagating an image of the Basij as a homogeneous group of pious citizens committed to Islamic ideology and willing to sacrifice their lives to defend the Islamic Republic of Iran. On the other hand, the opposition has depicted the Basij as group of brutal, amoral thugs focused on materialistic spoils, not piety. What is the true nature of the Basij and its members' motivation? It is difficult to determine, for when it came to the Basij and its members, there were many questions but few answers.

Although the number of studies of the Basij and its branches is growing,[1] a lack of understanding remains about the demographic and ideological underpinnings of the group, its members' incentives, socioeconomic backgrounds, and mentalities.[2] Many questions are too often ignored, including the following: What drives individuals to join the Basij? What common socioeconomic or ideological characteristics do Basij members share, if any? What are the motivations of Basij members? To what extent is the Basij royal to the Islamic Republic? In this chapter I attempt to fill the gap in academic knowledge about the Basij by shedding new light on the biggest militia in the world by exploring the aforementioned questions and developing the understanding of why Iranian citizens choose to join the Basij. In addition, I discuss the social and political cleavages among the group's adherents and in doing so explore the various dimensions of Basij membership.

Conducting research in this field is especially challenging considering the dearth of preexisting studies on the topic and the sensitivity of the subject. I use a variety of data and resources in this chapter, including publications in Persian and English. The study incorporates a number of academic dissertations on the Basij as well as the main Islamic Revolutionary Guard Corps (IRGC) publication, *Sobh-e Sadegh*. Online sources, including websites and blogs written by Basij members, are also a component of this study. Combining such a diversity of sources made it possible to take a comprehensive look at this complicated institution.

Some of the results presented here are based on a study I conducted a few years ago while studying and teaching at Iranian universities. While there, I was able to communicate with Basij members—students and lecturers—and study the organization more closely. These personal, informal communications have also enabled me to better understand the Basij and learn about its training, inner structures, functions, and recent transformations.

In 2006–2007, I conducted small surveys in Basij Mosque Resistance Bases in southeastern Tehran and the student Basij Resistance Base at Islamic Azad University. Of the 126 questionnaires I distributed, 92 were returned. Due to the risk of conducting such studies I focused the surveys only on basic questions about the socioeconomic background of Basijis (members of the Basij) and their reasons for joining. I also conducted thirteen individual interviews with Basij members in different bases in Tehran and two smaller cities, one in eastern Tehran province and one in the Central (Markazi) province. In fact, some of my information is rooted in these observations made as a scholar of politics. Wherever possible, I tested the reliability of my data using ancillary sources.

I divide this chapter into three main sections. The first section presents a brief history of the Basij and its increasing role in Iranian politics over the last thirty years. The second section explains the Basij membership and organizational structure to show the different levels of Basij membership. Finally, I analyze the Basij members' socioeconomic backgrounds and motivations for joining the Basij.

History and Transformation of the Basij (1980–2009)

The Organization for the Mobilization of the Oppressed or Downtrodden, commonly referred to as the Basij (Sazaman-e Basij-e Mostazafan), is one of the most important mass organizations founded after Iran's transformative Islamic Revolution of 1979. Created in the early 1980s on the command of Ayatollah Ruhollah Khomeini, the objective of the Basij, broadly defined, has been to confront internal and external threats to the Islamic Republic.

The Islamic Revolutionary Council approved the formation of the organization, originally named Basij-e Melli (National Mobilization) in May 1980 under the supervision of the Ministry of the Interior.[3] In 1981 the Basij was combined with the IRGC as the corps' tenth unit, and its name was changed to "Unit for the Mobilization of the Oppressed" of the IRGC or Vahed-e Basij-e Mostazafan of the Sepah-e Pasdaran.[4] Since then, the Basij began playing an important role in recruiting, organizing, and deploying volunteers to the Iran-Iraq War front, starting in September 1980.[5]

The end of the war and the death of Ayatollah Khomeini were milestones in the history of the Islamic Republic. Ayatollah Ali Khamenei, the Iranian religious cleric, replaced Khomeini as supreme leader. By Khamenei's order, as the commander in chief, in 1990 the Unit for the Mobilization of the Oppressed of the IRGC changed its name to the Basij Resistance Force, or BRF (Niru-ye Moqavemat-e Basij), and experienced an upgrade, becoming one of the five main forces of the IRGC. (The other four are the air force, army, navy, and the Quds [Jerusalem] Force.)[6]

In addition to these transformations, one of the most significant structural changes in the Basij was the establishment of its new battalions in 1990, units comprising war veterans and aimed at addressing civil unrest. The Ashura battalions were all men; Al Zahra battalions were made up of women. These battalions, which were responsible for local defense and the internal security of the regime, were employed quickly after their establishment and were an active part of the government's attempts to quell social revolts from 1992 to 1994, during Ali Akbar Hashemi Rafsanjani's second term as president, in cities including Qazvin, Eslamshahr, Mashhad, and Akbarabad.[7]

Theologian and reformist politician Seyyed Mohammad Khatami claimed an unexpected and shocking victory in the 1997 presidential election. His victory was seen as a sign of the Iranian people's discontent with the prevailing political system and its conservative institutions. In response to Khatami's victory, Ayatollah Khamenei asked the Basij to get more involved in politics to confront the reformists and create obstacles for Khatami's presidential plans. Also, the Basij increased ideological-political training efforts for their members, so as to shield them from the reformists' ideas.[8]

In addition to the conservative political camp's policies that served as an obstacle to the reformists, the inefficiency and passivity of Khatami and the reformists disappointed Iranian youth and led them to withdraw their support for the reform movement and to boycott such city councils and parliamentary elections since 2001.[9] Realizing this opportunity, political hard-liners mobilized Basij members, especially in Tehran, to take an active part in the second city council election in favor of their candidates. With the Basij's support, hard-liner political candidates won the majority of the seats on Tehran's city council.[10]

That the hard-liners won the 2004 parliamentary elections in such a setting was not surprising. During this election, while several reformist candidates were disqualified by the Guardian Council, many hard-line candidates were selected as Parliament members with the support of the Basij members. Of the 152 new members of Parliament, ninety-one had a background in the Guards or Basij.[11]

In the 2005 presidential election, a group of IRGC and Basij commanders, especially in Tehran, used the Basij to win the contest. Under the Basirat project, Basij members were tasked not only with convincing their families and friends that Ahmadinejad was the best candidate but also with bringing their relatives, especially those who were illiterate, to the polls to vote for him. These strategies allowed Mahmoud Ahmadinejad to win 14 percent of the votes and emerge as the second among nine candidates. In the second round of the election, Ahmadinejad defeated Rafsanjani. The systematic role of the Basij in making the victory possible was criticized by the other presidential candidate, Mehdi Karroubi, but the supreme leader rejected his criticisms.

The use of Basij's network to propagate and mobilize their families to vote in favor of the hard-line candidates was an evident tactic used in elections following 2005, including parliamentary elections in 2008 and 2012. Many Basij commanders were selected as parliamentary members, including Mehdi Kuchakzadeh, Hossein Najabat, 'Alireza Zakani, Mohammad Khowshchehreh, Hamid-Reza Fowladgar, Fazlollah Mousavi, and others. However, the most visible and systematic mobilization of the Basij members in elections occurred during the presidential election in 2009. The result was a highly disputed win for Ahmadinejad. As Iranians poured into the streets to contest the results, the Basij forces, along with other security forces, suppressed protestors, attacking and jailing many.

In the aftermath of the disputed 2009 election, the Islamic Republic radically modified the structure of the Basij. The Basij resistance force's name changed once again to the Organization of the Mobilization of the

Oppressed (or Downtrodden) (Sazeman-e Basij-e Mostazafan), or OBO. Their focus shifted more heavily to internal political control and defending the Islamic Republic against the alleged "soft war" or "cultural war."

In spite of the close relationship between Ahmadinejad and the Basij, the Basij officially took Ayatollah Khamenei's side during the power struggle between the supreme leader and the president in 2011. As a result, a gap emerged within the Basij. While a small group of Basijis supported Ahmadinejad, many of them criticized his behavior and for not totally subordinating himself to Khamenei.[12] Many Basij members announced their complete submission to the supreme leader and emphasized the fact that they only follow the Ayatollah's orders.

The Basij members were again divided during the 2013 presidential elections, where six conservative candidates competed with two political moderates. Although some Basijis and most of the IRGC's members supported General Mohammad Ghalibaf, an ex-IRGC commander, most of the younger Basijis supported the hard-line candidate Saeed Jalili, who was a Basij member during the Iran-Iraq War. In this election, Jalili promoted a platform best described as "resistance discourse" (*ghofteman-e moqavemat*), due to his emphasis on Iran's revolutionary values and a confrontational attitude toward the West. A group of the Basij members, mainly the young and more radical of the organization, hailed him as the quintessential Basij candidate. Such Jajili supporters contrasted their candidate to Ghalibaf, whom they saw as a politician more reliant on technocrats than Basijis. Ultimately, Hassan Rouhani, a moderate candidate, won the presidency with 50.7 percent of the vote. It is, however, worth noting that Ghalibaf, with 6.1 million votes (16.46 percent), was second to Rouhani, and Saeed Jalili, with nearly 4.2 million votes (11.31 percent), was third.

Immediately after Rouhani's victory, the Basij began criticizing him and his administration. The gap between the Basij, which supports more radical and religious policies internally and externally, and the Rouhani government, which is more pragmatic and less ideological, has widened since the election. The Basij members became increasingly vocal in the public sphere and via the Internet in their critiques of Rouhani's administration. From their point of view, the Rouhani government's negotiations with the P5+1 (five permanent members of the UN Security Council, namely, the United States, Russia, china, the United Kingdom, and France, plus Germany) regarding Iran's nuclear programs undermine Iranian independence. Domestically, they also criticize Rouhani for opening political and culture spaces and marginalizing hard-liners.

Basij Membership and Organization

One facet of the Basij that has confused many Iran watchers is the organization's internal hierarchy. According to the Basij constitution, its members are classified into four groups: regular, active, cadre, and special. This is based on the training they undergo, the extent of their cooperation with the Basij, and their level of ideological commitment.

Regular membership is the basic form of Basij membership. The regular members usually have little connection to the Basij organization and only undergo basic training. Legally, a regular Basiji must be at least eleven years old. Beyond the age limit, there is no other limitation on people joining as a regular member. In fact, becoming a regular member is very easy; legally, any citizen can join the Basij regardless of age (after age eleven), gender, religion, ethnicity, or education. They only need to fill out a form in a Basij office and pass the first stage of Basij general training, which is a compulsory two- or three-day program.[13] According to a Basij regular member, joining the organization is informal and quick: "I used to go to the mosque for congregational prayers. One day, a guy who was a member of the mosque's board of trustees asked me why I hadn't joined the Basij. I asked him how I could become a member, and he told me of a meeting following afternoon prayers [at the mosque] and that if I wished I could attend. I stayed [for the meeting]. . . . The next day, they took my photograph and I became a Basij member."[14] Legally, after six months of collaboration with the Basij, members who are fifteen or older can apply for active membership status, the second level of the Basij membership hierarchy. In order to do so, candidates simply have to fill out necessary forms and apply for a status upgrade. After initial approval by their base commanders, their files are then reviewed by an ideological and political selection committee comprising the representative of the supreme leader in the Basij, the commander of the intelligence section, and some other Basij commanders. According to a Basij member, "[These committees] are investigations on everything. It starts with your school, where you went, the kinds of things you did, how you dressed, what your personal opinions and views are, whether you go to the mosque or not, your reputation around your neighborhood, etc. They investigate all these things."[15]

Once the committee decides that the members are qualified, they then undergo the second stage of general Basij training, a one-week program. High school students who pass the course of defense readiness (*amadegi-e defa' i*) are exempt from this training. According to new regulations, they should spend six hours per month in their bases and collaborate with the Basij as volunteers. These active members are usually used for less sensitive positions, such as cultural and educational affairs, due to their limited military and ideological training. In addition to organizing in resistance bases, some active Basijis are simultaneously organized in the Basij combat organizations (*sazeman-e razm*). To be a member of these battalions, Basij pledges must undergo a forty-five-day training program. Active members are assigned to Basij combat battalions such as the Resistance Battalions (Ashura for men and Al Zahra for women), and Imam Hossein Battalions.[16]

A small selection of active Basijis may also be promoted to the third rank, called the cadre Basij. They must be older than sixteen and pass more intensified ideological and political training. After passing these courses, cadre Basijis become the main part of these base organizations and can occupy some sensitive positions. Many of the cadre members are employed by the Basij organization under short-term contracts (usually three to five years). It means they are full-time Basij members and on the payroll. These members also shape the main skeleton of the Basij's structure and its military units.

The highest rank of the Basij is made up of the special Basij. These members possess military skills and ideological qualities similar to those of IRGC members. They become part of the organization after passing special military and ideological courses and commit to serving in the IRGC full-time.[17] Special Basijis have to join the IRGC military academy and undergo a specialized and rigorous training routine, similar to that of regular members of the IRGC. Special Basij members are placed in the upper echelons of the organization, such as in Basij headquarters. Since special Basijis are full-time members and undergo specialized training in light arms, mid-heavy arms, and ideology and politics, they usually hold more positions of higher responsibility—for example, as commanders and deputy commanders in Basij battalions.

The Basij's Structure

All Basij members are organized into the Basij hierarchal network. From the bottom-up view, the Basij members are organized in the Basij bases, as the lowest level of the Basij organization, which are spread throughout Iran's society. According to the Basij commander, General Kazem Yazdani, there were 47,000 Basij bases located in neighborhoods, schools, universities, bureaus, factories, and so on throughout Iran in 2013.[18] Basij resistance bases have separate units for males and females, and according to the commander of the women's Basij, 12,000 of all bases are for women and the rest are for men.[19]

Groups of ten to fifteen Basij bases are directed by one Basij resistance district (*hozehha-ye moqavamat-e basij*). According to the deputy commander of the IRGC, the number of these offices was around 4,000 in 2005.[20] Like the resistance base, there are separate districts for male and female Basiji. Eight hundred of these districts belong to women, and the rest are for men, according to a former commander of the Basij.[21]

Several Basij districts are under the control of one Basij resistance region (*nahieh-e moqavemat-e basij*). The number of Basij regions per city depends on the city's size and population. While small cities are controlled at least by one Basij region, big cities have several Basij regions. The precise number of the Basij regional offices is difficult to verify, but according to one of the Basij commanders, there were 1,000 regional offices throughout Iran in 2013.

Basij regional offices in each province are under the control of the IRGC provincial command (*sepah-e ostani*). IRGC provincial commands are responsible for all the IRGC and Basij forces in their provinces. In total, there are thirty-two IRGC commands across the country. The Basij resistance regions are simultaneously directed by the Organization for the Mobilization of the Oppressed or Downtrodden, which is subordinated to the IRGC as part of Iran's military establishment. The OBO has more than twenty different suborganizations, including those for secondary school students, university students, the guilds, medical associations, nomadic tribes, engineers, university professors, artists, and lawyers. There are also Basij organizations for women, athletes, retired people, and so on.

The Number of Basijis

There is no reliable data on the number of Basij members or the proportion of different membership types. According to Islamic Republic propaganda, the Basij had 13,639,722 members in 2008.[22] The Basij commander recently claimed that the number of Basij members passed more than 20 million in 2013.[23] Nevertheless, the official statistics are not only exaggerated but also contradictory.[24] Moreover, according to the organization's regulations, every member is allowed to be in only one Basij group at a time. But for various reasons, such as confusion with older records, some Basijis are accidentally overcounted, making the organization appear larger than it actually is.[25]

A possible solution for getting at real membership statistics is to focus on the organizational structure of the Basij, the numbers of Basij resistance bases and districts, and the population. According to the representative of the supreme leader of the IRGC, every Basij resistance base has around 100 members.[26] With approximately 40,000 to 47,000 bases in the country, Basij membership should be between 4 million and 5 million. Alternatively, since there are about 4,000 to 4,500 resistance zones, and each district includes around 1,000 people, Basij membership should be approximately 5 million. Taking into account the "ideal chart of the twenty-million-member army," which shows the ideal distribution of regular, active, and special members, I estimate that the Basij membership is as follows: more than 3 to 4 million regular members, about 1 million active members, and 200,000 cadre and special members.

The Sociology of the Basij

According to a report by its human resources division, the Basij ideally wants to recruit 20 million members, out of whom 25 percent should be women. However, the chief of the Women's Basij announced that the number of female Basij members was about 5.5 million in 2009,[27] or 37 percent of the current Basij (which she claimed numbered over 13 million). It seems that women usually have a more positive attitude toward Basij resistance bases in mosques and welcome Basij membership more often than men, especially in certain social groups.[28] This could be due to women's widespread interest in higher education and employment and the advantages that Basij membership brings them in those areas. On November 4, 2003, a huge OBO maneuver brought together about 50,000 students, 57 percent of whom were women.[29] According to the Basij's human resources division, the breakdown of each Basij group should be as follows: student Basij should comprise 55 percent; rural and tribal Basij, 20 percent; worker Basij, 10 percent; guild Basij, 7.5 percent; university Basij, 3.5 percent; office Basij, 2.5 percent; medical Basij, 1.25 percent; and seminary Basij, 0.25 percent.[30] According to this report, children and teenagers between the ages of eleven and eighteen should make up more than half of Basij members.

The idea of recruiting teenagers can be traced back to the initial years of the organization. During the early years of the Revolution, the Revolutionary Guards absorbed a large proportion of the country's youth, particularly those with a deep religious inclination. Youth who could not join the guard became members of the Basij. As a result, around 550,000 students participated in the Iran-Iraq War, out of whom

36,000 were killed.[31] Despite all their efforts, an analysis of recent official Basij statistics shows a lack of success in recruiting teenagers. According to the study, children and teenagers currently form only 4.6 million, or 30 percent, of the whole Basij population, which is 20 percent below the desired level.[32] Given Iran's youthful population (there are over 14 million students across the country), this shows that the Basij has not been very successful recently with its youth recruitment initiatives.

During the second and third decades after the 1979 Revolution, the Basij made great efforts to recruit young adults and university students, which were more successful than recruiting teenagers. Although Basij policymakers had foreseen the recruitment of 700,000 university students in the initial program, the number later increased to 905,000, according to the Basij deputy commander.[33] Some researchers confirm that the majority of Basijis in some provinces, such as Sistan and Baluchestan, are young adults and university students.[34] For example, according to a study in 2002, 53.8 percent of female Basijis in Tehran were under twenty-four years old, and a majority of them (71 percent) had a high school diploma or less than a high school diploma.[35] In another study among Basiji women, 60 percent were between fifteen and twenty-five years old, 30 percent were between twenty-five and thirty-five years old, and just 10 percent were more than thirty-five years old.

Since there are no limitations on who can join the Basij (once a person is eleven years old), members come from different ethnic groups, including Azeris, Baluchs, and Arabs. Also, as there is no legal limitation preventing non-Muslims from joining the Basij as regular members, some of which are adherents to minority religions in Iran. For example, according to the head of the Women's Basij Organization, that group contains a number of Christian and Zoroastrian women.[36]

As for the social origins of Basij forces, the general view is that they come from the poorest and most marginalized segments of society. While this view does not fully reflect the entire picture, it has some merit. One reason for the popular perception of the Basij's socioeconomic roots can be found in the choice of titling the organization "Basij of the Oppressed [or Downtrodden]" at its establishment. If the Islamic Revolution was a revolt of the "barefooted" (*pa-berahneha*), the Basij was created to organize the previously marginalized oppressed so that they could defend the Revolution of 1979. The word *mostazafan* (oppressed) was repeatedly employed during the Revolution to describe the underprivileged and the poor who suffered exploitation at the hand of the upper classes. Perhaps for this reason, many of those who lived on the margins of society or belonged to the socioeconomically lower classes joined the Basij soon after it was established.

In the early 1990s its name was changed to the Basij Resistance Force, omitting the word "oppressed." However, the Basij still continued to rely on the inclusion of the lower social and economic classes as the major source of its membership. Indeed, the majority of Basij members still belong to the lower social and economic classes. Most of them also belong to religious and traditional families characterized by strong religious belief and the strict observance of religious rites.[37] According to my survey,[38] 95.6 percent of Basij respondents at the resistance bases in mosques around Tehran stated that their parents were strict in attending religious rites.[39] Moreover, 87 percent of respondents stated that their parents' levels of education were below high school diploma.[40] About 76 percent of the respondents also said that they belonged to large families with more than five children.[41] Another point worth mentioning is that of immigration from villages and towns to large cities. Some scholars have pointed out that most Basij members are originally from rural areas.[42] My study confirmed this: about 88 percent of Basij respondents in Tehran were from families that had migrated into urban settings such as Tehran in the past thirty years.[43] Many of the Basij members who joined in the second and third decades after the 1979 Revolution were from families that had migrated to large cities shortly before or after the Revolution. Other statistics show that people in small cities and rural areas join the Basij more frequently than people in larger cities like Tehran. For example, among the 1.2 million school students in Tehran, only 180,000 have joined the Basij, according to Colonel Jafer Layqe Haqigi, an IRGC commander, while in some smaller cities and towns more than 50 percent of students join the Basij.[44]

An analysis of the Basijis' economic backgrounds indicates that a majority of them belong to the lower-income and working classes. More than 55.4 percent of the Basiji respondents in Tehran stated that they belonged to the working class, 43.4 percent to the lower middle class, and 2.2 percent to the upper middle class.[45] In fact, Iran's "oppressed" appear to be the major source of recruitment for the Basij organization. Their poverty and strong religious beliefs make these individuals better candidates for membership in an ideological militia organization than the middle and upper classes. The results also show that, during the past two decades, the Basij has been recruiting some of its members from middle-class families. My observations show that the parents of these members, especially those at the student and university bases, are usually small business owners. This is particularly evident in the traditional areas of large cities, such as the eastern and southern areas of Tehran.

Basijis' Motivations

Investigating the motives for joining the Basij is of the utmost importance. For instance, it is questionable whether people who join the Basij really believe in the Islamic Republic or if they join for purely economic or opportunistic reasons. Two major hypotheses are set forth by scholars in addressing this issue. The Islamic Republic claims that the main reason for Basij membership is ideological. Many researchers argue to the contrary: that alternative motives, including university entrance quota privileges, military service reductions, and employment priorities, are the major reasons why people join the organization.

It is widely accepted that the most important motive for many people joining the Basij during the first decade after the Revolution was belief in the Islamic Republic and its leader, Ayatollah Khomeini. Basij members included young and middle-aged people who joined willing to defend the newly established Islamic system and to accept the call of the leader, serving on the war front without any special training. But when the war ended, the previously ideological atmosphere began to fade. Iranians started to redefine their social values, and in the process many believe that ideological commitments to the state began to decline in this period, even among regime advocates. In response, the Islamic Republic developed nonideological and financial incentives to encourage citizens to join. The laws passed in support of Basijis in the decades following the 1979 Revolution are a sign of this trend.[46] Some laws were promulgated for specific Basiji groups, and others were available to all groups. For example, university admission privileges, exemptions from military training, and reductions in military service target high school and university students. Employment priorities, supporting legal cases, and welfare services, including free or discounted recreational and pilgrimage trips, were offered to all Basijis. According to the law passed on July 19, 1998, services that have been presented to the Basijis shall be composed of

- Hiring and being given job opportunities
- The enjoyment of housing facilities
- The enjoyment of loan facilities

- The enjoyment of welfare and cultural services
- Access to special educational and training facilities for studies in and entering centers of higher education[47]

These incentives became the main motivation for joining the Basij in the decades following 1979. Interestingly, not only a majority of Iranians, but many Basijis themselves announced that materialistic incentives, such as "giving discounts to [members of the] Basij and exemptions from the compulsory military services motivated unemployed Iranians who otherwise would not be interested in the Basij to join this organization."[48] According to a study conducted in Basij bases in 2006–2007, around 66.3 percent of Basij members reported reasons other than ideology as why their "friends" joined the Basij. Meanwhile, 96.7 percent of the same respondents reported "ideology" as their own most important reason for signing on with the Basij, showing that members are afraid to admit their own materialistic reasons for joining. Examples of ideological reasons include obeying the orders of Imam Khomeini and the current supreme leader as well as defending Islam and the Islamic Republic.[49] Interviews with Basijis at the centers also indicate that most of them believe that "others" joined the Basij to benefit from its privileges, not due to beliefs in its ideals. These statistics are parallel to general Iranian public opinion. Even an official study by the Basij organization confirms[50] that 62 percent of Iranians (Basijis and non-Basijis) believe that material reasons are the key motivating factor for joining.[51] According to a Basij veteran, "Nowadays, the number of those who join the Basij because of their beliefs is very small. In the past, for example during the time of Imam Khomeini, maybe 90 percent of the Basijis had joined because of their beliefs. However, now there are less than 10 percent of people who join for their beliefs and the rest are here for benefits and the advantages of being in the Basij."[52]

Yet these statistics also show that a small number of people still join the Basij for genuine ideological and religious reasons, such as "promoting values of the revolution" or "implementing Imam Khomeini's ideas."[53] These members mostly include teenagers who are recruited from religious families, peer groups, schools, or mosques. As one Basiji teenager said, "For me, being a part of Basij means love, love of the regime and the supreme leader. We will give our life for the supreme leader."[54] But while the Islamic Republic tries to show that people join the Basij only for the purposes of "saving Islam," "obeying the commands of Imam Khomeini and the supreme leader," and "honoring the martyrs' blood," only a small number join the Basij purely for ideological reasons.

In addition to ideological motivations, several mechanisms offer incentives for particular social strata to join the Basij. For example, for school students, educational privileges are one of these motives. The Basij sponsors a plan called "Verses of Civilization" (Ayehey-e Tamadon) that encourages more school students to join the organization by promising to improve recruits' access to educational support. Through this plan, the school student Basij organization identifies the top-ranked middle and high school students through rigorous exams and then recruits them to the Basij. The Basij supports the students who are recruited through this plan during their studies and helps prepare them for the national entrance exam (Concour).

Aside from these incentives, some young students and teenagers join the Basij for other reasons, such as pursuing an opportunity for adventure. According to a recent study of the Basij, the adventure-seeking spirit is stronger among young Basiji students than Basijis from other social groups.[55] Recognizing this desire for action and adventure, the Islamic regime has used a defense readiness course to recruit Iranian youth. About 78 percent of Iranian school students have found a defense readiness course, which has been implemented by the Basij, desirable. Half of those students who actually passed the course developed a more positive attitude toward the Basij.[56]

Additionally, some scholars argue that many teenagers and young adults join the Basij because they find the idea of war and fighting exciting. In the words of one such member, "You must know Hatamikia's work [referring to Ebrahim Hatamikia, an Iranian film director who has made several films about war and the role of the Basij in war]. He is my idol, he is the whole reason I wanted to be a Basiji."[57] As members of the Basij, youth complete several military trainings that include basic firearms training, participation in war games, and attending camps. All of these activities give the youth, especially males, a good incentive to join. The Basij uses the excitement of the military as a motivation to recruit.

Moreover, teenagers often join the Basij for the individual feeling of power that membership provides. First, the symbols associated with the Basij, such as the uniform and baton, provide young conscripts a heightened sense of importance. Also, many Basiji youth feel more influential from their participation in Basij moral control missions, stopping civilians to search their cars or arresting civilians on the grounds of morality violations.[58] One Basij member recalls the following: "I was only fifteen years old, a teenager with a little beard and mustache. I thoroughly enjoyed when people older than me called me Haji (a respectful name given to people who completed the Hajj) and asked me to release them." General Afshar, the former Basij commander, acknowledges that the Basij's checkpoints and patrolling have been one of the main reasons for youth enrollment in the Basij.[59]

Additionally, Basij membership offers a sense of empowerment to marginalized strata within Iranian society. According to one Iranian scholar, the temptation of power is especially attractive to the socioeconomically powerless, which is one of the reasons Basij recruitment is so successful among the poor. Young Basijis raised in poor communities feel overwhelmed with the power that comes from being part of the Basij. One Basiji describes the thrill of targeting wealthier young people as follows: "It was just to have fun to tease a rich *sousol* (effeminate) kid of north Tehran. With some of my other Basiji friends we jumped in a car and drove to *Sharake Gharb* or *Miydan Mohseni*, we put a stop checkpoint sign up and annoyed 'rich kids' in their *Kharji* (foreign) cars. If one had a beautiful girl in his car, we teased him even more. Sometimes, if we didn't like one, we cut his hair to belittle him before the girl."[60] The level of authority the Basij possess provides members with a sense of being above common civilians (regardless of class) in the power structure of the state, a feeling that proves alluring to many young Iranians.

However, research shows that the motivations for the majority of Basij members are more practical and opportunistic, and less ideological and religious.[61] In fact, the older the person is at the time of joining the Basij, the weaker his ideological motives tend to be. According to one member, "The only reason I stay in the Basij is for the money . . . many of my friends in the Basij are unhappy with the government."[62] Undoubtedly, money and other financial factors serve as solid materialistic motives for some Iranians to join the Basij. Nevertheless, according to the Basij constitution, only special members who are officially employed by the Basij receive monthly salaries like other IRGC members, whose salaries are higher in comparison to other governmental employees. In addition, some of the cadre members, who are hired by the Basij under short-term contracts lasting three to five years, receive monthly salaries. While many Basijis (regular and even active) don't receive a direct salary, the government grants special bonuses to some of the active members who are in charge of Basij bases. Usually these Basijis were paid around $100 to $150 per month in 2008. That's a fairly significant sum, considering that $800 a month is the poverty line in large Iranian cities.[63] The Basij provides additional financial advantages for its members. It offers loans between $700 and $1,000 at low interest rates for regular and active Basijis (4 percent, compared to the general rate of 20 percent) and low monthly payments (as low as \$49).[64] According to a study done by the Basij, 41 percent of members believed that the salary was an important reason for them to join the Basij and 79 percent of them agreed that financial issues are an important reason not to cut their relationship with the Basij.[65] There is anecdotal evidence that Basijis are paid cash prizes during crises and unrest—for example, after their active role in suppressing the Green Movement in 2009.[66] There are rumors about money paid to Basijis who are active in cyberspace and who try to identify and confront potential cyberthreats. According to this rumor, the Islamic Republic of Iran, following in the footsteps of the Chinese government, is paying Basiji bloggers for each post in favor of the regime.[67]

Also, Basijis receive discount coupons for movie tickets and other entertainment, public swimming pools, books, food, and traveling to holy cities. Several recreational facilities and entertainment clubs are state-owned, and Basijis receive membership discounts for these establishments (30 percent for active members and 20 percent for regular members). Since 1995 the Basij has established many youth clubs throughout Iran that primarily offer services to its members, such as educational and cultural classes. These classes are popular among poorer Basijis and create solidarity among its members. Since Basijis from lower classes use these services more than those from middle and upper classes, these services are a significant method for maintaining the unity of the people within the Basij.[68]

The opportunity to travel and visit various religious sites and cities is a key incentive for many to join the Basij, particularly people in the poorer socioeconomic strata. The Basij sends thousands of Basijis and their families on religious and cultural tours to holy cities such as Mashhad and Qom and to the Iran-Iraq War battlefields in the southwest. One Basiji said, "I became a member of the Basij of my workplace because I wanted to go to Karbala [for pilgrimage]. The story is that one day some people from my office were taking a pilgrimage to Karbala. I asked why they were not taking ordinary employees and I was told that only Basij members were able to go. I asked how I could join the Basij and . . . became a member."[69] Many Basijis from lower socioeconomic classes take advantage of these tours since they are inexpensive. Moreover, because these trips are conducted by women counterparts, women from more religious and conservative families have the unique opportunity of traveling without their male relatives.

The neighborhoods from which most Basiji members come are poor, have high crime rates, and are generally difficult places, especially for teenagers and women. These areas often lack opportunities for employment or state welfare. Securing safety is therefore another crucial incentive for some female Basij members, especially widows and divorced women. As a widow living in a suburb of northeast Tehran explained, "I joined the Basij to protect myself and my sons from the intrusive thugs in my neighborhood."[70]

In addition to economic benefits, many other privileges exist for those who join the Basij. These include legal support, educational privileges, insurance discounts, and social support, all of which are not usually accessible to the lower classes. For example, many high school and university students join the organization to benefit from its educational privileges, including a quota for the university entrance exam and postgraduate admissions. According to Iranian law, at least 40 percent of undergraduate admissions and 20 percent of postgraduate admissions must be allocated to active Basij members.[71] During the Khatami era, only Azad (private) universities applied this quota for Basiji members, but since 2005, Ahmadinejad's administration implemented this quota for entrance into all the state universities. According to Abdullah Jasbai, the former head of Azad University, more than 300,000 Basiji have used the regulation to enter different colleges in Azad University since 1998.[72]

Moreover, there are privileges for employment in the public sector. Under the law, priority is given to active and cadre Basijis, particularly active members of the military and security battalions, in all employment exams. The same applies to permanent employment in the OBO itself, which is one of the limited options for unemployed youth with little education. It has been estimated that 65 percent of government employees were members of Basij organizations in 2003.[73] Many employees in the public sector decide to become members in order to benefit from the job security that the Basij grants its members. Not only is it difficult to fire Basijis, but Basij membership is an essential factor in employee promotions.

Also, some Iranians join the Basij to use the Basij network to satisfy political and social ambitions. According to research on female Basiji students, there is a positive correlation between political aspirations and their Basij membership.[74] Since success in the Basij is directly connected to an ideological commitment to the Islamic regime and the supreme leader himself, people can quickly climb up the political ladder without any specific scientific, technical, or even ethical qualifications as long as they prove their commitment to the regime. Therefore, those looking for quick social and political upward mobility but are lacking the appropriate social status or experience to gain it often join the Basij as an easy alternative. This ability to move rapidly up the political and social hierarchy is especially appealing to students. Basij membership offers a range of privileges for students, especially to those from lower socioeconomic backgrounds. One example is Mehrdad Bazarpash, the previous head of the student Basij at Sharif University. Through Bazarpash's relatively fast movement up the political ladder, he has become the vice president for national youth organizations, a member of Parliament, and the head of one of the biggest automakers in Iran.

Joining the Basij also provides members with a sense of social inclusion. As Mehran Kamrava explains, membership in the militia not only provides the experience of belonging and political efficacy, but more importantly, it presents them with the possibility of upward mobility in a society where few other opportunities are open to them.[75]

In certain situations, the Basij also protects members against the law. In a society where the morality police are always trying to control, supervise, and penalize citizens for "wrongdoings," being a Basiji is an easy way of avoiding trouble. All Basijis need to do is show their membership cards to avoid being questioned or detained. A young Basiji put it this way: "I joined the Basij only because I wanted to get its membership card. So when I am going outside with my girlfriend, if authorities want to bother me about my relationship with her, I can show them my membership card and then they don't bother me anymore."[76] In a magazine published by a Basiji, one Basij member wrote about how his Armenian friend got an active Basij membership card to be able to flirt with girls (*dokhtar bazi*) without fearing the Basij's response.[77]

In an interview in 2008, another Basiji told me, "Because I have to carry satellite equipment [currently illegal in Iran] in my car, I decided to become a member of the Basij and get a membership card so I can carry my tools easily. If somebody wants to stop me and search my car, I will show them my card and that will solve everything."[78]

While one may wonder if the Basij members quoted here accurately represent the broader demographic of Basij conscripts, an official report suggests that their responses are the norm, not the exception. According to the study conducted by the Basij Study and Research Institute in 2005, 79 percent of Basij members claimed that the advantages of receiving a Basij membership card influenced their decision to join the Basij, and 81 percent said their motivation included being able to wear a Basij uniform. Giving public service has been another factor influencing the decision of 75 percent of Basijis to join the organization.[79] The fact that people join the Basij for material or security gains means that an increasing number of Basij members are not driven by the theocratic ideology of the Islamic republic. This is not a very recent phenomenon: In fact, a published study conducted by the Basij organization as early as 1995 showed that only 35 percent of Basij members in resistance bases agreed with the statement that "a majority of Basijis believe in the culture of Basij and its values and live according to these beliefs."[80] One Basiji even said, "There are not any real Basiji, just hypocrites. They go out and arrest people wearing *Titanic* [movie] t-shirts and then brag to me about how many times they have watched *Titanic*. I ask them, why do you watch it if it is illegal? And they say they need to know what it is in order to judge its value. Sure—but do they have to watch it five times?"[81]

Perhaps because of all these issues, many Iranians don't have a positive view of the Basij and its members.[82] They think that most Basijis are inexperienced, dishonest (*hoghe baz*), prejudiced, irrational, unreliable, and arrogant.[83] According to the 1995 study conducted by the Basij, youth and people in the middle and upper classes have a more negative attitude toward the Basij than members of other socioeconomic groups. Many Iranians have a less-than-positive view of the Basij. According to a 1995 survey of female Basijis across different strata, only 40 percent were happy to be members.[84] According to a young female Basiji, "Many husbands ask their wives what they get out of being in the Basij."[85]

Iranian public perception of the Basij became particularly negative following the organization's aggressive role in suppressing the 2009 Green Movement. During and after the Green Movement, Basiji members became increasingly anxious about how they were being perceived, especially given that many Iranians believe that a majority of Basij work as informers and agents. Because of this anxiety, which increased during the Basij's suppression of the Green Movement, many Basijis now avoid revealing themselves as members of the Basij. One female Basiji said, "I do not expose that I'm a Basiji for fear that people will think I am a spy."[86] In some cases, families have been ripped apart because some were part of the Basij and some were not. One such instance was documented by a journalist interviewing a Basiji who was active in controlling dissidents in 2009. His fiancée asked him to choose between living with her and being a member of the Basij. "She said to me, 'Go beat other people's children then,' and 'I don't want to have anything to do with you,' and hung up on me." According to the interviewed Basij, his ex-fiancée returned her engagement ring and cut off all correspondence.[87]

The Basij and the Issue of Loyalty

Considering the numerous motivations that impel individuals to join the Basij, we must then question whether Basij members support the political regime unconditionally. If we take into account the major motives for conscription—ideological, economic, and opportunistic—we can divide Basijis into three main groups: the believers, the opportunists, and the thugs. The "believers" are those who join the Basij for religious and ideological reasons or whose beliefs are strongly reinforced by Basij ideological and doctrinal training. These members believe in the righteousness of the Islamic Republic and its supreme leader; a few even believe that the leader is somehow sinless (*masoumiat-e ektesabi*) and therefore obey his orders unconditionally. Despite their strong belief in the Islamic Republic and its leadership, at times these Basijis encounter ethical and religious dilemmas when suppressing other Muslims in their own society.

In fact, some Basijis refused to actively participate in the street violence following the 2009 presidential election. One such Basiji said, "I went to the streets because my commander asked me to, but I couldn't beat people, beat my brothers and sisters, so I tried to escape from the scene and went back home. When I couldn't escape, I decided to stay back and only watch people."[88] The clerical establishment tries to justify the suppression of the opposition by dehumanizing them as infidels, Baha'i, and so on. For example, during Ashura in 2009, the Basij mobilized several religious clubs to go the streets and suppress the protesters. To justify this, they accused the protesters of insulting Muharram and the Imam Hussein.[89]

While they might not like to be involved in internal repression, these members are the Islamic Republic's major loyalists when it comes to dealing with international threats. Thanks to their ideological beliefs, they value defending the Islamic Republic and martyrdom for God. Some of this stratum of the Basij has traveled to Syria to fight against the Wahhabis and Sunni extremists (religious militants understood as enemies of the Shia). Reviewing the motivations of these religiously ideological Basij shows how they see the pursuit of martyrdom and jihad against enemies of their sect as justification for their actions.

The second group of members, which in fact constitutes the majority of Basij forces, is made up of those who join the Basij for materialistic and opportunistic reasons. These people, who can be called the "opportunists," lack strong ideological beliefs. The majority of them are high school and university students seeking admission to higher education or employment opportunities. Moreover, some of them are looking for rapid and easy paths into the political power structure. Because of their ambitions and personalities, they usually occupy top positions in the organization. That is why some Basijis believe that "the problem of the Basij is that the people who are in power in this organization are not Basiji, and don't believe in its ideas."[90] This group's loyalty to the Islamic Republic, therefore, depends on the regime's ability to keep the members motivated to stay. In other words, as long as the state fulfills this function, they will support it. Should they feel the Islamic Republic has an insecure future, they would quickly start thinking about safer and more attractive alternatives. Consequently, the opportunistic Basijis cannot be relied upon for either suppressing internal riots or confronting international threats. For example, during the first months of the 2009 crisis, the Basij failed to mobilize even a few thousand members around Tehran to show support for the government. But once things quieted down in Tehran, they were again seen participating in pro-government demonstrations. These members are suitable only for participating in the Islamic regime's show of popularity. They can be organized to demonstrate in the streets in favor of the Islamic Republic, but the majority will not be involved in coercively responding to the opposition.

The last group of Basij members includes those considered thugs or ruffians (*owbāš*), a segment of the Basij that serves as a special force for the Iranian regime. The use of thugs by politicians and the clergy is not a new phenomenon; it goes back centuries. But the most widespread use of this group by a regime occurred in Iran after the 1979 Revolution. "Many thugs who in the past would have joined the ranks of the *luti* (vigilantes) have now become official agents of the government in the guise of members of the Basij."[91] During the past three decades, this group of Basijis has been one of the most important tools of the clergy when seeking to marginalize their opponents. In fact, the role of thugs has increased in Iranian society through the growing involvement of the Basij in the regime. Although these Basij appear to believe in Islamic rites and mores, they lack ideological, religious, and even ethical beliefs, and that is why they are hated by many devout Muslims. A Basiji who managed a mosque in southeast Tehran told me in 2008, "They are savage. They attack each other and steal everything, even from mosques, if they can."[92] Like the opportunists and security seekers, it is predictable that they would also withdraw their support for the Islamic Republic in the event that its authority was seriously threatened. This was clear in the aftermath of the disputed 2009 election, where photographers caught these Basij masking their faces, a sign of their fear of being recognized. Although this force is one of the regime's main tools of internal repression, the state cannot rely on it for confronting foreign military attacks, given its members' lack of ideological commitment.

Conclusion

Since the Basij's inception in 1980, the Islamic Republic has used Basij members to tighten its control over Iranian society. However, the Basij as a mass organization is not homogeneous; in fact, the Basij comprises Iranians with diverse demographic backgrounds and various motivations. Since many Basij members are young and from marginalized, poor, and lower-middle-class society, they are more susceptible to radicalism and the appeal of the populist slogans of political hard-liners, particularly appeals to socioeconomic equality and social justice. That is why they strongly supported Ahmadinejad and his political agenda, which emphasized social justice, supporting the oppressed, and hostility toward the middle class.

While ideology and religion can induce a small group of people to join to the Basij, many Basij members join because of materialistic and opportunistic incentives: to find a job, to get promoted, to take advantage of educational training opportunities, to improve one's chances at acceptance to a more accredited university, and so on. The Islamic Republic has tried to combat this issue by intensifying Basij ideological and political training. Although many of these ideological trainings fail to change mentalities among the Basij universally, such trainings have resulted in the heavy indoctrination of a small group of Basij members. During these ideological trainings, some Basiji became simultaneously more radical and conservative. While they grew more conservative in their zeal for defending the Islamic Republic's traditional and religious values, they also became more supportive of radical methods of implementing Islamic social and political policies, including the promotion of force as a means of implementing sharia.

Such extremists further alienate the Basij from more progressive segments of the Iranian citizenry, which has led to social polarization and intensifying anger and hatred of these two groups toward each other. Taking into account the presence of at least several million people in the Basij and the spread of this organization all over the country and throughout society, nobody can remain indifferent to changes within the Basij and their implications for Iran's future. A proper knowledge of

Iranian society and politics is impossible without knowledge of the Basij. Consequently, further study of this organization and its branches is critical for enhancing our understanding of Iranian society and the Islamic establishment.

Notes

1. See, for example, Martonosi, "The Basij: A Major Factor in Iranian Security"; Ostovar, "Iran's Basij"; Golkar, "The Paramilitarization of the Economy."

2. Ostovar, "Iran's Basij."

3. Torabi and Roohi, *Basij dar Partow-e Qanun*, pp. 40–41.

4. *Vahed-e Basij-e Mostazafan of the Sepah-e Pasdaran* is translated as Islamic Revolutionary Guards Corps.

5. Wehrey et al., *The Rise of the Pasdaran*, p. 27.

6. For the first time, *Bekargiri* ("using the Basijis") became part of the constitution of the Basij, and Bekargiri became one of the Basij's responsibilities, besides recruitment, training, and organizing.

7. Bayat, *Life as Politics,* p. 69.

8. Golkar, "The Ideological-Political Training of Iran's Basij."

9. In Tehran city council elections in March 2003, only 562,022 people took part, out of the 4,681,000 who were eligible to vote.

10. Golkar, "The Paramilitarization of the Economy."

11. Wehrey et al., *The Rise of the Pasdaran.* p. 13.

12. Press TV, "Basij, IRGC Support Iranian Government."

13. Ghasemiyan, *Akhlaq va Adab-e Moashera-te Basij*, p. 8.

14. Ostovar, "Iran's Basij," p. 353.

15. Ibid., p. 352.

16. Imam Hussein (*Seyed Al Shohada*) Battalions are trained and directed by IRGC ground forces to prepare a group of Basij members for future wars based on the strategy of scattered and mosaic warfare. See Golkar, "Organization of Oppressed or Organization for Oppressing."

17. Rafiehi, "Conversation with Director of the Deputy of Preparing the Textbooks of Islamic Research Institute of IRGC," p. 175.

18. Fars News, "Educating of 17,000 Sport Coaches at the Sport Basij Organization."

19. Golkar, "The Feminization of Control."

20. Zolqadr, "News and Analysis" (Akhbar va Tahlilha).

21. Babakhanian, "Sisters Basij and Intelligent Defense with Soft Threats," p. 16.

22. Taeb, "ISNA Interview with Commander of Basij."

23. Fars News, "The Organized Basij Member Passed Twenty Millions."

24. For instance, in 2003, while the commander of IRGC announced that the population of Basij was around 7 million (*Sobh-e Sadeq*, no. 103, June 2, 2003, p. 5), the commander of the BRF talked about 8,597,000 members (*Hejazi*, 2003), and according to the deputy of the force (Ahmadi Moqaddam) it was about 10 million (65 percent of 20 million soldiers will be realized by the next year), *Sobh-e Sadeq*, no. 123, October 20, 2003, p. 1.

25. Naqdi, "Lebas shakhsi."

26. Ayatollah Movahdi Kermani, *Sobh-e Sadeq,* no. 51, April 23, 2002, p. 15.

27. Aslani, "Empowering Female Managers Is the Core of the Women's Basij Organization's Activities."

28. Parchami, "Measuring Public Attitudes Toward the Basij," p. 88.

29. "The Biggest Educational Drill of Student Basij," *Sobh-e Sadeq,* no. 132, October 23, 2003, p. 5.

30. Afshar, "Ashena'i ba tashkilat va mamuriyatha-ye Basij," p. 21.

31. Kile, *Europe and Iran,* p. 54.

32. Political Research Deputy of Islamic Republic of Iran, *Basiji Teenager,* p. 14.

33. Taeb, "ISNA Interview with Commander of Basij."

34. Tila and Ranjbar, "A Study of the Function of the Basij in the Province of Sistan and Baluchestan and Suggestions for Its Development."

35. Shirazi, "The Study of Recalling and Usage Methods of Sisters Basijis," p. 79.

36. Golkar, "The Feminization of Control."

37. Fathalizadeh, "Forces to Reckon With," p. 9.

38. Although I know I cannot generalize this data to all Basij members, my observations as a scholar who lived in Iran and who worked on the Basij for a few years support these statistics.

39. Author's surveys conducted in 2006–2007.

40. Ibid.

41. Ibid.

42. Schahgaldian and Barkhordarian, *The Iranian Military Under the Islamic Republic,* p. 95.

43. Author's surveys conducted in 2006–2007.

44. Young Journalists Club, "A Comprehensive Information System Should Establish for Identifying Veteran Students."

45. Author's surveys conducted in 2006–2007.

46. Torabi and Roohi, *Basij dar Partow-e Qanun,* chap. 3.

47. Princeton University, "Revolutionary Guards Employment Law."

48. Gholami, "A Basiji's Opinion on the Pathology of the Basij."

49. Author's surveys conducted in 2006–2007. People are clearly very careful about how they answer such controversial questions, due to distrust of people in the military force and concerns about security issues. Also, the Shiite custom of *taghiye,* by which believers are entitled to lie in defense of their lives, must be taken into consideration.

50. Since these statistics were published by the Basij organization, the actual numbers are probably higher.

51. Parchami, "Measuring Public Attitudes Toward the Basij," p. 79.

52. Ostovar, "Iran's Basij," p. 353.

53. Tila and Ranjbar, "A Study of the Function of the Basij."

54. Varzi, *Warring Souls,* p. 178.

55. Zianali, "Sanjesh-e Angizeh-e Ghaleb Aghshar-e basij."

56. "Nazaersanji az Danshe amouzan Piramzon Dars-e Amadeghi-e defai," p. 11.

57. Varzi, *Warring Souls,* p. 178.

58. Golkar, "Politics of Piety, Moral Control of Iranian Society."

59. There has been propaganda against the Basij (Afshar, "Interview with General Ali Reza Afshar," p. 29).

60. Khosravi, *Young and Defiant in Tehran*, p. 39.

61. Eisenstadt, "The Security Forces of the Islamic Republic and the Fate of the Opposition."

62. Wehrey et al., *The Rise of the Pasdaran*, p. 68.

63. Faruru News Agency, "Khat faghr dar Iran."

64. A Basiji's opinion in a social network discussion about giving privileges to Basiji, September 28, 2009, www.cloob.com/club/post/show/clubname/Basij 2000000/topicid/1821815/wrapper/true, accessed July 13, 2014.

65. Torbi, *Influential Factors on Recruiting the Basijis,* summary report, Basij Study and Research Institute, July 20, 2006, www.bro.ir/PrDetail.asp ?ItemID=361, accessed March 20, 2011.

66. Alfoneh, "The Basij Resistance Force."

67. Golkar, "Liberation or Suppression Technologies?"

68. Ghasami, "The Study of Basij Sport."

69. Ostovar, "Iran's Basij," p. 354.

70. Author's interview with a female Basij, Tehran, October 2008.

71. Golkar, "The Reign of Hard-line Students in Iranian Universities," pp. 21–29.

72. Golkar, "Cultural Engineering Under Authoritarian Regimes," p. 12.

73. Mahdavi, "The Study of Governmental Employees About the Position of Basij in Offices," pp. 117–120.

74. Yadoallahi, *Barsi ellal va anghizehah jameh shankhti ozyat dokhtern dansh amoz dar Basij dansh amoozi.*

75. Kamrava, "Military Professionalization and Civil-Military Relations in the Middle East," p. 84.

76. Author's interview with a teenage Basiji in Tehran, August 23, 2008.

77. Hosseini, "A Good Basiji Is Not Usually a Member of the Basij."

78. Author's interview with a satellite-dish installer in Tehran, June 16, 2009.

79. Torbi, *Influential Factors on Recruiting the Basijis.*

80. Mahbobi, "Investigating of Factors Affecting the Declining or Increasing Activities of Basij Resistance Bases."

81. Varzi, *Warring Souls,* p. 178.

82. For example, while the Basij was defined as "the sincere army of God [*Basij-e Lashkar-e Mokhless Khodast*]" by the government, many sardonically refer to the Basij as the "Mokh-less" (stupid) army of God.

83. Parchami, "Measuring Public Attitudes Toward the Basij," pp. 67–69.

84. Mobin, "The Study of Opinion of Sisters Basijis."

85. Sadeghi, "Foot Soldiers of the Islamic Republic's 'Culture of Modesty.'"

86. Ibid.

87. Fassihi, "Inside the Iranian Crackdown."

88. Author's interview with a special Basiji who has responsibility at a resistance base in southeast Tehran, July 12, 2009.

89. Hadadian, "Dialogue with Raja News."

90. A Basiji's opinion on the pathology of the Basij, at Ehsan Heshmati, website of the Supporters of Supreme Leadership (Hamian-e-velayat), January 23, 2010.

91. Floor, "*Luti*, a Persian Term with a Variety of Meanings."

92. Author's conversation with a manager of a mosque in southeast Tehran, August 8, 2008.

6

A Portrait of
the Persian Blogosphere

John Kelly and Bruce Etling

If one follows Iran, or follows the global phenomenon of blogs, a story emerges across numerous articles, reports, and interviews. The conventional wisdom is that the Iranian blogosphere[1] is a dissident space dominated by young, would-be democrats opposed to the ruling regime.[2] The difficulty with this story is not its veracity. Aside from some grand claims regarding the rank order of Persian among the world's blogging languages, there is little in the story that does not merit considerable confidence. It is the story of brave people yearning for freedom and democracy. Quite understandably, many people want to hear this story, but it is not the whole story. If the Iranian blogosphere is a place where women speak out for their rights, reformists press for change, and dissidents press for revolution, it is also a place where the supreme leader is praised, the Holocaust denied, the Islamic Revolution defended, Hezbollah celebrated, Islamist student groups mobilized, and pro-establishment leaders, including President Mahmoud Ahmadinejad, reach out to their very real constituencies within the Iranian public. Furthermore, a great deal of the discourse in the Iranian blogosphere has little to do with an outside observer's preconceived list of key issues. Religion is a major topic for bloggers, and not predominantly in its overtly political aspects, but more often in its historical, theological, and deeply personal ones. Persian culture and history, including music, visual arts, and performance, but most especially poetry, are very big topics. Sports are popular, too, as are movies. And as in the American blogosphere, a great many bloggers write simply about their day-to-day lives, seemingly with mnemonic rather than polemical purposes in mind.

To carry out this study, we used computational social network mapping in combination with human and automated content analysis.[3] Automated analysis was conducted from July 2007 to March 2008, and human coding of blogs by Persian-speaking researchers took place between November 2007 and March 2008. Our research indicates that the Iranian blogosphere is a large discussion space of approximately 60,000 routinely updated blogs featuring a rich and varied mix of bloggers. Social network analysis reveals the Iranian blogosphere to be dominated by four major network formations, or poles, with identifiable subclusters of bloggers within those poles. We label the poles as (1) *secular/reformist*; (2) *conservative/religious*; (3) *Persian poetry and literature*; and (4) *mixed networks*. The secular/reformist pole contains expatriates, as well as Iranians living in Iran, and features discourse about Iranian politics, among many other issues. The conservative/religious pole contains three distinct subclusters, two focused principally on religious issues and one on politics and current affairs. Given the repressive political and media environment, and high-profile arrests and harassment of bloggers, one might not expect to find much political contestation in the blogosphere. However, we identified a subset of the secular/reformist pole focused intently on politics and current affairs and mainly comprising bloggers living inside Iran, which is linked in contentious dialogue with the conservative political subcluster. Blocking of blogs is less pervasive than we had assumed, even though the Iranian government is a vigorous Internet censor. Most of the blogosphere network is visible inside Iran, although the most frequently blocked blogs are clearly those in the secular/reformist pole. We also include findings of the OpenNet Initiative, which show what parts of this discourse network are visible inside Iran, as well as the reach of domestic and foreign news sources in the Iranian blogosphere. We conclude that, given the repressive media environment in Iran today, blogs may represent the most open public communications platform for political discourse, in part because the peer-to-peer architecture of the blogosphere is more resistant to capture or control by the state than the older hub-and-spoke architecture of the mass media model.

Structure of the Iranian Blogosphere

Figure 6.1 is a network map of the Iranian blogosphere, in which each dot represents a blog. Understanding the map is the key to understanding the Iranian blogosphere. The size of the dot represents the number of other blogs that link to it, a measure of its popularity. The position of each dot is a function of its links with its neighbors. The diagram is drawn with a Fruchterman-Rheingold "physics model" algorithm. Imagine that there is a general force trying to push all blogs away from each other, like a wind blowing them off the map, and that a spring (or force of gravity) pulls together any two blogs that are linked online. Blogs are drawn together by their direct links, but more importantly by the links among their shared neighbors. Thus, large groups of blogs cluster into densely interlinked network neighborhoods. Blogs that share a lot of common neighbors will be close together in the map, even when they do not link directly to one another.

Figure 6.1   Social Network Map of the Iranian Blogosphere

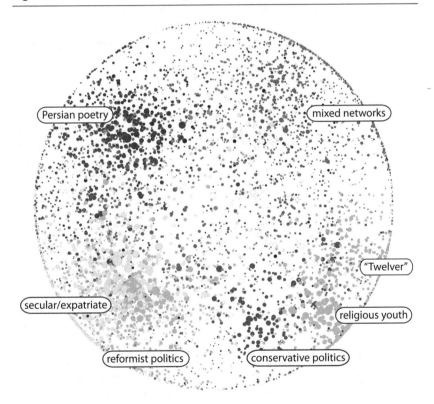

Note: This map represents the 6,018 most prominent blogs in the blogosphere based on the number of links to each blog.

The shade of each dot on the map is determined through a different process. A large proportion of the links from blogs are not to other blogs but to online news, organizations, businesses, and various other Internet resources. In some areas of the blogosphere, particularly clusters attentive to news and public affairs, the majority of links are to things other than blogs. On this map, shade indicates the assignment of a blog to a particular *attentive cluster*, which is a group of blogs that link to similar online resources. *Attentive cluster analysis* looks at the full range of online resources linked by blogs and groups each with others that share a similar linking profile. Traditional audience measurement of mass media uses "soft" measures of attention, which estimate probable attention to media and messages based on inferences. If a person subscribes to a certain magazine, or has the television tuned to a certain channel at a certain time, researchers infer the likelihood that a particular advertisement was seen. In blogs, linking to something represents a hard measure of the blogger's attention, which is why a statistical correlation in linking patterns among a number of bloggers is interpreted here as an *attentive* cluster. We see clear patterns in what bloggers are paying attention to across the network. *Network neighborhoods* and *attentive clusters* usually overlap a great deal, but it is important to understand that they represent two different (though highly correlated) things. The first is the direct linking among bloggers, that is, who is close to whom in the online newsroom; the second is where they are linking to in the Internet at large, that is, who is looking in the same direction, statistically speaking.

The analytic approach of this study is based on the principle that macrostructure arises from the tendency of individuals to link more frequently to things in which they are interested. This phenomenon is an extension into blogging practices of social behaviors that are well understood in other social-scientific contexts. Sociology has an extensive literature on *homophily*, the tendency of social actors to forms ties with similar others.[4] Communications research has identified complex processes of *selective exposure*, by which people choose what media to experience, interpret what is experienced, and remember or forget the experience according to their prior interests and beliefs.[5]

Research on blog networks bears out the intuition that large-scale online communities are structurally reflected in higher-density network neighborhoods.[6] The shape of a network that emerges from the billions of individual writing and linking choices made by millions of individual authors reflects large trends in what interests them. Online behavior is conditioned by the users' preferences in conscious and unconscious ways. In the blogosphere, these preferences express themselves as choices about what to read, write about, link to, and comment upon. The result of this online activity is a *discourse network*, tractable to empirical research as a massive corpus of text and hyperlinks created by millions of people and stored on thousands of the world's Internet servers. By mapping this network and using the map to view these bloggers' communicative activity, we achieve something like an fMRI of the social mind.

The Iranian blogosphere is dominated by four major network formations, each with its own interesting structural and social characteristics. With the notable exception of Mahmoud Ahmadinejad, most Western (e.g., academic, think tank, and journalistic) discussion about the Iranian blogosphere refers to bloggers who are found within just one of these structures, a large group dominated by expatriates and reformists and featuring frequent criticism of the Iranian regime and its political values and philosophy. It is often difficult to judge where a blogger is physically located, especially since Iranian bloggers inside and outside Iran use the same Persian-language blog-hosting services, but our analysis suggests that a significant proportion of the bloggers in what is thus popularly understood to be the Iranian blogosphere do not live in Iran. Blogs in the remaining three groups appear to be authored almost exclusively by people living inside Iran and reflect a diversity of interests and concerns that our analyses have identified and located to particular sectors of the map.

We refer to the four major regions of the Iranian blogosphere, which appear in separate quadrants of the social network map, as poles. In this complex network, each pole has its own structural characteristics, and these reflect important characteristics of the communities of bloggers found there. Our various analyses tell aspects of the same story. We look at each of these in turn, but first, in summary, the four poles of the Iranian blogosphere are (1) the secular/reformist sector (includes *secular/expatriate* [*secPat*] and *reformist politics* [*refPol*]), which contains most of the well-known Iranian bloggers, including notable dissidents and journalists who have left Iran in recent years, as well as long-time expatriates and critics of the government; (2) the conservative/religious sector (includes *conservative politics* [*conPol*], *religious youth* [*relYth*], and *"Twelver"* [*12er*]), which features bloggers who are very supportive of the Iranian Revolution, Islamist political philosophy, and certain threads of Shia belief; (3) the *Persian poetry and literature* sector (*poet*), which is devoted mainly to poetry, an important form of Persian cultural expression, with some broader literary content as well; and (4) the mixed networks (*mixNet*) sector, which is different from the first three in that its structure is looser and less centralized. The mixed networks sector does not represent any particular issue or ideology, but rather the loosely interconnected agglomeration of many smaller communities of interest and social networks, such as those that exist around sports, celebrity, minority cultures, and popular media.

While the four corners of the Iranian blogosphere each require their own interpretation, some general insights emerge from the basic data collected on bloggers in the major clusters. The secular/reformist and conservative/religious poles each contain subgroups, which were profiled independently in the collection of basic data on blogger location, gender, and anonymity. These subgroups are described in more detail below, but some differences among them can be observed in the basic data. These data are the results of human researchers making judgments based on reading blogs sampled from the clusters; in many cases the researchers did not feel confident to make a determination and answered "don't know" (*dk*). Figures 6.2–6.5 include these *dk* values. Several observations stand out, as follows.

Figure 6.2   Blogger Location

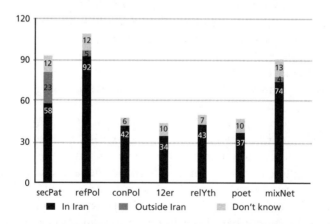

Note: With the exception of the first *secular/expatriate cluster* (*secPat*), which contains a significant number of expatriate bloggers, the vast majority of bloggers live inside Iran.

Figure 6.3 **Blogger Gender**

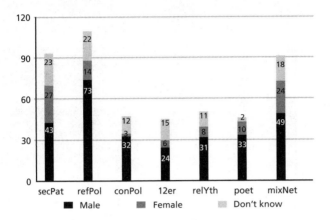

Note: The majority of the bloggers in all clusters are men, but some clusters feature a large minority of women, principally *secPat* and *poet,* and to a lesser degree *mixNet* and the *12er* subcluster of the *conservative* pole.

Figure 6.4 **Blogger Anonymity**

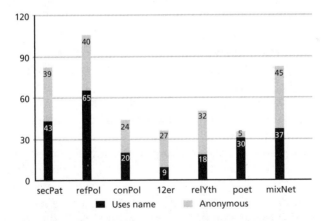

Notes: There are interesting variations in the balance of bloggers using what appears to be their name versus those who are blogging anonymously or under an obvious pseudonym. Our hypothesis had been that *secular/reformist* bloggers, especially those living inside Iran, would be the most likely to blog anonymously, yet the opposite is true. Conservative bloggers write anonymously far more frequently, as do bloggers in the *mixNet*. One possible explanation for the high frequency of anonymity among conservative bloggers is the value placed on modesty in Islam, as opposed to any fear of retribution by authorities. Only the poets are more likely to use what appear to be real names.

Figure 6.5 Blogger Age

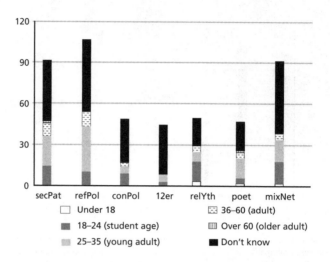

Notes: The researchers were usually unable to estimate the bloggers' ages, and we consider this data very unreliable. However, in qualitative discussions about blog content, researchers repeatedly made observations that confirmed the general indication that the *conservative* pole, most especially the cluster we call *religious youth (relYth)*, contains younger bloggers on average than other parts of the map.

Pole Profiles

Poetry and Mixed Networks

The following sections present the findings of several distinct analyses, all of which help to illuminate the political dimensions of the Iranian blogosphere. These analyses are preceded by a brief introduction to the major parts of the Iranian blogosphere, including descriptions of sub-clusters used in the analysis.

The poetry pole is focused almost completely on a single topic or activity. Most of the blogs feature poems (original, quoted, and histori-cal) as well as analysis and discussion of poetry, with a particular focus on love poetry and Ghazal, a traditional poetic genre. Poetry is a major form of cultural production in Iran, historically and, unlike in the West, today as well. By contrast, the mixed networks pole is a patchwork of small subnetworks discussing a plethora of issues and topics. It has no A-list of stars, nor any discernable center of gravity. There are blogs about soccer, pop music, Zoroastrianism, political poems, a great many personal diaries, and various other things. Whereas the other clusters have clear patterns of concentration in their outlinks—meaning that they link preferentially to coherent sets of online resources (such as particular sets of news sites or nongovernmental organizations)—this group links to a wide variety of items in no clearly patterned way. This pole comprises a kind of loose tissue of very modestly popular blogs that are unaffiliated with larger political and cultural movements, as well as the "treetops" (the most popular bloggers) among these particular social networks of friends, students, and subcultures.

Secular/Reformist Pole

This pole comprises a single large structural cluster that contains a degree distribution (popularity curve) typical of emergently organized blogosphere structures, meaning that it arises from a great many bloggers making independent choices about whom to link to, but with substantial recognition of particular high-profile blogs (an A-list). This kind of structure is found in the liberal and conservative clusters of the US blogosphere, as well as much of the technology blogosphere. This cluster features a relatively high proportion of prominent women bloggers, which is notable since prominent bloggers in the other clusters are typically male. The blog network is well integrated, in the sense that the structure of links among bloggers forms a single large neighborhood. However, attentive cluster analysis shows patterns in the linking behavior of bloggers that reveal different dimensions of interests. While these blogs in general reflect a secular, often reformist point of view, one attentive cluster is particularly focused on politics and discusses news items, current affairs, and certain public figures with great frequency. More about the two attentive clusters:

• The *secular/expatriate* (*secPat*) cluster features a large proportion of women and expatriates. Common topics include women's rights and political prisoners. Many of these blogs discuss cultural issues, including cinema, journalism, books, and satire.

• The *reformist politics* (*refPol*) cluster focuses more intently on hard politics, including news and current affairs, journalism, and particular politicians and issues, including drug abuse and environmental degradation in Iran. Bloggers in this cluster are overwhelmingly male and live inside Iran. Counter to our expectation, given the risks that they face, most of these bloggers write under what appears to be their own name, as opposed to blogging anonymously or using a pseudonym.

The overwhelming majority of blogs in the conservative/religious pole are infused with religious references. Many of the blogs are primarily religious and not overtly political. Other blogs focus intensely on politics. Blogs in this cluster support the philosophy and legitimacy of the Islamic Republic and the supreme leader, if not always particular government policies and politicians. The conservative pole comprises three interlinked but structurally distinct subclusters, as follows:

• *Conservative politics (conPol)* focuses on power politics, in the sense of tracking news, issues, and current public affairs. It features discussion and criticism of particular politicians and policies. The focus is on domestic issues primarily, including the economy, but with attention to international news and foreign policy as well. Quotations from the speeches of politicians are very frequent. While some of its members support the current government absolutely, criticism of government institutions and political leaders, including Ahmadinejad, is common.

• The *twelver discourse (12er)* subcluster reflects the majority of Shii Muslims (approximately 89 percent in Iran) who believe that Muhammad ibn Hasan ibn Ali, or al-Mahdi, the Twelfth Imam (according to their line of succession, which other branches contest), has for over a millennium been in a state of occlusion, hidden and protected by God. He will return as the ultimate savior of mankind, creating a perfect Islamic society before a final day of resurrection. While Twelvers are the dominant Shii sect in Iran, some members focus much more intensely on the Mahdi's expected return, including some of the most radical political Islamists in the governing establishment. Ahmadinejad courted the approval of this group in frequent symbolic acts. To many conservatives, the entire purpose of the Islamic Republic is to prepare the way for the Twelfth Imam's imminent return. This cluster comprises several hundred devoted Twelver bloggers and is intensely concerned with religious matters.

• The *religious youth (relYth)* cluster contains bloggers who tend to be younger than those in other clusters, including a lot of students. Religion is a dominant topic of concern, and the cluster has structural properties (strong similarities in outlink profiles, relatively egalitarian in-cluster linking) that indicate possible institutional coordination. There are a number of putatively "grassroots" conservative student blogging associations in Iran, and they might account for this phenomenon.[7]

Content Analyses

To determine what the bloggers in different clusters care about, we conducted three separate content analyses, as described below. First, we used human researchers to identify key topics of posts and provide brief summary descriptions of blogs they read. Second, we analyzed relative frequencies in the use of terms found in blog posts across the various clusters. Third, we looked at groups of outlinks (news sources, websites, and other blogs) favored by particular parts of the Iranian blogosphere.

Human Coding

Our team of Persian speakers read and coded approximately 500 blogs, sampled from across our chosen clusters of interest. They used two questionnaires, a basic questionnaire that captured a set of essential data on blogger location, gender, anonymity, and estimated age, and an extended questionnaire that asked for researchers to indicate when bloggers wrote about certain categories of issues such as news, politics, religion, and personal life.[8] In addition to our standard issue questions, researchers were able to add their own issues to the questionnaire on the fly. This was not expected to produce reliable results, but was intended simply to identify emerging or unexpected issues. The results from the basic questionnaire (Figures 6.2–6.5) were reviewed previously. Figures 6.6–6.9 reveal some patterns.

Figure 6.6   Politics and Public Affairs Topics

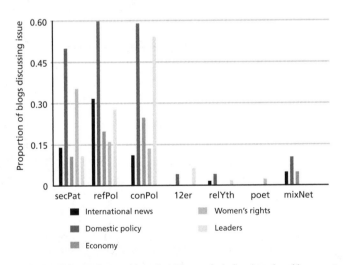

Notes: Public affairs are discussed broadly in the secular/reformist pole, with more attention to international news, the economy, and names of particular political leaders (mentioned by name) in *refPol*, and significantly more attention to women's right issues in *secPat*. Further, the *conPol* cluster of the conservative pole is intensely focused on public affairs, particularly domestic policy and certain leaders (mentioned by name). There is also discussion of women's rights issues, although from a conservative point of view. The *12er* and *relYth* clusters show comparatively much less attention to public affairs. Finally, the *poetry* and *mixNet* poles show very little attention to public affairs.

Figure 6.7 Islam and Religion Topics

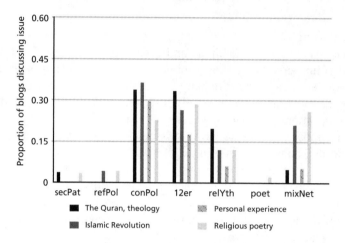

Notes: The *conservative* pole shows an intense focus on religion, particularly the *12er* cluster. Theology and the Quran are particularly important here. The *secular/reformist* pole shows little concern with religion, as is true also of the *poetry* pole. The *mixNet* pole contains religious posts, but less to do with the Quran and more to do with personal experience and poetry.

Figure 6.8 Personal-Life Topics

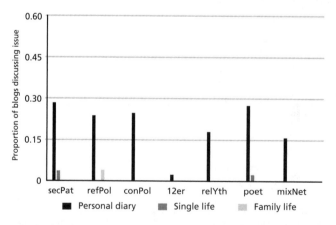

Notes: A minority of bloggers use the medium to make "personal diary" posts across the board, but with greater frequency in the *relYth* cluster and *poetry* pole. Strikingly, very few bloggers were found writing about single life (dating, relationships) and family life (marriage, children). This runs counter to descriptions of the Iranian blogosphere that emphasize dating behavior of rebellious youth. Presumably such activity among young singles uses more private modes of online communication (Mahdavi, "The Sexual Revolution.").

Figure 6.9   Specific Topics

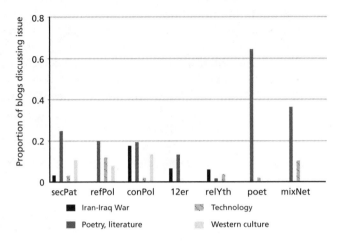

Iran-Iraq War ■   Technology

Poetry, literature ■   Western culture

Notes: Posts about the Iran-Iraq War were noted in all clusters of the *conservative/religious* pole, and not much elsewhere. Poetry and literature are, unsurprisingly, dominant topics in the *poetry* pole, but were also found to a lesser degree in other regions. Technology is not a major topic, but is seen more in *relYth* than elsewhere. Western culture and values are not major topics of discussion, but such discussion as there is occurs in the *conPol* cluster of the *conservatives* pole and in the *secular/reformist* pole.

In addition to the standard topics, the researchers identified 130 other issues. Issues occurring more frequently in the conservative pole included quotations from the speeches of leaders, criticism of the media, admiration of Ayatollah Khamenei, and Ahmadinejad's visit to Columbia University. Topics found more in the secular/reformist pole included journalism, the crackdown on university students, and political prisoners. Interestingly, the *conPol* cluster contained criticism of Ahmadinejad's government, as well as analysis of major problems they face, like Iran's poor economic condition, gas prices and rationing, and the nuclear issue. A range of opinion and analysis is present in the *conPol* cluster, including support and criticism of Ahmadinejad's leadership. This was a surprise to find, initially. However, more qualitative work with the researchers helped make sense of it.

In addition to the topic coding, Persian-speaking researchers working on the extended questionnaire were asked to write a short, one- to three-sentence description of the blog.[9] These descriptions were illuminative. Descriptions of blogs in the secular/reformist pole were often what one might expect—for example:

• *secPat*: "Blogger surveys women's freedom, or lack thereof, in comparison to men's rights in Iran. She criticizes capital punishment in Iran."

• *secPat*: "Blogger believes that Iran lacks basic freedoms and democracy and posts articles, poems, and pictures to reflect his beliefs."

• *refPol*: "This blog satirically addresses student issues like drug addiction, imprisonment, lack of political freedom, and general political issues."

• *refPol*: "The blog is published by one of Iran's most popular political parties, 'Jebheh Mosharekat.' Students and intellectuals are the party's base of support. In this site people can read and discuss the mistakes and mismanagements of the current administration."

Descriptions of blogs in the *conPol* cluster of the conservative pole were often what you might expect as well:

• *conPol*: "The blog is devoted to supporting the regime, its founder (Khomeini), and its current leadership, and their government policies and record."

• *conPol*: "This blog reviews political events and news and has a general disdain for liberals in Iran and admires the extremists like Ahmadinejad."

• *conPol*: "This blog is devoted to supporting the government and its leadership as the blogger believes they represent God and Shiite figures."

• *conPol*: "This blog analyzes speeches and political activities of Iranian liberals from a right-wing extremist standpoint. Additionally, the blogger supports Islamic rules and regulations in Iran."

However, many of the descriptions sound like those in *secPat*:

• *conPol*: "The blog directly analyzes the rampant inflation that is wreaking havoc on Iran's middle class and blue collar class of the society, leading women and young girls to prostitution. This site also talks about other issues and problems caused by the regime, using slang and indirect logic."

• *conPol*: "This is an intellectual site analyzing important events, activities, and mistakes of the Iranian regime in detail using persuasive logic."

• *conPol*: "Blog denounces the regime's corruption and lack of respect for the law of the land. Blogger also discusses the student movement and criticizes some media outlets."

• *conPol*: "This blog talks about the regime's mistakes and problems and criticizes the regime and the leaders by indirectly questioning the veracity of government facts and statistics."

If randomly sorted together with descriptions of blogs in the secular/ reformist pole, one would assume they belonged there. Some other descriptions help understand the nature of this criticism:

- *conPol*: "This blog both criticizes and admires Ahmadinejad in different instances."
- *conPol*: "This blog admires Islam and Islamic leaders like Ayatollah Khamenei and Ahmadinejad. Concurrently, the blog criticizes the regime on women's issues, some of its leaders, Israel, and U.S. policies in the region."
- *conPol*: "This blog supports the Ahmadinejad regime while criticizing the court system and the seemingly arbitrary nature of political arrests."

Conservative political bloggers make distinctions between various institutions, people, and policies of the Iranian government, and will praise some and criticize others. Support for figures like Ahmadinejad can be partial, and criticism can be from a "friendly" perspective, much the way an American politician can face criticism from members of his or her own party. The discourse in *conPol,* the conservative politics cluster, looks like "democratic" discourse, full of invective, opinion, and critique of friends and foes alike, rather than parroting of a party line. Descriptions of blogs in the other two conservative clusters were in general less surprising:

- *12er*: "All about the memorization of the Quran."
- *12er*: "The author of this blog explicitly states in his introduction that this blog does not intend to get involved in the partisan scene of politics and that it is only an attempt to reflect feelings about the 12th Imam of the Shias, who will one day appear in the world."
- *relYth*: "Devoted to religion, pictures of Khamenei and Ahmadinejad."
- *relYth*: "The writer is writing against reformists and criticizing them, while defending the ninth president, namely Ahmadinejad."

However, even these clusters had their surprises:

- *12er*: "This blog mostly entails religious poems about Islam, Shiite figures, and the martyrs of Iran-Iraq War. Interestingly enough, the blog poetically criticizes the mismanagement of some of the regime's leadership without specifically mentioning any names."
- *relYth*: "Religious but also seemingly liberal and has interests in the supernatural."

Term and List Frequencies

A second way we approached understanding the different modes of discourse across the map was with automated text frequency analysis. Here, rather than human researchers, we used computers to mine the full text of blog posts. We identified over 3,000 English-language Wikipedia articles on Iran-related topics of interest to us, of which approximately 1,700 had Persian-language translations of the term (article names of people, places, and things, such as *al-Mahdi, Mohsen Rezaee, Baba Taher, Evin Prison*, etc.) that we could extract algorithmically. Furthermore, these terms are organized by Wikipedia into large, overlapping sets of lists, such as "Iranian Politicians," which could include members of the list "Iranian Ayatollahs" as well as members of "Women members of the Majlis." Using the extracted Persian terms, we scanned the full text of blog posts harvested from the Iranian blogosphere over a period of about seven months (beginning July 2007) and found all occurrences of the terms. We then calculated the relative frequencies of hits across our target clusters. The results reveal which individual terms and which lists were more frequently cited by particular clusters. Since the source of the terms was Wikipedia, we could open the articles and read about these differentially cited items. For individual terms and for lists, some very interesting patterns emerged.

First, in general for terms and lists, some things are of interest more to one cluster than to others. For example, the *12ers* preferentially wrote the Persian text for *al-Mahdi*, the Twelfth Imam (term); *Allamah al-Majlisi*, a major historical Twelver cleric (term); *Shaykh Tusi*, a historical Twelver scholar (term); and *'Ajam*, a common Arab term for Iranians and other non-Arabs (term).

The *conPol* cluster uses a number of terms more than any others, including *Palestine* (term); *Mohsen Rezaee*, a powerful conservative official, linked to the 1994 AMIA bombing in Argentina (term); *Hassan Rouhani*, at the time a major politician and cleric and nuclear negotiator (term); *Hojjatieh*, a secretive, radical, anti-Baha'i religious group, which Ahmadinejad is accused of sympathizing with (term); Iranian religious leaders (list); and Iranian military personnel of the Iran-Iraq War (list).

Poet and *mixNet* bloggers, respectively, preferred the terms (Persian text) for *Baba Taher*, a major eleventh-century Persian poet (*poet*); *Behistun Inscription*, an ancient stone inscription, which is central to a famous mythical Persian love story (*poet*); *Shahab Hosseini*, a film and TV actor (*mixNet*); and *Mahasti*, an expat pop singer who died in 2007 (*mixNet*).

More commonly, however, certain terms or lists receive more hits not from individual clusters but from pairs of them, and there are very interesting patterns in which pairs of clusters use particular terms and listed aggregations. Significantly, the most common pairing is the *refPol* and *conPol* clusters, which preferentially write about such things as *Haleh Esfandiari*, an Iranian American academic, held by Iran in 2007 (term); *Amir Kabir*, a historical (1807–1852) reformist (term); *Gholamhossein Karbaschi*, an ally of Ali Akbar Hashemi Rafsanjani, imprisoned by hard-liners (term); *Akbar Hashemi Rafsanjani*, the pragmatic conservative former president (term); *Special Clerical Court,* Iran's "Star Chamber" court for trying clerics (term); Iranian clerics (list); Iranian law (list); Iranian political organizations (list); Iranian women in politics (list); and Iranian Majlis representatives (list).

Here, and with many more terms and lists from the analysis, we see that these two clusters focus on a discourse of power politics, from opposite sides of the ideological divide—one more secular and reformist, the other more religious and conservative. Not all political terms and lists are preferred by this pairing; some are preferred by another common pairing—*secPat* and *refPol*—who cite *Prison 59,* a Revolutionary Guard prison (term); *Evin Prison*, a prison in Tehran where political prisoners are kept (term); *Saeed Mortazavi,* a hard-line judge who closed reformist newspapers and is implicated in the death of Canadian journalist Zahra Kazemi in 2003 (term); Iranian prisoners and detainees (list); Iranian secularists (list); Iranian Jews (list); Iranian bloggers (list); and Iranian women's rights activists (list).

Here we see the kinds of politics that secularists and expatriates like to write about, but their conservative opponents would rather not. A final common pairing has little to do with politics but rather is cultural and entertainment-oriented. The *refPol* cluster (most all of whom are in Iran) shares a number of interests with bloggers in the *mixNet,* including *Zoroaster*, a prophet for Zoroastrians and Baha'is (term); *Shahab Hosseini*, a film and TV actor (term); *Siavash Shams*, an expatriate pop singer (term); *Afshin,* a pop singer (term); Olympic footballers of Iran (list); Iranian television actors (list); and Iranian classical musicians (list).

The patterns we see in the text analysis results contribute to the understanding gained from the human blog coding. We see large ideological formations: again, one that is more reformist and secular, the other more conservative and religious in outlook, each with subgroups (*refPol* and *conPol*) that are particularly attentive to the contentious politics of power. We see clusters in the secular/reformist pole concerned about things that the conservatives are less interested in talking about, like political prisons and conservative officials linked to terrorism. We also see a cultural affinity, built around sports and popular entertainment, between part of the secular/reformist side concentrated in Iran (*refPol*) and broader, unpoliticized members of the *mixNet* cluster.

Outlink Analysis and News Sources

Our third analysis aims to understand how various parts of the Iranian blogosphere relate to the broader ecology of online media—in particular, news sources and Web 2.0 sites. Iranian bloggers tend to link most frequently to domestic news sources such as Fars News and the Iranian Student News Agency. The most prominent foreign news source is BBC Persian Service, which is nonetheless significantly less cited than mainstream Iranian sources. Bloggers in the *secPat* and *refPol* clusters, where politics is a major focus, link more heavily to online news sources than do other parts of the network, with the exception of *conPol*. In contrast, *Poet* bloggers link heavily to other poetry blogs and a handful of websites about poetry, and *MixNet* does not link coherently to any particular bundles of websites.

US-funded Radio Farda is referenced by far fewer bloggers than the BBC or domestic news services, and its audience is almost exclusively limited to the secular/expatriate pole. Interestingly, Web 2.0 services based in the West like Wikipedia and YouTube are referenced more widely across the network than foreign-based Persian-language news services. Furthermore, government-mandated filtering of the Internet disproportionately targets those parts of the network that most frequently cite foreign news.

Filtering and Blocking of Persian Blogs

While we cannot know whether the Iranian blogosphere would feature additional contentious political discourse if it were not for government repression of bloggers, there is clearly a great deal of such discourse now. A key question then becomes how much of this discourse is visible to Iranians inside the country. To a reader in Tabriz, it may matter little whether the political blog post they read was authored in Tehran or Los Angeles, and in fact they would very often not be able to tell. What matters to that reader is whether the blog is visible at all or blocked by the government. The OpenNet Initiative (ONI) collects data on which websites are blocked in nations that filter citizen access to the Internet.

There are no metrics for defining how much blocking is a lot. From the standpoint of basic principles of free speech and open access to information, any blocking is too much. Blocking by Iranian authorities is clearly focused on blogs in the secular/reformist pole, though there are blogs blocked in the other poles as well, including the religious/conservative one. But a view of Figures 6.2–6.9 and Table 6.1 show that a minority of blogs are blocked. Furthermore, the large majority of secular/reformist pole blogs are visible to Iranians, including 79 percent of *secPat* and 89 percent of *refPol,* which is especially interesting given the latter's focus on political affairs.

ONI assigned a Persian-speaking researcher to review a number of blocked blogs to investigate why various blogs, including those outside the secular/reformist pole, might be blocked. The researcher found discussion of women's rights, temporary marriages, erotic poetry, offensive language, racism, and open source code. It was impossible to guess why some of the blogs were blocked, and the bloggers themselves were sometimes aware that they were blocked and confused as to why. Following are some examples. The question posed was, "This blog is blocked by the government. Based on the blogger and their writing, why do you think they would be blocked?"

In the *secPat* cluster:

• "The blogger is a law student. Her blog explicitly addresses feminist themes."
• "This is mostly an innocuous personal blog. In one post, however, the writer describes her new workplace favorably because 'men and women' are not separated and are able to interact together in a positive atmosphere. She also praises the management of her new office for not bothering women and not questioning them about hijab norms."
• "Written in an affectionate, familiar tone, the blog offers romantic/relationship advice to readers, deemed offensive by the regime."

Table 6.1   Blocked Sites by Cluster

Cluster	Percentage Blocked	Percentage Visible	Visible	Blocked	Total
secPat	21	79	650	178	828
refPol	11	89	663	86	749
conPol	2	98	252	6	258
12er	1	99	301	3	304
relYth	0	100	297	0	297
Poet	2	98	312	6	318
mixNet	8	92	1,667	139	1,806

In the *Poet* cluster:

• "Although his poetry and criticism are generally apolitical, some of his verses contain obscene language ('shit,' 'fuck')."
• "The blogger posts mostly verse, some by notable Iranian poets and some by him. The themes of most of these are typically Iranian: '*eshq*' (love), '*mey*' (wine), etc., etc. Others hint more directly at the erotic."

In the *conPol* cluster:

• "The blog is devoted to media criticism, especially film, television, and video games. . . . Most posts dissect western media, the Harry Potter series for example, through an 'anti-Zionist,' anti-imperialist prism. . . . [A recent post] is devoted to condemning Rupert Murdoch's 'Zionist' media empire. . . . [H]e sounds off-message because the regime makes it a point not to condemn world Jewry directly. The blogger also has a Persian ultranationalist take on pan-Turkish and pan-Arabist movements, claiming these movements are Zionist in origin and designed to divide and undermine the Muslim Umma."

And in the mixed networks pole:

• "The blogger is a programmer. His posts mostly consist of JavaScript tools and other web and blog related widgets and tools. In this case, I suspect the regime is trying to restrict access to open source code."
• "The blogger—a devoutly religious young man—is singularly devoted to advancing the cause of traditional temporary marriages ('*siqeh*'). The author believes that this institution is currently misunderstood by Iranian society as a way to legitimize temporary sexual relationships, when really it is a well-established, responsible Islamic tradition that helps those who are unprepared for permanent marriages reach out to the opposite sex and fulfill their healthy sexual needs."

ONI continues to analyze the data on blocking in the Iranian blogosphere, and we make no claims here about the processes or intent behind current regime efforts. We note only our surprise that such a large proportion of that part of the blogosphere, which the regime must consider oppositional, is in fact visible within Iran. The implication is that despite periodic persecution of bloggers, the Iranian blogosphere remains a viable arena of political contestation and forum for viewpoints challenging the ruling ideology of the Islamic Republic. In this sense, it remains a robust platform for democratic discourse for a society with severely curtailed modes of political participation.

Conclusion

Social network mapping and content analysis provide more systematic methods for analyzing blogs than those used in previous studies of the Iranian blogosphere. Our research reveals that the Persian blogosphere is a large discourse network, featuring a rich variety of discussions among many different groups of Iranians. Early conventional wisdom held that bloggers were mainly young democrats critical of the regime, but we found conversations including not just on politics and human rights but also on poetry, religion, pop culture, and many other topics. Given the repressive media environment and high-profile arrests and harassment of bloggers in recent years, one might not expect to find much open political contestation among bloggers living in Iran. Yet oppositional discourse is robust, particularly between the two politically focused clusters on either side of the ideological divide between the secular/reformist and conservative/religious poles. Blocking of blogs by the government, particularly within the secular/reformist pole, is less pervasive than we had assumed. It is uncertain whether the visibility of 80 percent to 90 percent of secular/reformist blogs inside Iran is a function of limits to the government's intent to block oppositional discourse, or its ability to do so.

Given the repressive media environment in Iran today, blogs may represent the most open public communications platform for political discourse. The peer-to-peer architecture of the blogosphere is more resistant to capture or control by the state than the older, hub-and-spoke architecture of the mass media model, and if Yochai Benkler's theory about the networked public sphere is correct in relation to blogs, then the most salient political and social issues for Iranians will find expression and some manner of synthesis in the Iranian blogosphere. In our view, the question at hand is not whether the Iranian blogosphere provides a samizdat to the regime's politburo, but whether a new infrastructure of the social nervous system, which is changing politics in the United States and around the world, will also change politics in Iran—and perhaps move its hybrid authoritarian/democratic system in a direction that is more liberal in the sense of modes of public discourse, if not necessarily in a direction that is more liberal in the sense of political ideology.[10]

In the four years since this research was initially conducted, our analysis of the Iranian blogosphere has continued. Each year we applied the same analytic method to mapping the blog discussion network using current data. We also conducted a special mapping on the eve of the 2009 Iranian presidential election. Over this period the network has evolved in some ways, and remained very much the same in others. In each of these mappings, the macrostructure of the network is essentially the same: large centers of density representing secular/oppositional and religious/conservative poles, each containing some more political and some more cultural clusters. Outside of this polarized landscape, a loose tissue of minor bloggers avoids the schism by focusing on pop culture, technology, domestic life, and other similar topics. Interestingly, this structural continuity exists despite the fact that the majority of the blogs themselves are different. Only about 15 percent of the blogs in the 2012 map are also in the original 2008 map. Perhaps in part because of government efforts to censor blogs, there is a high level of churn in the Iranian blogosphere. This point highlights the importance of taking a meso-level approach to analysis of social media networks. Individual fish arise, grow, and die, but the school continues.

Against this backdrop of structural continuity, several major evolutionary trends have taken place in the Iranian blogosphere. These are almost certainly related to government efforts to suppress dissent and bolster pro-regime online discourse. The key trends include:

• A large increase in conservative blogs since 2008, particularly of the religious and often Basij-affiliated "CyberShia" bloggers (called *Twelver* in this chapter). Some of this increase was due to a specific campaign by the Basij to promote blogging among its members and supporters.

• Migration of political opposition from Iranian blog platforms (like blogfa.com) to international platforms (like blogspot.com and wordpress.com). This migration accelerated after the 2009 elections, when the government began forcing blogfa.com to close particular blogs, whereas previously they had just blocked them at the ISP level.

• Particularly in the 2012 data, a reduction in the level of blogging among the political opposition. Oppositional blogs continue to exist, but they are not the vibrant network they were in 2008. Some observers speculate that oppositional activity has largely migrated to Facebook.

• Particularly in the 2012 map, an increase in blogs about food, parenting, and other aspects of domestic life. This is consistent with the claim that since the 2009 crackdown, many liberal Iranians have retreated from politics into the private sphere.

Our initial 2008 project has thus continued to bear fruit, allowing an ongoing view of the evolving relationship between social media networks and Iranian politics and society. The Iranian case has demonstrated clearly that early optimism around the fusion of new media and politics in repressive societies was overly simplistic. Nevertheless, as the events of the Arab Spring have demonstrated, these technologies change the playing field on which political actors contest power. The Iranian story has certainly not yet reached its last chapter.

Notes

1. We use the term *Iranian blogosphere* throughout this chapter, since that is the more popular description of the universe of bloggers in Iran, even though a more accurate description for the network we analyzed would be *Persian-language blogosphere*. To capture the entire blogosphere of Iran would also require minority languages and English-language blogs by Iranians.

2. This popular view of the Iranian blogosphere has been supported by sources such as Alavi, *We Are Iran*, a collection of translated Iranian blogs, and the *New York Times* op-ed piece that argued, "Bloggers tend to be young, well educated and not very supportive of President Ahmadinejad, who typically attracts followers from the urban poor" (Parker, "Blogging Ahmadinejad in Tehran").

3. For a full description of the methodology, see Appendix B of the Berkman Center case study from which this chapter was drawn, http://cyber.law.harvard .edu/publications/2008/Mapping_Irans_Online_Public, accessed July 8, 2014.

4. McPherson et al., "Birds of a Feather."

5. Sears and Freedman, "Selective Exposure to Information." See also Frey, "Recent Research on Selective Exposure to Information," as well as Chaffee and Miyo, "Selective Exposure and the Reinforcement Hypothesis."

6. Kumar et al., "Trawling the Web for Emerging Cyber-Communities." See also Adamic and Glance, "The Political Blogosphere and the 2004 Election."

7. Tehrani, "Iranian Muslim Bloggers."

8. Both questionnaires are included in Appendix A of the Berkman Center case study, http://cyber.law.harvard.edu/publications/2008/Mapping_Irans _Online_Public, accessed July 8, 2014.

9. Detailed notes on methodology, copies of the questionnaires used in the study, and additional researcher comments for each attentive cluster are available in the appendices of the working paper, "Mapping Iran's Online Public," http://cyber.law.harvard.edu/sites/cyber.law.harvard.edu/files/Kelly&Etling _Mapping_Irans_Online_Public_2008.pdf, accessed July 8, 2014.

10. Benkler, *The Wealth of Networks*, pp. 180–185, 212–213.

7

The Role of Social Media: Myth and Reality

Mehdi Yahyanejad

S ocial media played a significant role in the creation, evolution, and suspension—if not the dissolution—of the Green Movement in the course of the disputed 2009 presidential election in Iran. In this chapter I highlight the impact of social media on the opposition up until February 11, 2010, when, as the world held its breath, the street protests— and, with them, the movement's dynamic momentum—came to an end.

Facebook and a number of Iranian websites were used to share information inside Iran and globally. Twitter had relatively few readers in Iran but helped a number of journalists and activists reach the international audience. Given the slow Internet connections in Iran, YouTube was not easy to access, but Iranians were able to view the videos on BBC Persian and Voice of America (VOA) satellite programs. (See Figures 7.1 and 7.2.)

The Many Roles of the Internet

The Birth of the Persian Blogosphere

In 2000, toward the end of Mohammad Khatami's first term as president, the Iranian government severely curtailed freedom of the press, shutting down many print media outlets and intimidating and arresting journalists who resisted self-censorship. The crackdown drove many reporters and activists to the Internet. This change of venue coincided with emerging blogging platforms that supported Unicode, which in turn allowed users to blog freely without technological restrictions.

The Persian blogosphere grew exponentially as a result and by 2006 ranked tenth in the world. Conversations revolved mainly around democracy, pluralism, and tolerance, generating discussions about civil society, personal freedom, social and political reform, and the rule of

Figure 7.1 The Function of Internet Platforms During the 2009 Iranian Presidential Election

Internet Platform	Description
Video platforms	Video websites provided evidence of demonstrations and exposed brutality and killings by security and paramilitary forces. YouTube, the most popular video sharing website, highlighted the Iranian protests on the front page of its CitizenTube during the demonstrations.
Social networks	Unblocking Facebook before the presidential election allowed rapid user growth and political activism. Facebook allowed information to go into and out of Iran.
Microblogging platforms	Twitter did not have a large following in Iran. A handful of Iranian activists and journalists tweeted what they read in Iranian sources, which allowed international audiences and reporters to track the events.
Political campaign websites in Iran	Political websites based in Iran were influential in creating Internet activity on social networks by providing content to be shared and discussed.
	GhalamNews and Kaleme, Mir-Hossein Mousavi's official websites, were the reference point for many of his supporters.
	Mowj-e Sevvom, the campaign website of reformist candidates, played an important role in bringing former president Mohammad Khatami back to the campaign scene. One of its petitions was signed by 450,000 people.
Blogs in Iran	Blogs were a continuous source of new ideas for the Green Movement and a channel for exposing human rights violations by the Iranian government.
	Balatarin—a link-sharing aggregator of blogs and news that allows members to vote on the postings—served to amplify the voice of the bloggers and became the most widely used site for sharing news and views, and for organizing protests. Several nonviolent protest activities had their origins in posts or discussions taking place on Balatarin.
News websites outside Iran	A number of news websites based outside Iran played an important role in exposing human rights violations and compiling daily updates, among them, Roozonline, Gooya News, and Radio Farda.
Blogs in major English-language news outlets	Blogging in major outlets such as the *New York Times, The Guardian,* and the Huffington Post allowed quick reporting on what citizen journalists produced.
Mailing groups and chain emails	These were among the most reliable ways of distributing news or protest calls in Iran.

Figure 7.2   Other Digital Communication Channels or Devices That Played an Important Role in the Iranian Presidential Election

Communication Channel	Description
SMS (text messaging)	SMS has a much broader reach in Iran than the Internet and was used widely to share information until the government blocked access.
Satellite broadcasts	BBC Persian and Voice of America (VOA) have a large audience in Iran that far surpasses the reach of the Internet but does not elicit the same level of engagement.
Cell phone videos and photos	Video footage and photographs captured on cell phones and circulated in Iran and internationally provided some of the most important content on the Web.

law—activities that had started during a period of relative freedom in the early years of Khatami's presidency (1997–2005). The Internet served as a marketplace for new ideas and an open forum for dialogue among bloggers, as well as an increasing number of Internet users.

By spring 2009, reformist activists began using social media to promote their favorite presidential candidates. During the three months leading to the June election, the presidential campaigns, especially of the frontrunners, Mir-Hossein Mousavi and Mehdi Karroubi, but also of the third candidate, Mohsen Rezaee, took place on blogs; political websites; social news aggregators—the focal site being Balatarin; microblogging tools such as FriendFeed and Twitter; and social networks, primarily Facebook.

Presidential Messages and Social Media

When Mousavi, a reformist who had served as prime minister from 1981 to 1989, announced his candidacy for the presidency, he had been away from politics for more than twenty years and had less than three months to campaign. There is no independent television in Iran, and most of the reformist media that might have backed him under normal circumstances had been shut down in the previous years, yet it took him only a short time to achieve popular support among youth, students, and middle-class Iranians in particular.

Mousavi was running against the incumbent Mahmoud Ahmadinejad. In the months leading up to the election, Iran's populist president had substantially increased retiree pension payments, distributed shares of state-owned companies among villagers and the poor, and promised additional future dividends. When campaigning, he blamed Mousavi for the past failures of the Islamic Republic and publicly denounced one of Mousavi's prominent supporters, former president Ali Akbar Hashemi Rafsanjani, as corrupt.

An online poll asked supporters of the four presidential candidates the main reasons for their choice of candidate. Ahmadinejad supporters mentioned his interest in fighting corruption, producing nuclear energy, and helping the poor. Supporters of Mousavi, Karroubi, and Rezaee, on the other hand, mentioned their hope for increased social freedoms, improved relations with the West, and democratization as the main reasons for their choice.

It is not too much of a stretch to equate the medium with the message. The candidates who contested the status quo were those who made most use of social media for being open, equalizing, innovative, urban, global, and democratic by design.

Cyberactivism on the Eve of the Election

In January 2009 the Iranian government unblocked Facebook and Twitter. Surprised, large numbers of Internet users wasted no time to sign up for these services. In less than a month, Facebook became the fifteenth-most-visited website in Iran. Twitter did not enjoy the same success, likely because FriendFeed, a microblogging platform more suited to conversations and content sharing from other sites, was already popular in Iran.

The reason the Iranian government freed access to Facebook and Twitter remains a mystery. At the time, some speculated that it was to generate more excitement for the approaching presidential election and boost voter participation. Others disagreed, saying that Facebook and Twitter were far less effective as political tools than reformist and opposition websites such as Gooya News, Roozonline, and Balatarin.

Perhaps by allowing access to Facebook and Twitter, platforms that the Iranian government perceived to be apolitical, the authorities tried to divert attention from more overtly political sites. Another explanation could be that the Iranian government wanted to collect information on Facebook users by taking snapshots of their and their friends' profiles. This move was technically feasible, given that Facebook did not support encrypted access to its website.

The unblocking of Facebook and Twitter coincided with the hacking of Balatarin. Bloggers had used the link-sharing website to expose corruption and wrongdoing within the ranks of Ahmadinejad's government, and by 2009 the site had emerged as the central hub of Iranian bloggers, journalists, and dissidents.

The political activism of the pro-reform camp in Iran was initiated by the Third Wave (Mowj-e Sevvom), an activist website. In their campaign, the activists petitioned former president Khatami to run against Ahmadinejad, collecting more than 450,000 signatures calling on him to run. On February 8, 2009, Khatami agreed, acknowledging the role of the online campaign in his decision, although five weeks later, he withdrew in favor of his longtime friend Mousavi when the latter announced his candidacy.

Following Mousavi's nomination, the political campaign heated up in record time. The media-savvy Mousavi, who had served as editor in chief of *Jomhuri-ye Eslami*, the official newspaper of the Islamic Republican Party in the early years of the 1979 Revolution, ran an active campaign website called Ghalam News, while his wife, Zahra Rahnavard, who soon proved to be a strong campaign partner, had a Facebook page. Mousavi's campaign slogan, *Har Irani yek resaneh* (Every Iranian a Media), called on his supporters to use the Internet to broadcast his message.

The other reformist candidate, Mehdi Karroubi, chairman of the National Trust Party who had also run in the 2005 presidential election, was also active on the Internet. His party's newspaper, *Etemad-e Melli*, was also published online; his campaign manager, Gholamhossein Karbaschi, created and maintained an active Twitter account.

In short, candidates for the 2009 presidential election in Iran understood the power of the Internet to mobilize support and tried to exploit it to their advantage. One campaign adviser recalled a strategy meeting where they looked for an associate with enough seniority points on Balatarin who would be able to create daily headlines more sympathetic to their campaign.

Proving the Raid on
Mousavi Headquarters via Live Video Feed

The day before the election, the militia raided Mousavi's campaign headquarters in Qeytarieh in northern Tehran. The campaign had set up a room on the fifth floor of the building to broadcast Internet-based video interviews with politicians and celebrities encouraging people to get out and vote.

Suddenly, the building was stormed by hostile bands of militia that charged up to the fifth floor and smashed the broadcasting equipment, disrupting the program. VahidOnline, an Internet celebrity who had remained anonymous until that day, happened to be in the building. He immediately posted news of the raid on his Twitter account and other web services. To underscore the severity of the raid, he also sent live video feed of the attack on a site called Qik using his mobile phone, providing undeniable proof of the criminal assault and its perpetrators. Because of VahidOnline, whose identity was now exposed, about 8,000 users saw the footage. Meanwhile, people put up resistance and were able to arrest four of the militia before calling the police.

The video of the raid that was broadcast live on Qik later aired on the BBC Persian evening newscast. The footage was one of the most important testimonials associating the election with militarization. Owing to the shadowy nature of the attack, the perception emerged that a silent coup had taken place, while government supporters claimed that security forces had visited Mousavi's headquarters to stop a broadcast that was in violation of campaign regulations. In any event, fearing for his life, VahidOnline went into hiding and later escaped from Iran. He posted an emotional statement on his blog titled "The Crime of Being Online" before crossing the border with the help of smugglers.

At 6:30 p.m., several hours before the polling stations closed, Fars News Agency, a website close to the Iranian Revolutionary Guard, projected that Ahmadinejad would win with 60 percent of the votes. The announcement elicited grim disbelief among online users and was posted to Balatarin with a modified title, "Is this credible: Mousavi 28%!! Ahmadinejad 69%? (the biggest fraud of the century)." The link was posted to Balatarin at 12:09 p.m. Tehran local time, only three hours after the polling stations closed. Social media had emerged as the pivotal forum for communication.

Election Day: Disputing the Vote Count

The presidential election on June 12, 2009, was marked by events unfolding so fast that they caught everyone by surprise. Mousavi's camp had stationed more than 20,000 observers at different polling locations; they were to report their observations or any irregularities to Mousavi's campaign headquarters by means of SMS messages. On that very day, however, the government disabled SMS services across the country. Later on, with the election results fiercely disputed by a massive number of incredulous and angry voters, the Mousavi campaign underlined the interruption of SMS services as one of the primary pieces of evidence in the election fraud. The government responded that, given the law prohibiting campaigning on Election Day, SMS service was interrupted to prevent its being used for campaign purposes.

Throughout the day, social media buzzed with rapid exchanges of news, commentary, hypotheses, statistics, and computations that questioned the integrity of the vote count giving Ahmadinejad a second term in office. The unresolved dispute led to massive antigovernment street protests and a brutal crackdown on the opposition—events that, among other consequences, bred a contingent of Internet-based citizen reporters.

Voicing Opposition on TV with a Million SMS Messages

The most-watched program on Iranian state-run TV is the sports show *90*. On occasion, the host invites viewers to vote on one of three answers to the question of the day via SMS. Given that the last choice was usually displayed in green, in early January 2010, activists asked the public to choose the third option at the next broadcast, regardless of the question. As it happened, the host displayed the third answer in yellow on that show; people voted for the third option nevertheless. The question was, "What is the main reason for the decline of soccer in Iran?" The optional answers were: (1) Poor management; (2) Unqualified coaches; and (3) Loss of the Golden Generation. More than a million Iranians voted for the third option—which was not the right answer—by sending SMS messages to a sports program on state-run TV to show their support for the Green Movement.

Most Iranian viewers, whose favorite sport is soccer, were well aware that poor management was to blame for the decline of Iranian soccer. Yet, of the more than 1.8 million people who voted on the program that night, a whopping 75 percent chose the third option, the least sensible answer. This demonstrated that at least 1 million Iranians were willing to follow Green Movement campaign tactics, regardless, to show their dislike of the government.

Placing the Green Movement on the Global Map

The rise of the Green Movement to the top of world news was the result of the effectiveness of Iranian activists in getting the news out of Iran and into the hands of the right audience in the fastest possible way. The most memorable example of this process is the haunting video of twenty-six-year-old Neda Aghasoltan bleeding to death before the frantic eyes of bystanders after being shot by the Basij militia in Tehran on June 20, 2009. The footage, captured on a cell phone by a protester, was originally posted to Facebook. In less than an hour, it was posted on Balatarin, and in less than fifteen minutes, it was voted straight up to the front page. From there, the video went viral, generating worldwide sympathy for the Iranian protesters and rallying support for the Green Movement. It is difficult to imagine such a development without citizen journalists posting videos to social media websites.

Calling for Action
Many people using the phrase "Twitter Revolution" imagined Iranian activists scuttling along the streets coordinating demonstrations using their mobile phones. This never happened. As mentioned earlier, Twitter users in Iran were few, and the Iranian government had disabled SMS. However, social media were used in a number of ways to call for action, including brainstorming and refining ideas before publicizing them further.

This activity mostly took place in blogs and on Balatarin. Once these ideas were ready, they were publicized widely by groups of activists connected through blogs, Balatarin, Facebook, and chain emails. I know of at least two groups that had built mailing lists with tens of thousands of email addresses and were distributing news or action calls to people around the country.

Email proved to be the most resilient way to communicate on the Internet. Many of the ideas developed on the Web were also broadcast to Iran by Mohsen Sazegara and Alireza Nourizadeh. They were guests and political analysts of a weekly TV program on the US-based VOA. While discussing political issues, they always took the opportunity to point out the locations of the coming demonstrations. The show's moderator would often interrupt them with a reminder that sharing such information detracted from VOA's neutrality.

Most protests were planned to coincide with anniversaries of historical, political, or religious events where state-sponsored pro-government rallies were expected to be held. The Green Movement activists planned their demonstrations on the same days to lower the risk of being isolated and targeted. Major demonstrations took place on Qods ("Jerusalem") Day, Student Day, University Student Day, Ashura (the Shiite day of mourning marking the martyrdom of Imam Husayn on the tenth day of Muharram), and February 11 (twenty-second day of Bahman), which is the anniversary of the victory of the 1979 Islamic Revolution.

Sealing a Turning Point Online: The Qods Day Rallies
In 1979 Ayatollah Khomeini named the last Friday of Ramadan Qods Day, marking an anti-Israeli platform as the central feature of his foreign policy. Since then, state-sponsored rallies had been organized to commemorate Qods Day. In summer 2009 the violent crackdown on the

postelection protests and shocking reports of the rape and torture of prisoners filled the air with a sense of fear and foreboding, leading the government to believe that the days of street demonstrations were over. Nevertheless, several weeks ahead of Qods Day, online activists called for Green supporters to attend the rallies and to protest the crackdown. The Iranian opposition figures did not initially support this idea. The Green Movement activists called it "Qods Day, the Green Day of Iran." Many of them were hesitant to use the demonstrations against Israel to protest against the Iranian government. Only in the days close to Qods Day did Mehdi Karroubi, one of the opposition leaders, respond to the calls of online activists. Mousavi waited until the last day to announce his participation. The Qods Day demonstration was thus an idea that was born on the Internet and spread mainly through the Web.

The Iranian government disrupted Internet services on Qods Day. For several hours after the demonstrations, there were no YouTube videos of the activism. BBC News published an article that read, "Reformist opponents of the controversially re-elected President Ahmadinejad seem to have been massively outnumbered by system loyalists eager to demonstrate their support for the president and his patron, the Supreme Leader, Ayatollah Ali Khamenei." Balatarin users posted a link with the title, "Bizarre claim by international media that turnout by Green Movement activists on Qods Day was low; need to send pictures." Soon, photos were linked up and new videos were posted on YouTube attesting to a very large opposition turnout. The BBC website updated the article without acknowledging its original mistake: "Thousands of opposition supporters have clashed with security forces during a government-sponsored rally in Tehran."[1]

Qods Day may be summed up as the moment when the Green protesters subverted the official government rallies and reinvigorated the opposition. The demonstrations may be said to have changed the course of events from an election protest to an enduring movement.

Mousavi was well aware of the significance of the day. He called it a turning point for the movement. In a speech following the demonstration, he also acknowledged social media's role:

> A virtual network exists today that operates efficiently when no other type of [independent] media is available. The social groups acting within this virtual space are less vulnerable. Members of these groups have infused the movement with dynamism, which renders us much more hopeful.
>
> Though the leaders of the movement did not officially call for it, we witnessed a great demonstration on Qods Day. This happened

despite the numerous threats over the past three months that drove many
families to stop their children from going [to the demonstrations]. This
could have not have been achieved without this [virtual] network.[2]

The success of social media on Qods Day resulted in overreliance
on these media as not only a means for communication but a place for
the public to collectively settle on a strategy, then publicize and act on
it. As can be seen from Mousavi's words here, the leaders of the Green
Movement had high hopes for the virtual network.

This virtual network was not only susceptible to cyberattacks by the
Iranian government, however, but as indicated by the events of the
Green Movement that followed, it also lacked a structure required for
expert decisionmaking and strategizing. To many observers, Mousavi
and other leaders of the Green Movement left too much of the strategy
and leadership to the loosely framed and fuzzy virtual world, with dev-
astating consequences for the democratic movement in Iran.

Debating Strategy Online:
How Freedom Square Failed to Go Green

Following the massive demonstrations on Ashura, Green Movement
activists looked forward to the opportunity to make a mark during the
anniversary celebrations of the 1979 Islamic Revolution on February
11. In the capital, the annual demonstration starts on a main street in
central Tehran and leads to Azadi ("Freedom") Square. This time, in
2010, the well-known satirist and blogger Ebrahim Nabavi suggested
that the protestors hide any green signs and paraphernalia until they
reached Azadi Square. Once there, they would be in a position to reveal
their allegiance to the Green Movement, take over the square, and dis-
rupt Ahmadinejad's speech.

Nabavi published this idea first on his blog and then on JARAS, a
Green Movement news website. The proposal was debated online.
Some criticized Nabavi's idea for being concentrated on Azadi Square,
believing that scattered demonstrations across Tehran would work best.
Most people were in favor, however. In a poll conducted the day before
the event, 80 percent of Balatarin readers said they believed the strategy
would succeed. Many activists saw it as the last push to overthrow the
regime, comparing it to the spontaneous show of furor by the crowd on
December 21, 1989, that led to the overthrow of Nicolae Ceauşescu,
Romania's last communist leader.

The actual events of February 11 showed that the Iranian government had long prepared for the day. Security forces were heavily

deployed in targeted areas and in total control of the streets; people were scared to leave their houses. The government bused large numbers of supporters from the provinces to Tehran and deposited them along the route leading to Azadi Square. Many protesters who made it to the rally found themselves surrounded by government supporters. Since the strategy called for the protesters to hide their green signs until they reached the destination, it was hard for them to identify their allies and build pockets of protest. People were barred from entering Azadi Square; only a select group were allowed, which then filled the front row near Ahmadinejad's podium.

The government broadcast the rally as proof that it still enjoyed wide popular support. Many Green Movement advocates were disappointed at the outcome and felt defeated. Online activists started looking for someone to blame. Having initiated the strategy, Nabavi was accused by some of treason, reckoning that he might have conspired with the Iranian government to push the approach taken. The truth was that the strategy had in fact been widely publicized and openly debated online for several weeks. The exposure meant that the Iranian government had plenty of time to plan for countermeasures.

A satellite picture of the rally taken by GeoEye showed exactly what had happened. Numerous buses had hauled government supporters to line the main route and dropped them off on Azadi Street, which ends at Azadi Square. Azadi Square itself was kept sparse to protect the podium where Ahmadinejad was scheduled to address the crowd. Based on the population density captured in the satellite pictures, government supporters numbered around 200,000, not millions as the government claimed. Regardless of the numbers, the government won the day, only because no major opposition protest took place.

The Trojan horse strategy had failed badly. The reason is that the Iranian government knew the intentions of the Green Movement supporters well in advance and had prepared accordingly. In hindsight, many activists realized that the strategy had not been such a great idea after all, and they had failed to think through the details of their plan and the government's likely response.

The case demonstrated that existing online platforms do not support the exploration, brainstorming, and selection of ideas in a systematic and methodical way. The open nature of these platforms further allows competitors to follow each other's tactics and strategies, which makes surreptitious missions impossible.

The failed demonstration by the Green Movement on February 11, 2010, was the last major attempt by the opposition to protest in the streets.

Winning Strategies by Analogy:
Kasparov vs. the World Team
The flaw in Nabavi's Trojan horse strategy was pointed out to me by a
Green Movement activist who had initially supported it but was later
disappointed by the outcome. He compared the process leading up to
the February 11 rallies to "Kasparov vs. the World," a game of chess
that was famously played over the Internet in 1999. Sponsored by the
Microsoft Network (MSN), the game pitted the reigning world chess
champion, Garry Kasparov, against the World Team—50,000 individuals from over seventy-five countries playing collectively. Four star players handpicked by MSN were to suggest moves, with input from the
community. The final options would then be debated in online forums
and voted on by the 50,000-member team.

It took Kasparov four months and sixty-two moves to beat the
World Team. With millions of people around the world watching, the
wisdom of the crowd shaped fluidly in the open proved no match for the
coherent strategy painstakingly crafted by a stealthy expert.

Members of the World Team had several disadvantages as the game
unfolded. First, every strategy, including future moves, was discussed in
a public forum. Not surprisingly, Kasparov took a peek. "Of course I
used it to my advantage to look around and follow the discussion on
MSN.com about the game," he remarked. But let us remember that,
important as it was for Kasparov to win, it was only a game of chess
after all. In the Iranian scene, by contrast, the government faced a challenge that it could not afford to lose; it played for survival. So it kept a
watchful eye on the planning process as Green Movement participants
discussed their moves and made decisions online.

Second, the World Team had difficulty agreeing on a coherent strategy against Kasparov. The discussions were not coordinated well; some
were emotionally heated and confrontational. As a result, more energy
was spent on flame wars than on analysis. There was too much noise.
Most of the 50,000 members were not expert chess players; they
brought little of real value to the table, and emotion often drove their
votes. A clear parallel exists here with the online discussions among the
Green Movement activists whose exchanges were often too emotionally
charged. Lacking a coolheaded analytical approach, the participants
often perceived realistic assessments as pessimism. Like the World
Team, propelled by an exciting momentum, they failed to forecast and
counter their adversary's lethal moves.

A critical point in the chess game was a 49 percent to 44 percent vote on move 58 that turned out to be disastrous for the World Team and led to a checkmate a few moves later. Decided in a public forum, the Green Movement's February 11, 2010, strategy had a similarly disastrous effect. The Green Movement lost its foothold on the balance and was never able again to organize demonstrations, even on a small scale.

Conclusion

The events surrounding the Iranian presidential election in June 2009 were marked and impacted by social media. Activists used the Internet—blogs, social networking and news sites, and microblogging platforms, as well as word of mouth, SMS, and satellite TV—to mobilize the grassroots against the government and demand change. At a time when being a card-carrying member of an opposition party carried a high risk of retribution, online activism lowered the cost of political dissent, giving the masses the option to protest at a relatively acceptable level of risk. For many who wanted to make a difference, the risk of joining a Green Movement Facebook group or a Web-based mailing list was an acceptable cost. But while these loose affiliations helped attract and grow the opposition, they also resulted in confusion at critical moments, when what was needed was the articulation of clear goals, thorough planning, skillful coordination, and discipline.

Overreliance on the Internet as a substitute for leadership and strategy had a terrible cost, best exemplified by the failure of the critically important demonstrations on February 11, 2010. The discussions that unfolded online raised unrealistic hopes among the opposition and proved to be a recipe for disappointment. Relatedly, the wisdom of the crowd failed to produce the best protest strategies for the simple reason that the average Internet user was not in a position to assess one proposal over another. Yet another downside was the overtransparency of the Internet-based decisionmaking process that handed the Iranian government plenty of information as well as adequate time to plan a countermove to defeat the opposition's strategy.

The main lesson here is that, to be effective, online activism needs to be balanced with rational leadership. Leadership cannot delegate strategic decisions to the wisdom of the crowd. Leaders should pay attention to their followers online but base their decisions on a thoughtful, methodical, and realistic approach on the ground—and, throughout the process, take responsibility for the outcome.

Notes

1. For the original BBC article, see http://feoline.blogspot.com/2009/09/rally
-attack-on-iran-opposition.html. For the Balatarin link, see https://www.balatarin
.com/permlink/2009/9/18/1761900. For the BBC article after the modifications,
due to the outrage of the social media activists, see http://news.bbc.co.uk/2/hi
/8262273.stm.

2. Author's translation from Russian news agency website, http://pe.rian.ru
/foreign/parties/20091001/123323488-print.html.

8

The Revolution and Music: A Personal Odyssey

Mohsen Namjoo

The Islamic government, consequence and fruit of the 1979 Islamic Revolution, was the inheritor of all the efforts for the transformation of the state in Iran from the early twentieth century (the constitutional period) on, whichever elite or political group had proposed them. Until a few months prior to their taking place, activist religious groups could scarcely have foreseen the Revolution, the fall of the shah's government, or their own acquisition of power, and indeed they had not necessarily desired them either. These groups had no systematic ideas about the transfer of power and were basically not interested in change at the infrastructural level. At that stage, their basic demands were the freedom to hold religious ceremonies; observance of religious appearances and rites in the public sphere; preventing the government from allowing immoral material to appear openly in the media; the nonimplementation of certain provisions of the White Revolution, including land reforms and military service for women; and, most importantly, recovering control of two institutions that the clergy had monopolized prior to the Constitutional Revolution: education and the administration of justice. That said, there were, of course, also religious groups that, in imitation of left-wing political groups, likewise sought justice and political freedoms, but over time most of these either shifted in the direction of the leftists or returned into the traditionalist religious fold.

All of this is to say that these groups had no road map for the new era. They had neither a party nor a manifesto—nor even (at least not in complete form) theoretical texts that would instruct their own people in Islamic government, the ideas and ideals of the Islamic society, its pro-

This chapter was translated from the Persian by Shervin Emami and Philip Grant.

cedures and methods. There were no sources or historical events to which they could refer in this area to help them make decisions. For this reason, the unexpected occurrence of so great a revolution left them facing as great a void. The only source the religious leaders of the Revolution could refer to was the critiques they had made of the shah's government and its various manifestations. The truth is that, in the final analysis, they only knew what they didn't want.

For that very reason, the policies, laws, and procedures adopted under such conditions were contradictory, both internally and in relation to other policies. Except for matters of law and justice, recourse to religious texts was not a way forward. When it came to explaining and solving other matters, referring to religious texts was of no use to a twentieth-century society, and indeed created major practical obstacles on the road to a religious government. The leader of the Revolution had declared "an Islamic republic: not one word more and not one word less." Accepting the dual Islamic and republican character of the new state only served to nourish these obstacles. This religious perspective on the entirety of social institutions and relations produced a whole host of problems and questions. Civil rights, democracy, freedom of expression, the justice system, the demands of women, and educational institutions: all of these are unquestionably part of the wheel of social life, interacting organically with the structures of power and government, and all of these social realities now needed to be redefined. And one of the largest obstacles was the question of art and artistic production.

On the one hand, according to the laws of sharia, any kind of activity in the figurative arts (whether painting, drawing, or sculpture) was considered a kind of polytheism.[1] Music likewise, especially if involving singing, was considered a frivolous pastime leading to debauchery and therefore sinful. This was the perspective of the traditionalist clergy, who did not have a favorable view of theater and cinema either. As far as they were concerned, artists were members of the community of Satan.

On the other hand, some of the leaders of the new government had a wider acquaintance with their society and times, and had realized that it is not possible to eliminate art from people's lives. In consequence, they sought a solution. First, a novel reading of sharia was necessary that might, in the coming years, render music, painting, and so on "permitted," to use a religious term (*mobâh*), which would take art out from under Satan's banner and bestow divinity upon it. At the time (the beginning of the Revolution), this new and subversive reading incorporated an ideological understanding of religion. This reading was not the result of a reconsideration of the basis and principles of religion; rather it came out of a process of drawing analogies between the commands of religion and modern revolutionary ideologies, and it led to the construction of a religious interpretation that was revolutionary and democratic and that sought justice and freedom.

The central criterion of this interpretation of art and artistic activity was its effectiveness. As a result, those who constructed this interpretation did not value art as the possibility of coming to grips with and knowing the world (which is what it is in reality); rather, they valued art as a tool to be utilized in service of specific social groups and classes (here, the Muslim community), in the dissemination of their thought and worldview, and ultimately as a way of consolidating the regime's authority. Since art is an instrument that can be engaged and put into service, it could also serve the religious ideals of the Revolution, even if in religious texts it is considered forbidden and sinful.

The next stage, which was naturally to take on a greater importance in the ensuing years, was to give practical form to this theory. In other words, the leaders of the Revolution gradually realized that, instead of trying to eliminate or isolate art, art could be used to explain and justify the ideals of the Revolution, and to stir up and mobilize the people. They quickly realized (from about the beginning of the "Imposed War")[2] that in order to keep the flame of the Revolution constantly kindled, to generate excitement and enthusiasm across the nation and engage the people, and to acquire for themselves a greater role in guiding public opinion, no slogan, speech, or sermon would be nearly so effective as, for example, a piece of music. Music could be transformed into a reliable revolutionary institution. Thus, because of the specific uses to which it could be put, the clear commandments of sharia with respect to music could be ignored—a sharia hat, so to speak, made for it—and the meaning of these commandments made dependent on personal interpretation.

Nonetheless it should not be forgotten that despite the opinion of political leaders of the Revolution that art (and, in particular, music) should have a public presence, a large section of the clergy, who also claimed leadership—as well as those religious forces that controlled various positions in state and religious institutions—considered music to be illicit, just as they had done previously, and constantly looked to eliminate it.

As a result of this state of affairs, for thirty years music has remained betwixt and between. Music has been like a child witnessing the ambiguous gaze of its father (the religious government) and never knowing for certain whether this serious, stern stare is one of approbation or reproach, because its father's reactions have always been contradictory. In daily life the child has sometimes sat beside the father without reprimand, or even at times seen kindness in his face; and yet the child has never been able to rule out the father's handing out a thrashing, whether a reason is given or not. The child, unable to live independently, has no choice but to coexist with the father, yet with such a father the child never has complete security of body or soul. As time passes, the child has learned, and continues to learn, to live with contradiction, to acknowledge the ambiguous and self-contradictory behavior of the father as inseparable from life—from life in Iran—and gradually to protect itself mentally and existentially from the dangers of life with such a father. For example, on the one hand, music has made up an important part of radio and television programs; on the other, never in all these years has the television screen shown an actual instrument. On the one hand, musical instruments have always been bought and sold in shops around Baharestan Square in Tehran and in many provincial locations, and no official order has ever closed this market down. Conversely, however, at various points in time, having an instrument in the street has been considered a defiance of social norms and customs; instruments have been confiscated and destroyed, and possessing one has been treated as a crime. Sometimes state officials, even the religious leader of the Revolution himself, encouraged a composer or singer to write a piece of music, even as in another location possessing a stereo system and listening to some songs at a wedding reception was enough to see all the guests hauled off to detention.

In the first years of the Revolution, musical production was extremely limited, and all those musicians and composers who had worked with radio and television were either sent on leave or fired. Consequently, very little was produced, and the broadcast media instead used either the revolutionary and folk music of other countries or Western classical music. Alternatively, they used the revolutionary anthems composed by various leftist groups. In these works, every style possible was present: traditional Iranian, folk, and pop. These works clearly reflected the ideas of these revolutionary groups, and although they shared ideals with the government, there was nonetheless no trace in the tone and language of these works of any religious discourse, or of religious figures and legends. The reason was that the religious groups had no prior history of musicmaking. In subsequent years the government slowly became aware of this lacuna, and works began to be produced reflecting the independent ideals of an Islamic government. The first music cassette produced after the Revolution was *Ney-Nava* (The Song of the Ney) and was released in 1980 or 1981 by the Artistic Committee of the recently established Organization for the Propagation of Islam. The singer was Hessam-od-Din Seraj; the composer, Mohsen Nafar; and the lyrics were poems in the Masnavi form written by Hamid Sabzevari. The album's contents were laments for the downtrodden of Lebanon and Palestine, aiming to stir up the listener to perpetual struggle with Israel and the liberation of Muslims. Musically speaking, the album was squarely in the traditional genre.

From this stage (the early 1980s) until the middle of the first decade of the twenty-first century, about twenty years passed, during which time the aforementioned child gradually figured out how to leave the house of the father and get on with an independent life. I do not focus on this period here. In this chapter, my intent is to discuss the development of independent music in Iran. That being said, it is not unhelpful to give an overview of this twenty-year period before moving on to the main discussion.

The twenty years can be divided up into four periods. Although this division has a political character and corresponds to the terms of three presidents of the republic, fundamental differences in policy are so apparent that it makes sense to relate these periods to developments in music. The four divisions are as follows:

1. Establishment of the government
2. War, prime ministership of Mir-Hossein Mousavi
3. Reconstruction, presidency of Ali Akbar Hashemi Rafsanjani
4. Reforms, presidency of Seyyed Mohammad Khatami (not including his second term in office, 2001–2005)

Elsewhere I give a detailed account of each of the musical styles in existence at the time of the Revolution. However, in order to establish the background for what we witness today, I consider the matter from the beginning in a different manner.

Establishment of the Government

During the first two or three years of the Revolution, as a wave of excitement and enthusiasm continued to sweep the country, there was no doubt that this excitement required musical accompaniment. At the same time, the official broadcast media, known in Persian as *Seda o*

Sima, had to try to fill its programming with music that, aside from stirring up revolutionary excitement, would not injure people's religious sensitivities, and, even as enthusiasm continued nationwide, would not offend the nation's religious beliefs. Various groups of people met these requirements. I divide them here into three principal groups.

Group A

This group was drawn to old archives and the productions of an earlier period. These productions included the following:

1. *Old pieces recorded before the Revolution*, which, although they did not reflect religious ideals, at least were not in conflict with the religious interpretations in wide circulation at the time. The best example here is the song "O Iran, O Bejewelled Frontier," written by Ruhollah Khaleqi with a poem by Gol-e Golab. The singer of the original version was Gholam-Hossein Banan, but there existed and exist many other versions.

2. *Western classical music*, particularly the work of nineteenth-century Romantic composers whose music had both the necessary excitement and, in the opinion of the founders of the Revolution, was far removed from the frivolous and diseased music of the diabolic corruption of the old regime.[3] In addition, the fact that in these pieces there was often no singer, in the strictest sense of the word (an independent voice declaiming poetry or lyrics), meant that the founders of *Seda o Sima* were not drawn into conflicts over the voice and style of the singer and whether or not there existed consistency with revolutionary ideals.

3. *The archive of anthems written by guerrilla groups* such as the Mojahedin-e Khalq and Fedaiyan-e Khalq and recorded by them, often in secret in their houses and with a low recording quality. The reason that these were able to find their way to the public broadcaster was that the differences between these ideologies and the religious revolutionaries were not yet as stark as they would soon become, and themes such as "The Blood of the Veins of the Plant Has Come to the Boil,"[4] "May Spring Be Auspicious," and "O Compatriot, the Time of Our Freedom Has Arrived" were themes common to all the revolutionaries, from Islamists to leftists.

Group B

This group was active in the domain of pop music and attempted to produce works that were consistent with the atmosphere of the times. A number of these songs were based on the revolutionary lyrics and melodies of other countries, particularly those of the Marxist revolutionaries of Latin America, and the most celebrated of these was "Rise Up and Tear Down the Enemy's Palace," written in imitation of a Chilean song attributed to Victor Jara. Of the original pop songs of this period, however, there is no doubt that "My Elementary School Pal" enjoyed and continues to enjoy a special place. Written by Mansur Tehrani, this was originally part of the soundtrack for *From Cry to Assassination*, a film he directed, but the song was far more memorable than the film or any other part of its music. It has become the anthem of choice for any demonstration in favor of rights and justice, from the Revolution to the postelection protests of 2009. I will consider the complicated reasons for its persistent place in popular memory in a future piece, approaching the question musically by way of an analysis of the progression of its melody in the minor mode.

Group C

This group was active in the sphere of traditional music; its youngest and most active members were musicians who had been deeply involved in the Center for the Preservation and Propagation of Traditional Music. At their head were Mohammad Reza Lotfi, Hossein Alizadeh, and Parviz Meshkatian, whose music, from the point of view of form and tone, bore no relation to the glum, conservative traditional music of the prerevolutionary era. Alizadeh's "The Dew Has Turned to Blood," Meshkatian's "Join Us, Dear Friend," and, most famously, Lotfi's "Iran, O Dwelling-Place of Hope" are examples of music in the traditional genre that reflected the enthusiasms of a large body of revolutionary listeners.

The War Era

Of all the groups mentioned above, the traditionalists were unique in their public presence and in making official recordings in the 1980s. Why and how was this?

Before I consider this point, however, note that alongside traditional music, *Seda o Sima* created and produced a new musical form—namely, revolutionary anthems or songs, although this nomenclature originally came from the Music Administration Office in the Ministry of Culture and Islamic Guidance; after the Revolution, the name of the Center for Music was changed to the Center for Revolutionary Anthems and Songs—as if music were nothing more than songs about revolution.

This cultural error aside, a new form, the "anthem," did indeed emerge in the 1980s; most examples were written and performed by the *Seda o Sima* orchestra, which, apart from the traditional musicians, had the most important presence in the musical field. Needless to say, all of these works were accompanied by lyrics, and almost all praised Islam and Muslims, or the sacrifices of soldiers at the front; condemned the great powers of East and West, especially the United States; lauded the downtrodden; and pilloried the arrogant oppressors. "The Cheer of Those Who Break the Line," "America, Shame on Your Tricks," and "I Am Iranian, My Ideal Is Martyrdom" are among the song titles that can be cited in this regard. What made these songs interesting, however, was that from the point of view of their sonority, they could not be fitted into any of the existing genres: traditional, pop, national (that is to say, with full orchestra), or folk. Musically, what gave them shape were the singers (with or without accompanying choir), military-style percussion, and brass instruments of the type used for military marches. The most active of the singers of this genre was Esfandiyar Gharabaghi, who had first been introduced to the artistic world in the 1971 film *Samad and the Demon's Steel Armour*, directed by Jalal Moghaddam and featuring the prominent prerevolutionary actor Parviz Sayyad; Gharabaghi played the role of the demon.

Gradually, once the new state was established, religious institutions had acquired new power, and religious commandments had gained authority over the organs of social life. Thus, the limitations imposed by the authorities increased in comparison to the 1979–1982 period, and their assessments of what was acceptable in music took on a more aggressively restrictive character. At this time, traditional music, despite its long-standing ties with poetry, literature, and mysticism—and therefore with religion, too—was not immune from suspicion. The new growth seen in traditional music, driven by a young and innovative generation of musicians, gradually withered and saw its hopes scattered to the wind. They were obliged to seek a safe haven where they might shelter and weather out the storm. As a result, the new traditional music sought ways of showing that its future involved a closer relationship with religion, and common ground between traditional music and religion was to be found in mysticism. After a period of stagnation, music was now being produced in Iran that could be termed "mystical music." Previously this kind of music had been confined to Sufi gatherings—circles of dervishes and the *sama'* ceremonies of the whirling dervishes[5]—and had received no recognition in official circles or on the public stage. Indeed, most people only came to know of the *daf,* a tambour like instrument used by Sufis and dervishes, during this period. This was also the first time in the history of Iranian music that the Ghazals of *Shams* by Rumi were put into song, accompanied by agitated, driven rhythms. It was clear that this music, because of the mystical and religious ideas in its lyrics, would be able to get past the beady eyes of the Ministry of Islamic Guidance. This music began with the cassette titled *The Sound of the Speech of Love*, the work of the Shams's Tambour group, with Shahram Nazeri the singer. However, once the war was over, other forms of music could take their place on the public stage. Along with social developments more generally, this meant that the music of mysticism saw its star wane.

Nonetheless, traditional music flourished in the 1980s as the turmoil of the Revolution receded, and perhaps also because the state guardians of art gradually distanced themselves from its initial excesses. Of course, when it came to their making peace with many musical forms, this distancing was never as great as it ought to have been. Even so, the distance that did exist was enough to allow the continuation, over several years, of one of the most complete, artistically endowed, and original periods in the history of Iranian music. The works in question involved the performance of a complete template for a particular musical mode (*dastgah* in Persian), and represented the climax of traditional musical forms: the prelude (*pish dar amad*), unmetered vocal section (*avaz*), ballad (*tasnif*), and instrumental (*reng*). In these years Mohammad Reza Shajarian, who before the Revolution had sung on the radio under the name "Siavash," made himself the undisputed master of traditional singing. During this period he, guided by Parviz Meshkatian, who also composed for him, presented to the public the greatest works of traditional Iranian music, including *"Bar Astan-e Janan," "Bidad,"* and *"Morakkab-khani."*

After the Revolution traditional music acquired a large audience. The number of music schools and students grew exponentially, as did the number of pieces presented to the public. Overall, however, this music, because of its fundamentally conservative nature—and the favor of the government notwithstanding, meaning fewer restrictions upon it—was never completely able to shed its skin and transgress its historical limits. As a result, this period saw the peak of its achievements.

Another important moment during this period was Ayatollah Khomeini's 1988 fatwa concerning music, which was interpreted in such a way that more space opened up for music in the media and in society more generally. The first positive consequences of this fatwa were seen in the introduction of music as a university subject, as well as in the opening of music schools for boys and girls, and state-run music classes. The present writer was among the first students of these schools, which opened in the Office of Culture and Islamic Guidance in every city. Another consequence was the revival of the Tehran Symphony Orchestra, as well as the reappearance of what had been prior to the Revolution its signature style: "national music." This became the only style of music we could hear after years of listening only to mystical music or revolutionary anthems. Composers such as Dehlavi and Fereydoun Naseri, and singers like Seraj and Mehrdad Kazemi, working with this orchestra as well as *Seda o Sima*'s large orchestra, announced the good news of the return of this style, and with great pride offered something whose content was not directly religious and whose form was not limited by a traditional framework. Of course, it did not go unremarked that this flourishing, at the beginning of the third period under consideration here, during the early 1990s, was precipitated by the state.

The Era of Reconstruction

The end of the war was followed swiftly by the death of Ayatollah Khomeini and twin changes in the makeup of the government. First, Ali Khamenei became the supreme leader, and an addendum was made to the Constitution whereby the "Guardianship of the Jurist" was changed into an "Absolute Guardianship of the Jurist" through the addition of conceptual and practical conditions.[6] Unfortunately, at the time no one among either the intellectuals or the mass of the people paid much attention to what was a fundamental change—unfortunately, because this modest footnote laid the foundations for the dictatorial rule we witness at present. Second, the post of prime minister was abolished and Ali Akbar Hashemi-Rafsanjani became president. Political analysts universally regarded him as espousing a more liberal creed than his colleague Khamenei, who had now been elevated to the most important post in the country. Even so, while Rafsanjani's presidency saw considerable economic development, the prospect of development in the cultural sphere was consigned to oblivion.

At this juncture (1989–1990), the government focused on (or was obliged to undertake) a transformation of the atmosphere within the country, something necessary and unavoidable, because by the time of Khomeini's death the government faced practically no opposition within the country itself, and had taken over all the organs of power. Subsequent to the Revolution, restrictions had daily become tighter, all thought of indulgence or permissiveness had been forgotten, and the government had substituted its ideals and values for those of the revolutionary people. The consequence of this radical surgery was sadness, despair, and a huge fall in people's hope in life. What is more, economic sanctions, the contractionist policies of the war period, and the absence of foreign investment meant that most people's standard of living returned to where it had been in the 1960s, prior to the oil boom. It seemed that banging on the drums of war to stir up and mobilize people no longer worked in every situation, forcing the politicians to agree to a cease-fire. Consequently, Rafsanjani's government embarked upon a program of reconstruction in the following ways: the activation of the labor markets, creation of employment, and stimulation of commerce; the opening of the borders to foreign-made goods; the raising of people's standard of living; and the creation of a social dynamic that meant people reacquired hope in life. In order to fund all this, the government resorted to foreign loans, thus deviating from the independence and self-sufficiency that were among the fundamental principles of the Revolution.

Another fundamental change, the need for which was widely felt in this period, was the rationalization and reorganization of various state institutions, and the bringing of political power under a single banner. The first measure taken in this regard was the consolidation under a single name and with one uniform of the various security services, with the intent of eliminating the influence of institutions and personalities operating outside the remit of central government. The government thus concentrated political authority in its own hands.

For our purposes, however, another important change was the stabilization of society's class structure. Why so? The first reason is that the Revolution had shaken this structure to the core, and the political and economic oligarchy that had emerged under the shah was swept aside. The revolutionary governing class was drawn from every level and class of society, transforming the principles of meritocracy. It included everyone from technocrats to bazaar merchants, from the educated urban middle classes to clerics, most of whom originated from villages and naturally retained the outlook of small rural proprietors; from menial workers to small traders. Moreover, the migration of large numbers of the rural population to the cities, especially Tehran, from the 1960s on, intensified these changes and the disturbances they provoked. Ways of earning a living, social positioning, outlooks, and ideals all underwent change. A society based on an ordered class system was transformed into a mass society in the full throes of upheaval and characterized by a loss of identity. The turmoil of the first postrevolutionary decade stemmed from the fact that class divisions were no longer based on income, mode of subsistence, level of education, or ethos, but on proximity to the Revolution and its leaders. A society whose structure is fluid and unorganized in this way may no doubt function effectively, but by the second decade of the Revolution (the period under consideration here), this was no longer the case.

Rafsanjani's government tried therefore to bring order to society and create a new middle class. The government increased the salaries of civil servants and made their lives easier in numerous ways; rebuilt cities and gave them a more attractive appearance; modernized transportation and communication; encouraged the manufacture and import of consumer goods, even beauty products; developed universities and other institutions of learning; modernized government offices; employed a more educated workforce; and made infrastructural improvements, including the construction of dams and airports.

Naturally, the appearance of this new middle class generated new cultural and social demands, and dealing with these was one of the challenges the government faced. This growing class, as it sought a higher standard of living, needed to travel, watch films, listen to music, read magazines and books, wear the latest fashions, and connect with cultural developments outside the country. The government acknowledged that clamping down or placing obstacles in the way of this development would not dampen people's desire to fulfill these needs; in addition, any such efforts would lead to people spending newly generated wealth in neighboring countries. As a result the government was obliged, up to a certain point at least, to create what people desired within Iran itself. Alongside the growth of state-run cultural spaces, and the state-sponsored growth of Islamic art, pop music was also enjoying growth, not least because attending pop concerts in Los Angeles was one motivation for people leaving the country. In this sense, the apparently contradictory expression "Islamic state pop" is not incorrect, since the music in question was supported by the state on the basis that it conformed to Islam, or at least did not contradict it; yet since it simply wasn't pop music, in another sense the expression is a misnomer.

Why Can't We Talk of Pop Music?

Answering this question requires examining two levels of discordant meaning.

1. The concept of "pop" arose, like any other modern phenomenon, in the West and is part of its mythology. It is a proven principle that every nation possesses riches of a kind whose roots lie in the history and mythology of that country. As far as we Iranians are concerned, the best example when it comes to cultural riches is poetry. Without our wealth of historical experience in this field, it would be impossible for us to have the kinds of brilliant works of poetry we have today, which take into account ancient forms even as they reflect the concerns of contemporary society. Without this support from historical traditions, we would have to accept that we would be capable only of producing something imitating imported forms.

Pop music's roots are to be found emerging from other symbols of popular culture, and those symbols themselves have roots in cultural forms that are extremely old, the fruit of experiences repeated time and time again. The common meaning of all these is a kind of collective joyfulness. In our Islamic Iranian culture, we have never had the profusion of joyful occasions that we can see in the culture of the West. Our greatest public carnivals, our grandest popular gatherings on particular days, are devoted to the sanctification of weeping. The most ancient roots of the mythology of collective joyfulness and celebration are in the cult of Dionysus, over two thousand years ago in Greece. Nothing similar in our mythology would lead us to expect an art consistent with it in the contemporary era.

The initial emergence of pop music in our country (before the Revolution) was, like many other cultural artifacts, the result of its being imported; and while it did respond to the needs generated by the urban middle classes, the causes that produced it, as well as the effects of those causes, lay outside the country. Nonetheless, because of the establishment of public media (radio and television), where sound was the preeminent material consumed, young musicians were very soon able to make this imported genre their own. In the same way, cinema and novels, providing as they did tools of expression and possessing a social base, gave rise to the Iranian novel and national cinema, concepts that were by no means void of sense. Iranian pop musicians, by using these Western tools (the singer, the band, composers, and songwriters), managed to "Iranize" (so to speak) the main concepts of this genre—at their forefront, earthly love. If the results were hardly revolutionary, they at least achieved parity with the mother forms of the West.

2. After about twenty years of the complete shutdown of this artistic genre, however, and uncontested hostility toward it, the era of reconstruction, for reasons already mentioned, felt the need to restart produc-

tion. At first, pop music production was restricted to songs describing religious leaders, the champions and legends of the faith of the Islamic state. Subsequently the bonds were loosened to some extent. Themes like chivalry,[7] sacrifice and solidarity in conserving moral values, or glorification of the idol-smashing and self-renunciation of the martyrs came to the fore. In the best case, singers mournfully sang of the sanctity of the family and relationships within it, praising the spouse in saccharine language, or particular models of the good wife for all times and places, like Fatemeh Zahra.[8]

Despite all this, it was once again possible that this new form of pop music, precisely because it was pop, might fall victim to the censor's scalpel. As a result, in order to obtain official permission, a great many musicians took care to include a song on their albums praising the Prophet or the Shii Imams, or one of the fundamental Shiite doctrines such as the return of the Twelfth Imam or their yearning for him during his period of occultation. In so doing they actually fooled both themselves and the authorities. Unfortunately this trickery quickly became the fashion of the day, and the first impression that hearing these songs generated in the mind of the listener, more than any other, was of being taken for a fool. Lies . . . big and official.

Because of the great gulf between pre- and postrevolutionary pop music—as well as the divergence between its roots and the causes of its emergence and the history of its development, on the one hand, and the way in which it took hold in Iran, on the other—most pop works, rather than reflecting people's contemporary and worldly lives, offered a kind of rootless musical collage. This collage not only bore no relation to the concerns of its own times, it also chased after the realization of a patchwork of superficial and romantic desires, one part of which was concerned with the social relations of a hundred years earlier, and another with the aspirations of fifteen centuries earlier. Its instruments, melodies, and rhythms were of the contemporary epoch, yet the landscape of its ideas and aspirations lay far off in the past. One reading of pop music says that it is the protest of people left behind and ailing by modernity. It is the cry of ordinary, contemporary people telling the tale of their loneliness, their misfortune, their failure; of them getting off their chest the oppression of the age, the way in which they have been uprooted and flung into urban life; of their betrayal by a beloved who is, like them, human; of the lack of solidarity their times have brought them, and so on. Which clear intellect will accept that such a person could sing songs in praise of religious legends (particularly Shiite ones)? Over these years, the reality is not that we have lived alongside contradictions as much as that we have lived the very contradictions themselves.

The music that the Islamic Republic produced under the name of "pop," then, was a phenomenon made up of the sorrow of a thousand types of contradictions, and entirely foreign to everything ever recorded in the history of Iranian music. But how did the state become the creator and preserver of this phenomenon?

* * *

Alongside the consideration of how the Islamic Republic supported what it termed "pop music," it is important to examine the roots of what in this chapter I call "independent music" from the middle of the third period, around the years 1993–1994. Thus, I address the rise and growth of other kinds of music in parallel. In this same period, the child was thinking about running away from his father's house.

On the Iranian New Year in 1993,[9] a satirical program was broadcast on television. Between each item on the show, a singer performed a type of music that at the time was unprecedented in Iran. I recall the time when, in the first years after the Revolution, houses that were, for whatever reason, deemed suspicious could be searched, and music counted as one possible crime. Every one of the various types of music that exist could be the subject of an accusation, but as far as the urban paramilitaries formed during the Revolution (the Committees of the Islamic Revolution) were concerned, one type of music above all was in the front row of those that should be charged—namely, any type of music cassette, of whatever style, containing the sound of a drum set, or, as they liked to call it, "the jazz." Simply having this sound was enough to criminalize both the music and its possessor. But after many years, on the program mentioned above, people could for the first time hear the sound of a drum set on the official airwaves. It is needless to remark that the lyrics sung by the singers in question were superficial numbers they had jotted down themselves, describing the spring and the people's revolutionary solidarity and so forth.

The state, whose initial response to music had been to repulse it, realized, in the period under consideration, for reasons already cited—at a time when sticking the label "Islamic" on any cultural or social phenomenon made it Islamic—that it could make use of pop music (or music of the kind that made the young happy) for the furtherance of its own objectives. As a result, it shifted from repelling music to instrumentalizing it. However, an atmosphere in which fear and hope were mixed together, where creativity was entangled with anxiety about its results being wiped away the following day, meant that there existed little motive to create works of the highest artistic quality, of the kind that would long endure. Instead, works were produced that had a specific objective or occasion for their production, fulfilling only the immediate needs of the day and coming with a best-before date. This government had discovered that the creation of the "Prophetic City" at the end of the twentieth century, in a country where people were at least half-modern, was a romantic and unrealizable dream. It had no choice other than to renege on its ideals, and the promotion of pop music was a glaring example of this. This renunciation, suspended between wanting and not wanting, between desire and the wish to refrain from desire, had twin roots. As I explain this phenomenon, it will become clearer why the Islamic state became the producer of the most appalling works of art, including musical ones, in the history of the last hundred years in Iran.

The Khatami Period, from the Reforms to Today

In June 1997 an unprecedented development took place within the institution of the state.[10] The inner circle of power was confronted with a demand that it had not predicted, and within a short space of time a cleric with an attractive record was transformed from a candidate for the presidency to the greatest hope of the nation.[11] His sphere of influence was clearly limited to the government in the strict sense of the word—other institutions, including the Assembly of Experts, the Guardians Council, the armed and security forces, and even parliament, lay outside his authority. And in the all-powerful sphere of the traditionalists were to be found the reactionary elements of the clergy, with the supreme leader Ali Khamenei at their head. Social and political developments are beyond remit, but it is helpful to note that the arrival in power of a government that claimed to be reformist added new challenges to existing problems, even if subsequently it was to lose, one by one, the support of the influential personalities and parties connected to it, and therefore the grip it had on power. These new challenges ran as follows: one official introduced freedoms, another closed them down. One issued a permit, another cancelled it. During this period, fundamental disagreements between the powerful and influential in Iran took shape, became apparent, and widened. Everyone acknowledged that the Islamic state was not, in truth, idealistic and ideological, but thoroughly pragmatic. For this reason, only the ceremonies and appearances of Islam retained an importance for it, rather than the realization of its ideals. It was concerned with how to preserve its power, and therefore any truth was acceptable to it to the extent that it did not call its power into question. Its only ideal was the preservation of power. As a result it was ready at any moment to tear up the rules of the game, opportunistically dissolving the hitherto-existing rules and order that it had itself put in place. Only those works (even pop music) that were completely sterile, insubstantial, and without identity had the right to appear in official media. That is to say, they could not help create any sort of movement or any sort of institution outside of the sphere of official influence.

Indeed, the authorities once again were thinking of giving order to the social structure and stimulating the growth of the urban middle classes, but they no longer wanted to put up with their demands. Therefore, the work that was begun was left half finished, lest when completed it create greater challenges still. During the reconstruction period, the authorities had decided to guide the people's demands by building cultural centers and music schools; but during the reformist period, the danger that they would lose hold on power was a serious one, especially because—with the election of Khatami's government—for the first time since the Revolution there was a government with a liberal ethos, and therefore the inner circles of power found they had no choice but to stop this movement in its tracks. The most important measure taken in this regard was Khamenei's issuing a fatwa just before the end of Rafsanjani's presidency, declaring that music education for those under eighteen was forbidden. With public instruction in music only available from age eighteen, all hope of a future generation that might know its music had become a bitter joke.

Important Events of Khatami's Presidency

Five events during Khatami's administration are notable.

1. Ataollah Mohajerani, minister of culture, in the vanguard of cultural reforms and reconciliation with music, called a meeting with leading figures in the musical world in order to evaluate, with their help, the various problems and challenges they faced. But the first problem was that he and his advisers did not really know whom to ask about these challenges. Therefore many of those who ought to have attended the meeting did not, and according to observers' reports, a large part of the meeting was devoted to fulsome praise of the minister and the favor he

had shown to music. Then a couple of the old masters of music complained bitterly of their own parlous situations, and these saviors of culture requested aid only for the alleviation of their own difficulties. It was then agreed that the musicians would meet with the minister on a regular biweekly basis. In fact, the fate of this arrangement was something else, since the next meeting took place not a fortnight but a month later, and at a moment's notice. Subsequently no more was heard of these meetings.

2. At the first Fajr Festival of Music during the reform era (winter 1998), a great deal of lobbying took place for the addition of new sections to the festival for the following year. Likewise it was announced that a festival would be inaugurated for young musicians. Ali Moradkhani, deputy minister of culture with responsibility for music, declared with great excitement that the following year's festival would last for one month and nine or ten days. Not one of these events occurred.

3. At the 1999 festival, thanks to an ill-thought-out measure (but as far as the authorities were concerned, no doubt quite creative!), because the event coincided with the twentieth anniversary of the Revolution, no musician more than twenty years of age was allowed to participate. Now, imagine a country where until the age of eighteen young people are not permitted to study music and where after the age of twenty they are not allowed to participate in its most important music festival!

4. Another of the ministry's initiatives was to put on the first festival of regional music (1998), also an event arranged in haste.

5. Some areas were beyond the control of Mohajerani and his ministry, namely the cultural centers and *Seda o Sima*. The first were under the control of the Tehran Municipality, and after Khamenei's fatwa, its music classes were closed and its spaces given over to classes in knitting, cooking, and other minor arts; to this day this contemptuous activity continues. Meanwhile *Seda o Sima*, which had become the founder of a new type of music (the pop music already cited), was not only outside of the ministry's control, it was also supposed to be a source of guidance for the ministry.

With the ending of the eight years of Khatami's powerless government, from its passing into history until today, restrictions have only found a wider scope, and a line has been drawn through any work showing even the least signs of thought or art, rendering it null and void. On the other hand, the funds earmarked for cultural development have been spent on the most ridiculous and characterless works of art. The musical works presented, and which continue to be presented, in official forums are for the most part butchered, or they are songs in which the morals and ethos of a minority of louts and street toughs of the 1920s, in Tehran and elsewhere, are celebrated and sanctified. Meanwhile, as these banalities were being produced, the state censorship apparatus did not hold back, straining to inject lies and institutionalize torpor, and more than 90 percent of the music played on radio and television is now of the sort that in earlier years was held to be a symbol of Western cultural invasion, the only difference being that today's music is several times weaker and more contemptible.

The religious state attacked whatever had a precisely delineated and meaningful content, hollowing out its meaning and piling its own meaning and identity in its place. The placing of Palestinian headdresses on figures of Achaemenid soldiers was just one example of this bizarre cultural cross-contamination. The reality is that the religious state is a supporter of tradition rather than an opponent of modernity. It is committed neither to religion nor morality, nor to ethnic and national identity. Rather it is a sort of charlatan, a shifty and unscrupulous individual prepared to stoop to the vilest level just to give itself the appearance of legitimacy. Neither God nor human has any importance for this religious state. It defends no truth and commits itself to no principle. For such a state, music is an essentially dubious and useless activity, which, since it was created for the purposes of pleasure, is fundamentally suspicious. The only music currently deemed worthy of support is the kind that serves as accompaniment to religious songs of lament and praise. Pieces are produced that are based on the weakest melodies taken from prerevolutionary street and bazaar songs, and then performed by Shiite praise singers with the ugliest voices imaginable. It is no accident that praise singers, particularly in recent years, have risen to high positions, including command of the Revolutionary Guard and as special advisers to the president and the supreme leader.

In the final analysis, over all this time, and particularly during recent years, all the offices at *Seda o Sima*, the Ministry of Culture and Islamic Guidance, and the Artistic Council for the Propagation of the Islamic Revolution charged with supporting and guiding music have expanded their field of operation, but in reality their principal raison d'être has been to earn their keep by finding fault with and creating problems for those involved in musical production. Even more interesting is that each one of these regards the others as incompetent and untrustworthy, believing that through their negligence (read "creation of fewer problems") they are leading society on the path toward corruption.

Independent Music

What we have explained so far has only been in relation to the music legitimized by the custodians of the state. Even though government support had its ups and downs over the years, it was never withheld completely. Therefore, a kind of state support existed for a certain type of music, one more or less aligned with the agenda of the Islamic Republic stylistically and thematically.

When we come to what I term "independent music," however, I am talking about the child who, gradually in the 1990s and especially in the early twenty-first century, learned to exist independently from its father's house (the government and its policies). Before I elaborate on this notion I should clarify a few points.

1. Art (particularly music) is, from the point of view of a religious state like the Islamic Republic, a fundamentally suspicious and potentially criminal phenomenon. At no stage in the history of the Revolution was music supported because it was music. Music's liberatory force; its psychological value; its ancient history, as old as humanity itself; the way in which it guides people to a nobler life than that actually existing—none of the inherent characteristics that have made it so important an art for humankind received the slightest bit of favor at the hands of the politicians and the official guardians of art. Music was for many of the founders of the Revolution the least of their priorities in life, when it was even part of life at all. Nowhere in the memoirs, oral or written, of these gentlemen is there any reference, however small or indirect, to the improving or even relaxing presence of music in their lives.

2. One of the supreme ironies of our times is that the supreme leader of the Islamic Republic, Ali Khamenei—who, mired in illusion, imagines himself appointed by heaven even as he presides over one of the worst and deadliest of dictatorships—was in his youth an avid musician. The bitter irony is that the very person whose fatwas have had the most negative impact on the development of music in Iran has had the experience of being a musician. That said, since his arm was paralyzed in a bomb explosion (an assassination attempt by an opposition group right after the Revolution), he cannot play a musical instrument, even were he not to show such animosity toward music. Who knows? Perhaps a full and independent psychological assessment would be able to tell us whether his antagonism toward music stems from this lost delight, the delight taken in playing an instrument that politics took from him forever.

My own experience of being a musician in Iran—with all that happened to me and to other musicians of various generations, all these attendant joyful and bitter memories that culminate in a sense of tragedy—leads me to state a truth: The main reason for hostility to music was not ideological concerns but a concern for power. For us there has been no experience clearer and more immediate than our striving to grow up living alongside the manifest contradictions in the ideals of the leaders of the Revolution. Today we can say quite clearly that most people in Iran have become inured to lies. We no longer hear them. That is to say, we don't make them out. It is rather like living for years with a foul odor: after a while one can no longer make out the stench. One of the most striking contradictions came from Ayatollah Mohammad Beheshti, one of the prime movers of the Revolution, who was assassinated and who had famously remarked that "we are enamored by service, not thirsty for power."[12] And the experiences in relation to music I have given an account of above have proved that thirst for power has subordinated everything, even the ideals of the Revolution, to its own will. The main concern was and remains power—not even Islam, which only serves to justify power. Musicians, the perpetually accused, must not be allowed to work—not lest Islam be shaken to the foundations, but so that the foundations of power be secured. And this poisonous idea that was always trying to camouflage itself behind the name of Islam became a flesh-eating virus that took hold of every part of the body of the state.[13] A minor official from the Ministry of Culture and Islamic Guidance in a small and insignificant provincial district who forbids a concert (of any kind of music) can hardly be or even want to be a guardian of the true Islamic life. The only thing that really concerns him and over which he has decisive influence is his own little sphere of power. Thus, if he refuses to give or annuls permission, it is not because of the ideals that, over the last thirty years, everyone including him has written off as irrelevant and ridiculous; it is so that he can keep hold of the desk he sits behind. Clearly, as we ascend the pyramid, maintaining one's power requires ever greater energy, therefore closing off all prospect of indulgence or moderation.

Defining Independent Music

Most of the definitions that come to one's mind with regard to independent music are broad terms that don't actually help a great deal. The most natural definition of *independent art* is that which is produced through the agency of the artist alone, a problematic definition since such an art does not exist.

First, no art has a purely independent existence. It is inconceivable that any form of art might be created in a vacuum, without recourse to any other human agent or any sort of tool. Setting aside expensive art forms like cinema, even the most personal forms of art—poetry, for instance—require funding in some form in order to reach an audience. Even if a poet funds printing and publication from her or his own pocket, the work still needs support from an audience, without which the artist may not sustain a livelihood. And if there is no audience (and there isn't for most poets), then the poet needs to be engaged in some other form of income-generating activity. Here again, there is a need for at least the simplest form of support mechanism. Furthermore, if the work is published without the required permits, the poet will be placing himself or herself in danger. Living in dangerous circumstances not only defies the common wish for a healthy and safe life, it also negates any logical reason for continuing to make art.

Second, a glance at history shows that those who have produced lasting works of art have always done so with the financial and political support of patrons. Even great talents like Johann Sebastian Bach produced their work as part of their duties within the context of employment for some institution—in his case, the church. The great and clear irony of the situation is that, if even a genius like Bach had fallen but a week behind on the path of divine inspiration, he would have forfeited his livelihood.

During these thirty years, the first requirement of all musical works was state support—that is to say, legal support in the form of the necessary permits. And even then, works that had received a hundred permits and been officially recognized still required the support of a producer and of an audience in order to be made and sold at all. When it came to a musical work being allocated government funds, only those works were eligible that were so in tune with the prevailing ideology that any artistic qualities were merely a secondary criterion. The fact of the matter was that financial support for these kinds of works wrote them even before their composers did, and that was clear from the start for what kinds of occasion they were made and what kind of ideas they were to put into musical form.

Another label applied to independent music in Iran in recent years is "underground music," once again a broad term that doesn't actually help a great deal. This music, from the perspective of the researchers and devotees—Iranian or not—who wrote and made documentaries about it, seemed to have a common characteristic—namely, it was produced in basements. This definition is not particularly helpful insofar as the underground quality of this music is something that all music produced in Iran since the Revolution (or under similar political and social conditions) could be said to possess—and, with only a little exaggeration, all music produced throughout our history. The essence of our music has always been something to be played in the corner of a room in solitude. Basically this music's mode of expression—based as it is on creative improvisation by one or more musicians—and even the physical and acoustic characteristics of the instruments and the playing environment have meant that it has had a historical tendency to restrict itself to the basements of houses and other confined, covered, and quiet spaces, rather than to courtyards or even large rooms. In another piece, I will show how the climatic conditions and the living environment of Muslim peoples—here meaning Iran—have a dialectical and reciprocal relationship with the theoretical characteristics of Iranian music, being each other's cause and effect. Thus, when traditional musical masters like Meshkatian or the Kamkars rehearsed their works in the 1980s, this too was considered to be underground music, even though stylistically their music was completely different from the music I am discussing in this section, and even though the results of these underground sessions constituted their official recorded output.

It would be better, then—indeed, it would make more sense—to leave out trying to come up with a single definition of independent music and move on to a consideration of its historical characteristics.

In the summer of 2003, a number of people who ran a website for culture and the arts by the name of Tehran Avenue felt the need to make the first-ever compilation of what would later become known as underground music. They had all heard the musical whispers of young people emanating from every nook and cranny of Tehran, as well as some other cities—people whose names and musical works were nowhere entered in the official register. About two or three years previously, it had become apparent to all music lovers that a kind of music was being created that was something other than the music sitting waiting for an answer to its requests for a permit in the corridors of the music building of the Ministry of Culture. The people making this music had no financial support and recorded it in their own houses using only digital tools (computers and music software) and a few cheap microphones. By this point most of their audience had figured out that the results were something more than simple personal experimentation and that these musicians were no longer making music simply to pass the time.

At that point I had just completed my military service, and while my own musical concerns were related to the space for music in Iran and new movements in Persian poetry, I also worked with a rock group as a singer and songwriter. At that time in Mashhad (the city where I had done my military service) there were, at least as far as we knew, three rock bands as well as a number of musicians who worked with all three of these groups. Some, like our group, rehearsed their own songs, while others had developed great musical skill through covering classic rock hits. Our group, Maad, was different from the other groups in that its founder, Abdi Behravan-Far, was an acoustic blues guitarist whose fingering was quite different from that of other guitarists. Another difference was the presence of a traditional Iranian instrument and a singer who sang in the traditional style alongside the instruments usually to be found in rock groups (acoustic and electric guitars, bass guitar, drums, and keyboards).[14] These two differences meant that the group had a rather different feel to it when compared to its peers. Nonetheless, all three groups had a common characteristic in that they had never been given full permission to appear on stage as rock groups. Setting aside certain one-off official or unofficial performances, the experience of playing and singing in houses (basements) cannot in general be compared to performing on stage.

Stage Performances

Often these groups did not have permits, or if they did—say, for three nights—it was common for the authorities to cancel the permit after the first night's performance. If the performance coincided with celebrations of a religious festival in Mashhad, the group might be allowed to appear on stage, but with conditions—for example, the electric guitar should not be too loud or the drummer could not get too worked up when playing, despite this being one of the requirements of a drummer in this style of music. When it came to those cases where what was played on stage bore no relation to what had previously been agreed offstage, these performances were not actually permitted. Now that I look back, I am much more surprised than I was at the time by the existence of this kind of music in the most important religious city in Iran. That said, I discuss below why today the very fact of that surprise is itself questionable.

When the first festival of underground music took place in the summer of 2003, no particular style was specified. Fifty works were presented. All participants were underground, without official permission and lacking the funds to record in a studio. The results form the basis of the following observations.

- About four songs could be classified as rap. The first artist to experiment with this style was Soroush Lasgari, known as Hichkas [No one] who, in my opinion, remains the best performer in this genre.
- Seven or eight pieces were in other styles, including pop, fusion, and alternative rock (including my own solo work).
- All the other pieces were firmly and squarely in the rock style.

This was the first time the runaway child had been somewhere where support was in place; the first place where the child's presence was important; the first time that this music, tired of its father's prejudices and of the way in which he always favored his other, backward, characterless, and talentless child (state Islamic pop), took its place and was well received there, even if the father took no pride in this achievement.

The person responsible for organizing this festival, so instrumental from the point of view of the history of Iranian music, was a man named Sohrab Mahdavi, founder of the Tehran Avenue website. Five songs were selected to receive help to produce them in a proper studio. All the same, it was obvious that no help could be expected from the official guardians of culture. This gesture was more one of friendly encouragement for the young musicians so that they might find hope and realize that their efforts at home had found an audience, however limited. The following summer (2004) saw the second iteration of the festival. Those artists whose work had been selected the previous year (myself included) were included on the festival jury. The results were unbelievable. Over the course of one year the number of works submitted had practically doubled, all of them sharing certain characteristics. Most involved guitars and singing. The musicians played tolerably well together. Themes of complaint and protest were omnipresent, and these themes were present in two guises. Either they were expressed in the lyrics, they came out in the screeching of electric guitars, or they were emitted from the singers' larynxes. As judges we wanted to know whether what we were dealing with was an artistic explosion. We had no doubt that it was, but its sound was so loud and piercing that all of us critics were prompted to investigate its roots.

In the first part of this chapter, I suggested that the roots of independent music could be traced back to the middle of the first term of Rafsanjani's presidency. This suggestion is based on the oral accounts of unofficial musicians and their circles, including their listeners, devoted followers, and serious collectors of their music. It is not at all unlikely that in the 1980s, during the height of the repression of music, there were rock bands getting together in the quiet and isolation of their homes to rehearse together, but there is no trace of any recording or other record of this. Indeed, even for officially recognized music and musicians, no trustworthy official source exists for research. Nonetheless, oral accounts for the period (1992–1993) are under consideration, indicating that various recordings of rock music were made at the time. One of the most prominent accounts was from a young man named Arash Mitoui, a songwriter whose mother was Sima Bina, the most active musician in folk music from the 1980s on. Her activities should also be considered part of the independent music scene. I will discuss her works in another piece, offering a complete description of postrevolutionary musical activity. Another personality worthy of mention here is Shahriyar Masrur, along with the members of his group, Raz-e Shab (the Secret of Night). They were the first musicians to contribute a large volume of material to the two aforementioned festivals, and their work was valuable in two main ways. First, they produced this work at a time when even traditional musicians lived a precarious existence on the margins. Not only did they not have a sponsor, any more than musicians do now, but they were active at a time when the very fact of musical activity was considered dangerous. Second, in their home studios they did not have all the possibilities available to them that the tens of groups who would appear a decade later had, with their digital recording equipment and software. In any case, these domestic activists grew and gained in experience until a point in 2003–2004 that they actually received official recognition. As the festival jury, however, we reached the answer to our question about the roots of this musical explosion in the following way.

Digital recording was growing; it was easier to work with and cheaper, and therefore available to a greater number of people. Analog recording was beyond the abilities of a handful of young people working from home and required specialists. Digital recording, on the other hand, used software that placed more or less on the same level the most professional studio, with its sound engineers, and a young person just beginning. No expertise was required that opening another window in the software couldn't achieve.

That said, the Internet was perhaps the most important factor in the growth of this music. Today we continue to witness how the Internet has altered the structure of social, economic, and even political relations.

Prior to this period, these young musicians had no forum for their work beyond what the state granted to them. You had to go through official channels in order to reach the public; no one had the power to present their work as an independent artist. True, you could record your work in a studio (at this point, home studios hadn't really taken off) and then, assuming you were prepared to take on the risk of working without a permit, produce copies and distribute them one by one to your audience by way of friends and family. But in that case you exposed your friends and family to danger, and at every moment ran the risk of one of the links in the chain being broken and your activities being revealed. One example of this danger is a singer named Saeed who recorded and distributed pop songs around the years 1988–1991, at a time when this music was banned. When one of the links in his distribution chain broke and those involved were arrested, he was forced to flee Iran. At that time, arrest was inevitable.

The usefulness of the Internet and that mode of distribution is clear here. The government's censors and controllers can see quite clearly that such and such a song is being progressively more widely distributed among people rather than being imported from abroad, as had been the case a few years earlier, and that it is a domestic production. Yet it is simple for whomever they suspect to shrug off the accusations, since no proof exists of their involvement.

I have been arrested and taken in for questioning on such a charge. My answer was as follows. "You are dealing with the phenomenon of the Internet, which has no owner and no institutional accountability. I take responsibility for the production of such-and-such banned song, but not for its distribution, because it wasn't me who distributed it." It is enough for someone, remaining anonymous, to make a copy of the work in question and, instead of passing it onto the next person, to put it on the Internet where thousands of people can access it instantly.

In any case, this music, like other cultural and social phenomena, had forged an independent path for itself. Sometimes it did so in reaction to the frameworks in place, in which case it generally took the form of rock music; sometimes it deviated more from the established norms, in which case it took the form of musical fusions. Either way, as the average age of the population fell and access to technology at home grew more widespread, this music became richer and its presence in society became undeniable. Large numbers of people recorded works or staged intimate concerts at home, but because of its recent arrival in the public sphere, this music had hardly been subject to critical attention. At the second independent music festival, another member of the jury and

I wanted to draw people's attention to this issue and, without wishing to construct a rigid framework for independent music, thought that it would be helpful for these musicians, who were more or less of the same generation as us, to offer a few observations in order to give this fresh musical activity some theoretical assistance. This move was important because, since they had reached a point of success after years with no support whatever, the main public reaction to them was simply to applaud and congratulate them. Thus it happened that my friend Saeed Ganji and I decided, alongside words of encouragement and respect, to offer some of our own thoughts on how not to stray from the path at the outset of the journey. Here it may be useful to reproduce our comments in the context of the present discussion.

One way to classify the concerns of today's musicians is in the following manner.

Preoccupation with style and genre. Style or musical genre is an ambiguous category, as defining it in a universal, catch-all manner is impossible. When an artist presubscribes to a given style, he or she imposes an unfortunate limitation, blocking the wellsprings of creativity. The naming, classification, and attribution of style are essentially the function of the critic. A work of art whose potential bubbles up from within, as yet unheard by any critic, has no name and fits in no genre. An artist's task is to create music. As an example, there is no reason for an artist who has written in her mind a piece of music for two guitars to then, when it comes to recording, engage a band merely in order to mold the work into a certain predefined style.

The fact that terms like *fusion*, *alternative rock*, *modern jazz*, and *world music* have become normal should not concern the artist. Being inspired by others' work, far from being something to shun, is in fact good and necessary. Musicians should know the definitions and characteristics of different musical styles, but when they come to compose a piece themselves, all raw data ought to be set aside. Listening is the best teacher for any musician, in any style. Creative musicians never turn their noses up at a particular style, individual, or group, and are never submerged into a single genre. Those musicians who are respected and the focus of attention produce work that is inspired by every single piece of music they have ever listened to or studied.

Playing or recording covers. Although covers previously existed in Iranian music, the expression itself came into our musical culture from the heart of Western rock and pop music. To "cover" simply means to perform a song that was originally written and performed by another artist. For example, Kurt Cobain performed a cover version of "The Man Who Sold the World," originally by David Bowie. We also have numerous examples of this in contemporary Iranian music. For example, Ebi made a cover version of "When I Fell in Love" by Hayedeh, and one of Ali Akbar Sheyda's songs has been covered on multiple occasions. In cases in which a composer provides a song to more than one artist, such interpretations may also be considered cover versions. In Iran, we call the latter *reinterpretation*, *copying*, or *rearrangement*. Of course, in cases where the original author is not credited, this practice is unethical, whether considered from the standpoint of copyright or of what is customary.

* * *

Over ten years have now passed since that first moment of celebration of independent music in Iran. During this decade, a few events worthy of mention occurred.

A short film called *The Flying Gentlemen* (*Aqayan-e Parandeh*) by Reza Bahrami-Nejad was released depicting a rock band in Bandar Anzali (a port town in northern Iran). This was the first time an independent rock band had been the subject of a documentary.

Another film, titled *The Sound of Silence* (*Seda-ye Sokut*), was made by a young filmmaker, Amir Hamz, who lived and had been educated in Germany. This documentary was about a handful of underground groups in which unofficial and official musicians were interviewed. Within its own genre this film was unique, because its stance was not an angry one, and it listened to these young people talking without making negative or positive judgments.

Several other films were made about the lives of independent musicians, the most famous of which was Bahman Ghobadi's *No One Knows About Persian Cats*, which received recognition worldwide. Offering a detailed examination of to what extent these films were sincere and accurate in their depiction is beyond the focus of my discussion. Suffice it to say that these films, especially those commissioned by foreign television channels, were made by people who knew the answers to the questions they were to ask of these young musicians the moment they set foot in Tehran Airport. Preconceived theories were superimposed on the interviews with musicians, which in turn served only as a means to confirm those theories. Most prominent among these theories was the separation of state and people into two distinct camps of good and evil. Government officials were depicted as hideous monsters who could commit nothing but injustice toward young people whose innocence had been announced at the outset. The good guys and the bad guys did not emerge through the films' narratives, but had been determined before the films were made. I criticized this approach severely at the time, and I continue to hold this opinion. The principal reason for my criticism was the hostile attitude of these foreign channels to culture in Iran, a hostility that took various forms.

In their opinion, all subjects in Iran must be approached from a political perspective. The main target subject of all their films was not Iranian culture or young musicians as part of that culture, but politics. Most deplorable is that these young people were, completely unaware, turned into actors in a political script devised by these channels, where they would, like parrots or wind-up dolls, trot out a list of the problems that the Islamic government created for them. They would fill the film canisters of foreign journalists with what the journalists wanted, and without receiving any reward (financial, spiritual, or moral), the musicians would be left to their plight. The child would be left helpless and without refuge, and the father grew angrier and angrier with every report or film he watched. This criticism does not mean to deny the government's frosty attitude or its lack of support for music, concerns that, after all, are the subject of this chapter. Rather, the criticism is a way of drawing attention to the bitter truth that none of those filmmakers from beyond the border are able to, or even intend to, mend the relationship between the father and his child. The filmmakers' aim in recording all these young people's criticisms of the state for not granting them permits was simply to carry out their duties, as specified in their working conditions, and not to save these musicians who, despite a lifetime's lack of support, had still achieved what they had. Unfortunately, as soon as these young musicians saw a European television camera they were unable to refrain from expressing their great enthusiasm at being the center of attention in the world beyond Iran's borders, and they therefore poured out whatever they had bottled up inside, imagining that this was the only forum they would ever have, and an excellent one at that.

I once made this point quite directly to a journalist from the Franco-German channel Arte. "I am aware of the clever and subtle game you want to draw me into. I know that you want to treat me and other musicians like me, not as musicians, but as musicians from a backward country. What attracts you to us is not that we are good musicians, because you do not have the knowledge to distinguish good music from bad. Rather you possess preconceived notions when it comes to my country, and you want to use modern art (in this case, rock music) to reinforce your own theories about our backwardness. Indeed, you suppose us to be like single-celled organisms that happen to play the electric guitar. The same sorts of young musicians exist elsewhere, but their existence in Iran is the subject of your report because you imagine that you have found gold among some abandoned ruins."

Journalists' lack of awareness stemmed from the superficial perspective they had on us. They found the fact that young Iranians were knowledgeable about 1970s American blues and rock to be quite unbelievable. This superficiality was at its height when they disregarded the possibilities afforded by modern social relations and the potential of contemporary media and means of communication. I will never forget the baffled look on the face of the European journalist who heard the names of Muddy Waters and Bessie Smith coming from a young Iranian. The slightest insight and intelligence would have led these journalists to understand that the availability of information to all is one of the fundamental characteristics of the contemporary world. Their baffled reaction was proof of their lack of understanding.

The Ministry of Culture and Islamic Guidance (Music House Division) once (and only once) held a daylong conference on underground music in Iran. This was in the spring of 2007. Holding such a conference was itself sufficient indication of the fact that the authorities were acknowledging the existence of something like underground music. Among the speakers were Mohammad Sarir and Davoud Ganjei from the ministry's music committee, as well as other of its members. Their audience, however, did not consist of well-known musicians experienced in well-established genres, people like Roshan Ravan, Alizadeh, and Zolfonoon; nor even did it consist of government-sponsored pop musicians. Rather, perhaps for the first time since the Revolution, the participants in that conference were young people between the ages of eighteen and twenty-five, whose interests were rap, rock, and heavy metal. Among my most profound and formative experiences in Iran was observing such contradictory situations, where I could clearly see that those behind the rostrum and those facing it did not subscribe to a single paradigm—as if they existed in two different worlds, belonging to two completely different planes of time. I was as amazed as I was preoccupied with the resolution and outcome of such profound contradictions. For me, yet another question mark was added to the series of question marks that dwelt in my being: When and how will this contradiction be solved? When it came to my turn to say a few words, I tried to combine my critical perspective on foreigners' reports about our country with my confusion at this contradiction and my excitement at the fact that such an unlikely conference was being held at all. I tried to argue that for us there was not much to choose between the indifference of the government establishment toward us musicians, and that of foreign reporters toward our culture, but that I personally preferred to deal with domestic repression rather than external. There is some sincerity in the cruelty of the father, however small, that is absent from the condescension of the foreign media. I wanted to impress upon all the young musicians gathered together for the first time at that conference that the sheer fact of existing underground, of being independent, gives them and their music an identity. I wanted to say that, for all we knew, perhaps the more we emerge from our underground, the greater the chance that our music will lose certain facets whose existence don't even occur to us—a transformation that we may not sense as it happens. Unfortunately, time was limited, and I didn't manage to make my meaning clear.

Our longstanding habit of dividing everything into black and white hinders our ability to think and analyze critically. Neither the officials nor the young attendees of that conference held a clear and definable position. The first group was preoccupied with justifying its position and its negligence over the years, passing over the deep and fundamental contradictions inherent to the ideals of the Revolution of whose cultural aspect they were the official representatives. Meanwhile, the second group—young, angry, and fatigued, confronted by repetition and a refusal to take on responsibility—was unable to set aside its anger and make use of that rare platform (like a single shoe found in the midst of a vast desert) in order to outline its demands and priorities, clearly presented using appropriate bureaucratic language and delivered by a group of representatives. What does not reach its destination remains simply a cry in the wilderness.

Today, many of the criteria of evaluation are fundamentally different from the period already discussed. Up until the end of this period, the existence of a father as a strict supervisor was accepted by all, whether those who collaborated with the state in order to make the fashionable music of the day, or those who sat in a corner at home and poured out all their repressed resentment into their irascible songs and styles. Consciously or not, everyone confirmed the father's presence. Some hoped and desired to earn the father's approval, while others sought to keep him as far off as possible. For both groups, however, that this father was the main sponsor of musicmaking was a sort of officially sanctioned taboo. I remember well myself that ten years ago the only way to live officially as a musician was to obtain a permit from the

Ministry of Culture. Every musician shared a single desire: to navigate safely past the obstacles laid out by the ministry, to be able to stand upright and not bow to the criteria they set, criteria that trampled under foot every musician's principles. Constant bargaining was necessary, and for your works to appear in the windows of officially approved book and cassette sellers, it was necessary to conform to the complicated principles of the struggle.

While the Internet has made offering musical work to an audience a great deal easier, distribution by this channel offers nothing in the way of financial or psychological returns—the latter being the sense of satisfaction gained from seeing an album pressed and on sale. To return to our familiar analogy, then, we were bold children who had gradually learned to live independently of our father's house, but every now and then, in order to get our father's approval, we paid him a visit. At least we entertained the thought of one day going back to live with him.

With the benefit of a few years' hindsight, however, and given the historically formative events, political and social, that took place on a grand scale across the country last summer, two important points can be made—two points, indeed, that could scarcely be considered separately from one another.[15]

First, the child—independent music, or, more broadly, independent art—has now completely forgotten the father and his house. When our generation, the first to have found forums outside of the father's house and which consequently became known for its audacity, courage, and innovation, looks at those who are today at the forefront of independent music, our generation sees more clearly how conservative it really was. For them, memories of the father's house and of the Ministry of Culture are fading fast on the road to oblivion. For them, living independently is no longer a source of pride. Since no one even acknowledges the house's existence, they can hardly live outside it. The Ministry of Culture is no longer considered the sole official source of art, and none of us care to spend a lifetime criticizing its activities.

When it comes to book publishing, a large number of collections of short stories have been produced in print runs of one or two thousand, not to mention the advent of the Web and literary sites with access to far greater numbers of readers and no longer under the supervision of the Ministry of Culture. These days any young person can write whatever she feels like, without having to be cautious, and can get her writings to her audience.

In the field of painting, a great many gallery owners hold exhibitions of painting or of video art with audacious and taboo-breaking subjects, without any official announcement or publicity; rather, they spread the news about their favored artists to their long-standing clients over the telephone. The supply and sale of art in these secret exhibitions present no problems and take place with a minimum of fuss.

Let us pass over the numerous private sessions and classes that take place in various branches of the human sciences and move on to our chosen subject—namely, music, which brings me on to the second point. As already discussed, under Khatami's government the growth of independent music, both in terms of quantity and quality, was in no way comparable to what we witnessed under the Ahmadinejad government. If we wish to explain this as simply as possible, we would note that under a government whose principal slogans were political and civil development and the freedom of art and artists, and whose minister of culture had a more liberal disposition when it came to matters of art and culture than any of his predecessors or successors, artists (here meaning musicians) could always be hopeful. It was a time when, in order to get something done, you always had your eyes on someone else, whose word was not entirely unreliable. At that juncture, hope always remained that the official sponsors of culture would—sooner or later, but in any case eventually—get around to removing the obstacles in its way. This hope meant that nobody was thinking particularly, however unconsciously, of making independent music, and, just as previously, people preferred to stay in the father's house rather than take the risk of going solo. Today, however, ever since 2005, we have a government in place that has thoroughly lost all legitimacy, especially since last year's events, and whose word is clearly worth little.[16] This government considers music to be among the least valuable cultural artifacts, and whatever is produced must be subjected to ideas that are, even in comparison to the original ideas of the Revolution, categorically several degrees more backward and reactionary. A government that spends a portion of its revenues preparing for the reappearance of a figure who is merely a historical legend quickly made it clear to artists what their duty was.[17]

This father is now a complete delusionary. As a result, remaining under his protection and looking to him for assistance in promoting and improving art is a futile exercise. This is how all these unofficial artistic forums took off, and the growth of so many independent music groups was likewise the consequence of the realization that there could be no hope of benevolence from such a father. Let us flee, then, his protection and his nest, and with that be safe from his baleful influence. This is the principal reason for the striking growth of these groups in recent years. The response of all these young people to a ministry that beats the drums of its own delusional desires and that has, from the very beginning, spent its budget on anything but true art is an authoritative step on the road to independence. We are talking here of a populist government from whose pores ooze the weakest and most reactionary forms of fundamentalist Islam—a government that after last year's events divides up even the clergy, the source of revolutionary legitimacy, into two parts: those who are with it and those who are against it (or to use its own vocabulary, the "American clergy" and the "Islamic clergy"). This government surrounds itself with the rawest, least educated, and least intelligent artists and thinkers, having driven away and delegitimized those artists and intellectuals who have been impartial for years and whose work is so highly regarded that friends and enemies alike agree on its qualities. Finally this is a government whose populist head is full of highly visible psychological complexes, who labeled a million people who took to the streets in order to ask a simple question "worthless scraps,"[18] and who has no shame in lying constantly on his path to absolute power. Such a government turns anyone who desires to breathe in the open air into its enemy.

Under such conditions, it is not only singing, making music, and playing an instrument that count as acts of protest and revolution, but the very fact of breathing. When a researcher came to interview me about musical developments subsequent to the political and social movement of the previous year, I answered as follows: When we were evaluating the groups that participated in those two festivals, groups that were subsequently active on the independent music scene, the one thing everybody agreed on was the presence of an element of protest in their works. This element of protest can be considered as a response to the harshness of the present period in a country where even its own revolutionary ideals are increasingly trampled underfoot; sometimes it is simply something inseparable from this kind of music, whether we are talking of rap (from the 1990s on) or, even more, rock music in its various forms ever since the 1960s and 1970s. In both cases, this generation had attained enough self-awareness that it was able to express its protest through the medium of its favorite kind of music.

Setting aside the play on words, I told the researcher that what we are witnessing today (meaning under the Ahmadinejad government and more specifically during the past year) is not so much a music of protest as a musical protest. That is to say, the very fact of living as an artist (a musician) is bound up with protest. This protest has thrust the covering of style aside and drawn into itself even the most joyful music, of the kind whose character, as well as that of its makers, is entirely one of blithe indifference to life's problems. As an example, in the past couple of years we have seen the emergence of something new in the kind of music that puts everyone in a happy mood at a party—namely, pop. Here I mean the young male pop singer Sasi Mankan. We can pass over the quality of the music, the recording, the videos, and the innovative way in which Persian lyrics are made to dance; from my point of view, this phenomenon is one of protest. And this was not a polite protest, as it might have been were it a rock song observing all the sonic rules of that style—no! It was an over-the-top protest, insolent, mad, tearing at chains wherever they were to be found, where they had for years bound joy, at all those governments who had been unable, one after another, to respond to the needs of the times, each year more lamentable than the previous one. The protest was tearing at all the spiritual and moral delusions, at the pathetic television music that, through a pop sonority, invited people to something entirely contrary to the spirit of that music, even contrary to the spirit of Los Angeles pop, which had been repeating itself for years and had thoroughly exhausted its audience.

At the time of this writing, all sorts of people, following and influenced by Sasi Mankan, are producing vast quantities of music of this absurdly and unreasonably joyful kind—hundreds of pop groups producing songs with the typically Iranian 6/8 time signature, all of whom are active inside Iran. In my opinion, the name "Sasi Mankan" has been transformed into a historically determinant event and reminds me of the old Persian saying that "the answer to a *haay* is a *huy*."[19]

As the projected image of these years of searching becomes clearer in my mind, I can also add the phenomenon of protest music to the mass of examples therein, all of which confirm the truth of the observation that all interpretations and concepts stabilize and shape their opposites. The great mass of young people whose protest has gone beyond their instruments and larynxes and that now mobilizes every fiber of their being—young people for whom the very substance of their existence is protest—is precisely and indisputably the product of a government that is charging down the path of reaction in greater haste than ever before. Any period that seeks to rein in people's everyday freedoms (particularly for the young) will likewise witness their response, which is to loosen the reins to an ever greater extent and with increasing creativity.

This generation has lived alongside danger and has had experiences invaluable in the breaking of taboos. This generation is also sensible enough to know to refrain from violence and courageous enough to know not to sacrifice hope in the future. For me, this generation teaches the audacity of hope.

Notes

1. Translators' note: *Sherk*, that is to say, association of others in God's divinity.

2. Translators' note: *Jang-e tahmili*, one of the standard terms in Iran used to describe the war with Iraq, which began in September 1980. From the Iranian perspective it was imposed because Saddam Hussein, tacitly encouraged by the United States and other foreign powers hostile to the Islamic Revolution, invaded Iran without provocation.

3. Translators' note: In Persian *taghut*, a term taken from the Quran and much used by the early clerical revolutionaries and their followers to describe the ostentatious lifestyle of those Westernized and arriviste groups who had made large amounts of money, generally from their proximity to the shah's court.

4. Translators' note: In Persian, the expression "plants have no veins" is applied to men perceived to lack *gheyrat*, the kind of highly gendered honor involved in defending one's family and by extension one's country or religion. Thus, for the nonexistent blood of plants to come to the boil means that the situation is so bad that even those who are normally uninterested in defending their honor are now stirred to action.

5. *Sama'* means "listening" in Arabic and is the name given to the rites especially of the Mowlaviyyat, the order of dervishes who follow the thirteenth-century poet and mystic Mowlana Jalal-od-Din, often known in the West as Rumi. Their "whirling" ceremonies are actually a stylized form of listening that draws them closer to God.

6. Translators' note: In the *velayat-e faqih*, the theory derived from Ayatollah Khomeini's lectures on Islamic government, one or a small group of the most eminent Shiite *faqih*s (high-ranking religious scholars) are selected by the Assembly of Experts (a body composed of both clerics and legal experts) to be the head of state. Supposed to remain above the political fray, this figure (the panel of jurists never having been realized practically) controls, among other things, the armed forces and the state-run media. He (for it cannot be a "she") is supposed to be distinguished not only by his religious knowledge and moral rectitude but also his revolutionary political commitment. When Ali Khamenei was elevated to this post, the emphasis was placed on the latter rather than the former, since he was only ever a *hojjat-ol-eslam* or mid-ranking cleric, although he was later retroactively promoted to the highest rank of the Shiite clergy.

7. Translators' note: Persian *javanmardi*. Literally "youngmanness," *javanmardi* is an ethos of generosity and looking out for others, especially those perceived as more vulnerable (including women), adopted by some men in urban neighborhoods, often less well-off ones, whose roots are in the Sufi brotherhoods of young tradesmen common in the western and central Islamic world in the Middle Ages. In Arabic this ethos was known as *futuwwa*.

8. Translators' note: Fatemeh Zahra (Arabic Fatima al-Zahra) was the

daughter of the Prophet Muhammad and wife of Ali ibn abi Tayyib, first Imam of the Shia.

9. That is to say March 20 or 21, the vernal equinox.

10. Translators' note: "Today" refers to the second presidency of Mahmoud Ahmadinejad (2009–2013), this chapter having been written prior to the election of Hassan Rouhani to the presidency and the reappearance of some hopes of reform.

11. Translators' note: Mohammad Khatami had been minister of Culture and Islamic Guidance early in Rafsanjani's presidency, where, before resigning, he had presided over some liberalizing measures much criticized by hard-liners.

12. Translators' note: The Persian is more mellifluous, on account of its internal rhymes: *ma shiftegan-e khedmat-im, na teshnegan-e qodrat.*

13. Translators' note: The writer actually talks of *jozam*, leprosy, which is caused by a bacterium and not a virus. Because the image of a virus is stronger than that of a bacterium, and because having leprosy has historically been bound up with social stigmatization, in the Iranian world as elsewhere, we have taken the liberty of altering this metaphor somewhat.

14. Translators' note: In Persian the words for guitar, acoustic, electric, rock, cover, drum, bass, and keyboard are all loanwords from English.

15. Translators' note: The events referred to are the massive protests of the second half of 2009 and the government crackdown thereon, triggered by the accusations of fraud leveled at the winner of the June presidential elections, Mahmoud Ahmadinejad, by two of his defeated rivals, Mir-Hossein Mousavi and Mehdi Karroubi.

16. Translators' note: See the previous note for details of these events. The administration in question left office in 2013.

17. The reference here is to the enthusiasm of former president Ahmadinejad and certain members of his circle with regard to the apparently imminent return of the twelfth Shiite Imam, considered to be in "occultation" since his disappearance in the ninth century AD. His return is part of the events of the end of the world and the final judgment. According to one version of the story, he will return at a place called Jamkaran near the Iranian holy city of Qom, and Ahmadinejad's government spent considerable sums of money on extending and beautifying the shrine complex there.

18. Translators' note: The question here is *ra'y-e man kojast* (Where is my vote?), the focus of the postelection protests.

19. Translators' note: That is to say, every action produces a reaction that in some sense completes it, even as the reaction remains distinct and diverges from the action that generated it.

9

Iran's
Democratic Movements

Abbas Milani

The quest for democracy in Iran is more than 150 years old. From the mid-nineteenth century a constant tumult began to shake the very foundations of political despotism, millenarian optimism, and dogmatic faith. The rise of new readings of Shiism (called the Sheihkiyeh); the emergence of the Babi movement and the Baha'i faith;[1] the early search for a more limited, constitutional monarchy; the rise of the first mass movement to resist a royal decree granting a tobacco monopoly to a foreign company; and the first signs of more assertive Iranian women were all early harbingers of Iran's nascent democratic movement.

The movement reached a new peak in the 1905–1909 period when Iran experienced what historians have come to call the Constitutional Revolution, the country's first overtly democratic movement. It was led by a coalition of secular intellectuals, members of the bazaar, parts of the burgeoning middle class, parts of the urban poor, newly formed social democratic and women's groups, and some of the Shiite clergy.

Iran's Shiite clergy were in fact sharply divided on how to respond to the Constitutional Revolution, and more generally to the many challenges of democracy and modernity.[2] Virtually all Iranian Shiites belong to the Twelver version of Shiism (Esna A'shari); they believe in Allah's decision to anoint twelve men, beginning with Ali, the prophet's son-in-law, as Imams, and ending with the Twelfth Imam, or the Mahdi, who has been in occultation for over a millennium and whose apocalyptic return promises to end corruption in the world and deliver salvation. Faced with the challenges of democracy, secularism, and modernity, the Shiite clergy became sharply divided in their response. Muslim thinkers in Turkey, no less than in Egypt, were faced with the same challenges and temptations. If in Egypt, for example, rejection of modernity begat the rise of the Muslim Brotherhood,[3] in Iran, the most strident arguments against constitutional democracy were initially offered by Sheikh Fazl Allah Nuri. In his view, what Iran needed was not a new constitution based on notions of popular sovereignty or rule of man-made (and eventually woman-made) laws, but a full implementation of the divine constitution—or sharia—and a rejection of Western ideas like equality, elections, nationalism, and popular sovereignty. These notions, he believed, were nothing but ideas intended to undermine Islam and the redemptive role of the clergy in managing social and political affairs.[4] Sovereignty, he said, belongs to Allah and no one else.

But transition to democracy in a country like Iran—where despotism is a 2,000-year-old reality and democracy a new dream and desire—is not, to use Hegel's words, a state of *being*, but a process of *becoming*. Studying such a process demands an approach that can account for the forces that begat the movement, but also those that have either resisted or deformed its trajectory. Such an approach, at once genealogical and historical, can shed light not only on the failed attempts of the past but on prospects for the democratic aspirations of the Iranian people in the future.

If the 1905–1909 efforts at democratization failed because of civil war and the absence of civil society, the 1979 Revolution failed to deliver democracy in no small measure because of an unusual array of domestic and international forces—from the shah's strategic misunderstanding of his friends and foes, to his failure to fully comprehend the consequences of the socioeconomic changes he himself had fostered in the 1960s and 1970s. Finally, his gross mismanagement of the crisis that began in 1977 allowed it to morph into the revolution that toppled him. In a meeting with the shah in October 1978, the British ambassador offered a surprisingly frank and insightful analysis of why Iran was in turmoil and the regime in crisis. The shah, Anthony Parsons said, "had kept the country under severe discipline for fifteen years while he had pursued his policy of rapid modernization. It was inevitable that when this discipline was relaxed, there would be a violent release of popular emotion. Thanks to the fact that the modernization program had ridden roughshod over the traditional forces in Iran, and thanks to the inequalities of wealth and appalling social conditions for the urban poor that had resulted from the boom, it was not surprising that this wave of emotion had become a wave of opposition."[5] In an earlier meeting, Parsons referred to the "massive influx into the cities from the rural areas," creating a "rootless urban proletariat of dimensions hitherto unknown in Iran." They had nothing to look forward to and "in this state of mind, it was natural for them to turn back to their traditional guides and leaders, the religious hierarchy."[6] The shah ignored the task of socializing this new urban class into the ethos of modernity. Nor was he willing to share power with them or the burgeoning middle classes. According to a CIA profile of the shah, he believed democracy "would impede economic development" in Iran.[7] He promised that the time for democracy would come in the future. He wagered that he, and only he, could and should determine the timetable for such a democratic transition; it was, he believed, a "gift" that only he could give to the nation. He lost the bet, and the result was the Revolution of 1979 and the failed transition to democracy.

This "majestic failure,"[8] some believed, was at least partially the result of the chasm that separated the shah's persona from his personality. He was, in the words of Ann Lambton, the eminent British scholar, "a dictator who could not dictate,"[9] a weak and vacillating man who pretended to have the authoritarian disposition of his charismatic father. In 1963, when Ayatollah Ruhollah Khomeini for the first time challenged the shah's attempt at reform, it was Assadollah Alam, the prime minister, who asked the shah for a "free hand" and used the full force of the military to brutally put down zealot supporters of the cleric. Ayatollah Khomeini had risen against land reform and the rights of women to vote as well as a Status of Forces Agreement (SOFA) with the United States, granting unusually expansive immunity to all US personnel working in Iran. Riots in many big cities threatened the regime. Many observers, including Alam himself, have opined that even in 1963, without his steely determination and iron hand, the shah might have caved.

In 1978, faced with the first signs of massive discontent, the shah shrugged it off, claiming dismissively that the cooks in his army could defeat the opposition. According to the CIA, the shah had a concept of "himself as a leader with a divinely blessed mission to lead his country from years of stagnation . . . to a major power, supported by a large military establishment."[10]

His success in consolidating in his hand the absolutist power of a potentate was particularly remarkable when understood in the context of monarchy's history at the moment he ascended the throne in 1941. By then, for more than a century, the institution of the Iranian monarchy had clearly been in a historic crisis. In Europe, the crisis had been even older. In Iran, since the 1850s, every king, save one, had been either assassinated or forced to live his last years eating "the bitter bread of banishment." The sole exception to this stark pattern, the only king who died in Iran and peacefully, was Mozzafer-al Din Shah who, not coincidentally, was the potentate who signed the decree marking the victory of the

1905–1907 Constitutional Revolution. In Europe, too, the only monarchies that survived the first, second, and third waves of democracy were those willing to accept a simply ceremonial role for the king or queen.

The last Iranian reminder of monarchy's institutional crisis was the fate of the shah's own father, who was forced to abdicate and died in exile, forlorn and heartbroken. It was a clear indication of the shah's concept of power that in spite of this historic pattern—and in spite of the fact that to celebrate 2,500 years of monarchy in Iran, he commissioned 2,500 books chronicling the accomplishments of his regime—he did not even once try to commission a serious substantive book that offered a convincing argument on the merits of monarchy for the modern age—a treatise that would answer the question of why monarchy was the best regime for Iran in the twentieth century. The failure to foster such an argument reveals the shah's authoritarian, even "divine right," conception of power. His first memoir was called *Mission for My Country*, and in it he unabashedly made the claim that his reign was divine in origin and his decisions divine in inspiration.[11] It was, he believed, simply "natural" for Iranians to accept his absolutist power.

In contrast, during the age when the British monarchy was experiencing a similar crisis, rooted in the political challenge of modernity, British kings and queens either wrote themselves or commissioned others to write virtually hundreds of monographs, essays, and books in defense of monarchy.[12] James I himself wrote dozens of treatises arguing why monarchy is the best system possible for England. The shah in stark comparison never articulated a theory about how and why monarchy can survive in the modern age. He only repeated his mantra that monarchy is a "natural system" and deeply rooted in the Persian *Geist*. Thirty years after the revolution, there is still no such treatise written by any of the Iranian royalists.

By the time the shah realized he had been wrong in his assessment of this *Geist*, and understood the gravity of the situation, the armed forces were in disarray, its generals were in despair, and the opposition was emboldened by what they perceived was the West's new critical disposition toward the shah. The concessions the regime had already made further encouraged the opposition. As is often the case with revolutionary movements, every concession by the beleaguered regime only fed the emboldened opposition's appetite for more, and in a vicious cycle that ends with the collapse of the regime, every concession also undermined the regime's cohesion and ability to survive. By December 1978, the British and US Embassies were both detecting "signs of dissension and disarray at the top of the armed forces." Commanders complained that the shah was infirm of purpose, suggesting that his father was made of sterner mettle and that such a crisis "would have never happened under Reza Shah." The commander of the air force, General Amir Hossein Rabii, went on to talk to the British ambassador "wildly about withdrawing the IIAF (Iranian Imperial Air Force) to the South" and fighting the revolution from there. But the threat was, in the view of the Embassy, no more than bombast, as they report that, "In the next breath he said his wife and children were in Florida and that if the shah left, he would be on the same plane."[13]

For years, in scholarly and diplomatic analysis of Iran it was surmised that the shah's main pillars of power were the military and the SAVAK (the acronym for the Persian name of the national security and intelligence organization.) The shah, these reports said, "would have to rely mainly on the loyalty and effectiveness of the security forces in the pursuit of his reforms."[14] While the shah believed he could use the promise of economic incentives and a rising standard of living to induce society, particularly the moderate middle classes, into accepting his authoritarian modernization, scholars and diplomats commonly believed that in reality it was the power of the military and the increasingly Procrustean demands of SAVAK that ensured the shah's ability to survive. Now the military was in disarray, and its leaders either increasingly doubted the shah's capacity for leadership, or on rare occasions were seeking to make a deal with the opposition. By the time of the Revolution in 1979, after the shah's departure, many top Iranian generals had at least some contact with some forces in the opposition, trying to make a private "pacted transition" that would at least guarantee the generals' own safety. By the end of 1978, the number of deserters in the military was also rapidly rising. The stories about the alleged "betrayal" of General Hossein Fardust, for fifty years one of the shah's closest friends and confidants and for a quarter century responsible for preparing the shah's daily intelligence briefs, was easily the most fantastic of these allegations.[15] It became evident that in the critical meeting of the top military brass—when they decided to declare that in the ongoing battles between people and the regime, the military is neutral and that its soldiers will be returning to their barracks (in those days the sure death knell of monarchy) General Fardust and his protégé, General Abbas Gharabi—then the chairman of the Joint Chiefs and virtual commander in chief of the armed forces—played critical roles. President Jimmy Carter's decision to send General Robert Huyser to Iran without telling the shah sapped any determination the shah or the military might have had to fight for a chance to regain a firm hold on power.[16]

At the same time, as a gesture to the opposition, SAVAK was initially purged of its most notorious leaders and agents, and then in December 1978 abolished altogether. Parviz Sabeti, the head of SAVAK's Third Division, in charge of domestic security, complained that "our hands were tied" by the shah and the human rights policies promoted by the West and implemented by some of the Iranian politicians. Moreover, in his mind, General Nasser Moghadam, the last head of SAVAK, had been covertly negotiating with the opposition and hoping to achieve a "pacted" transition that would save his own life. Even as late as November 1978, Sabeti still believed that his division could calm the situation with an iron-fist policy, reestablish law and order, and then "negotiate with the opposition from the position of strength."[17] The shah rejected the proposal, and before long Sabeti was himself relieved of his duties and allowed to leave Iran. To many in the opposition, dismissing Sabeti was a sure sign that the shah "had thrown in the towel" and was no longer even thinking of reestablishing his authority through force.

In spite of the role his own policies had in the creation of the crisis, particularly through his scorched-earth policy of eliminating all moderate and leftist sources from the political arena and allowing only Muslim forces to develop as an antidote to communism, the shah felt betrayed not just by the West but also by the people of Iran. Like a traditional Oriental potentate, he felt that the society owed him a debt of gratitude for the freedoms and the progress he had "given them." In reality, in the last fifteen years of his rule, there was unprecedented cultural and religious tolerance and freedom in Iran. Private lives were free from virtually any governmental interference. The only exception were the lives of those who in any way actively opposed the regime—in which case their phones were tapped, their mail was opened, their movements monitored, and in many cases they were arrested and even executed.[18] Jews and members of the Baha'i faith enjoyed virtual equality with Muslims—a fact unprecedented in much of Iran's twentieth century. But for most in Iran's opposition, these cultural freedoms were either a form of "decadent libertinism" or merely cosmetic to cover the more fundamental lack of political democracy. On the eve of the Revolution, this political freedom was, more than any other liberty, the focus of the democratic movement.

Moreover, most Iranians touched by modernity—and its notions about the natural rights of citizens—considered the freedoms that the shah thought he had "given" the people as their inalienable rights.[19] He was, in the words of a confidante, "like a man who had lavished everything on a beautiful woman for years, only to find that she had been unfaithful all along."[20] The authoritarian system the shah had established placed him as the sole "decider" for nearly every major economic, political, and military decision in the country. As a report by the State Department's Bureau of Intelligence and Research made clear,

> The Shah is not only king, he is de facto prime minister and is in operational command of the armed forces. He determines or approves all important governmental actions. No appointment to an important position in the bureaucracy is made without his approval. He personally directs the work of the internal security apparatus and controls the conduct of foreign affairs, including diplomatic assignment. No promotion in the armed forces from the rank of lieutenant up can be made without his explicit approval. Economic development proposals—whether to accept foreign credit or where to locate a particular factory—are referred to the shah for decision. He determines how the universities are administered, who is to be prosecuted for corruption, the selection of parliamentary deputies, the degree to which the opposition will be permitted, and what bills will pass the parliament.[21]

When his deteriorating mood and his failing grip on power rendered him incapable of making any decisions, as it did in late 1978, the entire machinery of the state came to a grinding halt. The shah felt that the West's decision to allow Iran to fall into the hands of what he called a group of "Marxists, terrorists, lunatics, and criminals" was a betrayal that far exceeded "the giveaway at Yalta."[22] Even in exile, many months after the fall of the monarchy, the shah refused to seriously appraise the role his own conflicted policies might have played in his demise, preferring instead the facile heuristic comfort of conspiracy theories. Such theories, eclipsing an individual's or society's role in determining their own fate and positing instead an omnipotent "other," are a curse of despotic societies. Conversely, critical self-scrutiny (individual and social) are important measures of democratic discourse in a society.

The shah's erratic policies in 1978 and his many practical lapses were more than matched by Ayatollah Khomeini's steely determination and his early appreciation of the democratic nature of the movement he had come to lead. The shah's paralysis—induced as much by his endogenous paranoia as by the medications he was taking while undergoing chemotherapy to fight his cancer—was more than matched by Khomeini's resolute and ruthless Machiavellian guile. By the time George Ball was dispatched to Iran by President Carter in December 1978 and entrusted with the task of appraising the shah's chances of survival, and by the time he concluded that the shah was not likely to survive, the British government too had, on October 30, 1978, decided that the shah did not have any chance to survive and that they "should start thinking about reinsuring."[23] When both countries began to "reinsure" and tried to establish ties with leaders of the opposition, the only force they found that could, in their judgment, keep the country from chaos or from falling into the Soviet orbit was Khomeini and his coterie of clerics. A surprisingly large number of democratic and even leftist activists were as blind as the shah to the power of the religious network of schools, clubs, publishing houses, mosques, and philanthropic organizations that had been allowed to grow during even the most despotic years of the shah's rule.

The 1979 Movement Against the Shah

The movement that overthrew the shah and brought Ayatollah Khomeini to power was democratic in nature and aspirations. Some 11 percent of the nation's total population of 37 million people participated in the movement, compared to 7 and 9, respectively, in the French and Russian Revolutions.[24] Slogans of the day were unmistakably democratic as well. Anywhere between 38 and 50 percent of the slogans were directed against the shah, while about 16 to 30 percent favored Khomeini personally. At best, 38 percent asked for an Islamic Republic (and none for a clerical regime).[25] The most common slogan was "Independence, Freedom, and an Islamic Republic."

In the months leading to the collapse of the shah's regime, Khomeini grabbed the mantle of a populist, even democratic, leader, and instead of espousing his own true intentions and ideology he took on the ideological guise befitting the leader of a democratic movement. He took on the persona of a Gandhi, but he had the goals of a Savonarola. He cleverly "out-Lenined" the Leninists of the Iranian left, particularly the Tudeh Party, who strongly supported him. He used them to destroy the democratic opposition, and then he destroyed them before they could mastermind their own people's democratic coup against him. The left apparently saw Ayatollah Khomeini as a Kerensky—someone who could easily be dislodged from power after he would get rid of the king—whereas the ayatollah had the determination of Lenin and the guile of Machiavelli. He also outmaneuvered the Iranian secular democrats, who either believed Khomeini's zany ideas ill-fitted to the complexities of Iranian society, or were mesmerized by his charisma and were co-opted by the promise of sharing power after the revolution (as with leaders of the National Front). In reality, most democrats believed that "the ascending of mullahs" will be a "passing phase . . . as they are not equipped to handle complex affairs."[26] Iranian democrats, as well as the Marxists, were children of modernity and both imbued with the spirit of Enlightenment. To them, religion was either an "opium of the masses," as Marx had prophesized, or at best a relic of a bygone era when revelation ruled reason. Modernity, according to both the Marxist and liberal democratic paradigms, had ushered in the age of reason and pushed what remained of religion to the private sphere.[27] Science and rationality would, as Enlightenment philosophers surmised and Iranian democrats believed, eclipse religion and superstition.

But Ayatollah Khomeini and his cohorts not only proved adept at handing "complex affairs" but also had elaborate designs of reestablishing the age of revelation and divine legitimacy, dismissing as flawed the rule of reason in human affairs, particularly the realm of law and jurisprudence. The battle for democracy in Iran, in other words, has not been just a political struggle over who rules the country but also a paradigmatic battle between reason and the rule of men and women on the one hand, and revelation and the rule of God (and his viceroys) on the other.

From his first book in Persian, written in the aftermath of the fall of Reza Shah, to the collection of his sermons on an Islamic government, compiled by his students in Najaf in the late 1960s, Ayatollah Khomeini had made it clear that in his mind the only genuine form of government is the absolute rule of the jurists who rule not in the name of people and for the goal of democracy but for implementing Islamic sharia.[28] He called the theory *"velayat-e faqih,"* or the Guardianship of the Supreme Jurist. Even in the annals of Shiite history, Khomeini's view was a minority, espoused only by a handful of ayatollahs.[29] In reality, the top Shiite clerics had, in 1905–1909, sided with the constitutionalists and the top clergy at the time, Ayatollah Mirza Muhammad Hossein Nai'ni argued that before the return of the Twelfth Imam (now in occultation), democracy is the best form of government. A minority of clerics sided with Ayatollah Fazlallah Nuri at the time, who advocated establishing an Islamic state, much in the spirit that Khomeini suggested.[30] In the months leading to the Revolution, however, Khomeini never referred to his own concept of *velayat-e faqih*. The fact that the shah and his SAVAK had banned Khomeini's books for decades made them unavailable to Iranian readers or critics. Moreover, Khomeini was nothing if not a disciplined politician. Even his book on the subject of *velayat-e faqih* was compiled by his students from their lecture notes, always affording him plausible deniability.

In the years after the clerical rise to power in 1979, some of the more conservative members of the clergy—such as Mesbah-Yazdi—have openly pointed to the incompatibility of democracy and *velayat-e faqih*, even conjuring such ideas as the "discovery" of the *faqih*, rather than his election or appointment, and of an "acquired" sacred sagacity once he is "discovered."[31]

But in the months before the Revolution, Khomeini exhibited exemplary discipline. Not only did he not refer to *velayat-e faqih,* but he repeated more than once that the next government after the shah will be democratic and that the clergy will have no role in any of its political institutions. There will be freedom for all, and coercion for none, he promised more than once. He could certainly find passages in the Quran to support this liberal proposition. For long now, it has been know that quranic verses have different dispositions. Those composed while the Prophet was in the city of Mecca, where he had few followers, are tolerant in attitude and poetic in tone. Those composed in Medina, where Mohammad was the head of state, were stern in disposition and tone. In Paris, Khomeini opted more for Meccaean verses. He quoted the verse in the Quran that conjures Jefferson's views on religious freedom: "There is no coercion in matters of faith."[32] Khomeini even claimed in an interview on November 7, 1978, "Personal desire, age, and my health do not allow me to personally have a role in running the country." On the same day, he told the German *Die Spiegel,* "Our future society will be a free society, and all the elements of oppression, cruelty, and force will be destroyed." A few days earlier, on October 25, he had said, "The ranking Shiite religious clergymen do not want to govern in Iran themselves," promising at the same time that women will "be free . . . in the selection of their activities, and their future and their clothing."[33] To add further poignancy to this democratic pose, Ayatollah Khomeini allowed a few ambitious Western-trained aides (like Abol-Hassan Bani-Sadr, Sadeq Gotb-Zadeh, and Ibrahim Yazdi)[34] to become in Paris the public face of his movement. At the same time, unbeknownst to much of the world, in Tehran Khomeini had already appointed a few trusted clerics—nearly all his students in earlier years—into a covert Revolutionary Committee that managed the day-to-day affairs of the unfolding revolution.

No sooner had Ayatollah Khomeini returned to Iran than these two sides of his operation, the public and the private, came into conflict. Even today, the battle between these two faces of clerical power continues in Iran and has become part of the regime's modus operandi. It is, in a sense, also a source of its vulnerability. It was a measure of the democratic nature of the movement in 1979 that the first draft of the new proposed constitution prepared in exile, as well as the one initially proposed after Khomeini's return home, still made no mention of *velayat-e faqih*. Iran was to be a republic, with all the democratic rights afforded the citizens of such polities. Even as late as the second presidential election, after Bani-Sadr was impeached as the first president, Khomeini still resisted efforts by the clergy, specifically Ali Khamenei, to run for the job of president.[35] But even then, behind the scenes, clerics were grabbing the reins of power more and more, organizing political parties, pressure groups, and militias and learning the management of a modern bureaucracy by assuming ostensibly second-tier positions in critical ministries—like defense, foreign affairs, and the treasury. From those very days, Ali Akbar Hashemi Rafsanjani, Khamenei, and a less-known cleric named Hassan Rouhani played crucial roles in these arenas.

Eventually, Khomeini's democratic promises transubstantiated into the clerical despotism of *velayat-e faqih*. There was in the style and substance of his Paris pronouncements an air of Chauncey Gardner—simple-minded innocence masquerading as profound saintly wisdom. But beneath this appealing, albeit disingenuous facade, there lurked the steely determination of a despot keen on riding a democratic wave to the deeply undemocratic shores of *velayat-e faqih*. Chauncey Gardner turned into a modern-day Savonarola, railing against the corruptions of modernity and democracy. When asked about this obvious transformation, and about the incongruence between the reality of his rule in Iran and the promises of his Paris period, he declared, with surprising nonchalance, that in Paris he had engaged in the Shiite practice of Tagiyeh—dissimulation in the service of the faith and the faithful. Akbar Ganji, an investigative journalist turned human rights activists and a onetime supporter of the clerical regime, has meticulously amassed these cases of dissimulation as well as other surprisingly undemocratic declarations of Ayatollah Khomeini.[36]

About six months after Khomeini's return home, the US Embassy in Tehran reported that he and a handful of clerics in Qom were "now making decisions [about] all matters of importance including public security, the press, commerce and the military."[37] In Iran, realizing the fracturing, feuding, and relative weakness of the democratic forces, and using a militant anti-US attitude as a motto to neutralize or co-opt many among the radical forces of the Iranian left—foremost among them the Soviet-backed Tudeh Party and the Maoist Ranjbaran Party—and finally using the chaos and crisis caused by Saddam Hussein's decision to attack Iran and by the occupation of the US Embassy by his ardent student supporters, Khomeini used a pliant Constituent Assembly to pass not the promised democratic constitution but a new one founded on his ideas about *velayat-e faqih*. In this constitution he was granted more despotic powers than arguably any despot in any constitutional government, and certainly more than the shah he had just replaced. In the new document, Allah, and not the people, was the sovereign.

As many recent memoirs, reports, and interviews by Iranian politicians of the time have revealed, it was Ayatollah Khomeini more than anyone else who prolonged the occupation of the US Embassy. According to Mir-Hossein Mousavi, for example, who in those days was an ardent supporter of Ayatollah Khomeini and today is a jailed leader of the Green Movement, it was Khomeini "who changed what was initially supposed by the students occupying the embassy to be a three- or four-day event into what he himself called a new 'second revolution.'"[38] The occupation of the embassy, along with the eight-year-long war with Iraq—which again Khomeini was instrumental in prolonging—allowed him to force through the constituent assembly a new constitution that was, in the words of one scholar, "the constitution of the hierocratically oriented Islamist camp, the product of a social stratum which, in the decades of modernization, had been forced to relinquish more and more of its positions of power and were, after the revolution, able to expand a scarcely hoped-for historical chance not only to retrieve lost ground" but to carve out for themselves more power than they had ever imagined.[39]

Iran's democratic dream was once again delayed. Revolutionary terror tried to deracinate the democratic flowering that had come about with the Revolution. In the months after the shah's fall, there was no censorship in the country. Hundreds of papers and magazines, each presenting a different perspective, were published. Books banned for the last thirty years suddenly flooded the society, in what came to be known as the "White Cover" series—for their use of simple white covers, free of any fancy designs. The series was heavy on translations of second-rate Soviet tracts and pamphlets written by radical underground groups, and light on democratic tracts. In cities and villages, no less than in governmental or private offices, committees elected by people took over the daily operation of the machinery of power and management. Political parties were free to operate. A "hundred flowers" were abloom, and it was precisely their power and promise that frightened Khomeini. Gradually and sometimes violently he dismantled the democratic machinery, replacing it instead with a complicated, despotic clerical structure. The committees that had been democratically elected by the people were replaced by committees dominated by clerics appointed by

Khomeini, invariably housed in mosques. Before long, these new committees were placed in charge of surveillance and suppression. In the country, as in each institution, a dual power structure emerged. There was a provincial government, with appointed ministers and managers, but real power was invariably in the hands of anointed "Imam's Representatives" (*Namayandeye Imam*). The regime's killing machine began by executing members of the ancient regime. When faced with criticism of the kangaroo courts, summary trials, and speedy executions, the same Ayatollah Khomeini who a few months earlier had promised the rule of law in a democratic Iran now declared stark disregard for both: "All one needs do with criminals is to establish their identity, and once this has been established, they should be killed right away."[40] The power and authority of these courts and committees were ensured by the growing military might of the newly created Islamic Revolutionary Guard Corps (IRGC). Instead of dismantling the predominantly royalist army—and creating 500,000 armed and trained potential foes of the regime—he kept the military intact, but simply retired, exiled, or executed nearly the entire class of generals. Younger, more zealous officers were placed in command positions. At the same time, more and more money and power were placed in the IRGC. Before long, poets and political activists were writing eulogies to the failed assay at democracy in Iran. Searching for reasons for this failed transition can shed light on the possible trajectory of a successful democratic transition in the future.

On the Roots of the 1979 Revolution

Democracy has been more than a 100-year-old dream in Iran. From its inception, the role of international forces figured prominently in the process. Iran's geostrategic importance—whether as a buffer state during the nineteenth-century days of the Great Game, a source of cheap oil for Western industrialization after 1908, a bastion against Communist encroachment after the 1917 Bolshevik Revolution in Russian, a center of democratic nationalism during the days of Mohammad Mossadeq (1951–1953), or the epicenter of radical Islam's resurgence after 1979—ensured the West and Russia's intense interest in political developments in Iran. If until World War II, Britain and the Soviet Union were the two dominant outside forces in Iran, after 1941 the United States became the clear dominant outsider.

The Persian malady of conspiracy theories, attributing every major event in the modern history of the country to some pernicious and pervasive foreign force—the British, the Freemasons, the Communists; in the last thirty years, the "Zionist-American" conspiracy; and more recently US institutions like Stanford University or George Soros's Open Society Foundation as instigators of the velvet-revolution conspiracy—has only added poignancy and confusion to the debate about the role of international forces in Iran's search for democracy.[41]

Belief in conspiracy theories, or "heated exaggerations, suspiciousness, and conspiratorial fantasy," is, as Richard Hofstadter has argued, founded on a "paranoid style of politics."[42] Such beliefs and theories are themselves an enemy of democracy. They posit and produce a passive citizenry, willing to accept that forces outside society shape and determine the political fate of the community.[43] A responsible citizenry, cognizant of its rights and responsibilities, is a foundational prerequisite for democracy, but conspiracy theories, at least inadvertently, absolve citizens of responsibility for their own action and fate, placing all the blame on the "Other."[44] The anticolonial rhetoric of the left, with its tendency to place all the blame on the "Orientalist" colonial West, helped nurture this "nativist" tendency to forgo self-criticism, opting instead to blame the other.[45] Ironically this conspiracy proclivity played an important role in even fomenting the failed 1979 attempt to bring democracy to Iran. As the British ambassador reported on September 25, 1978, everyone in Iran, from the shah and government officials to the common person in the streets, exaggerated Britain's "ability to direct events" in Iran. A few critical reports by the BBC were more than enough to convince the people and the regime that the shah was now vulnerable and that the West was out to get him. The shah was no less convinced that the BBC and the British government were the real instigators of the democratic movement. So pervasive was this presumption that, by September 1978, the British ambassador, in meetings with the shah and the prime minister (at the time Jafar Sharif-Emami), informed them of his decision to dispatch an "entirely trustworthy" emissary to meet with Ayatollah Kazem Shariat-Madari, "as leader of the most important moderate opposition," and reassure them that the BBC does not reflect official British policy and that Great Britain's "true position" was in fact full support for the shah.[46]

This "curious position of disproportionate influence" was not just afforded the British. The United States, too, was imagined to be an almost omnipotent outsider that controlled not just the Iranian economy, military, and politics but played a key role in determining the fate of the quest for democracy in the country. Even Khomeini was reported to have religiously listened to the nightly news broadcasts of BBC, Voice of America, and Radio Israel. Like their British counterparts, US Embassy officials also reported numerous meetings with the shah, other regime officials, and members of the opposition, when the main subject was the United States' alleged formative role in supporting and encouraging either the regime or the democratic forces in Iran. The US government took many steps to reassure the shah and regime officials of continued US support for the regime. But as Karl Popper has argued, an indispensable characteristic of all historicist[47] antidemocratic theories is that they are not falsifiable;[48] any attempt to offer empirical or rational proof critical of the theory is already "explained" and dismissed by the theory—and conspiracy theories become forms of historicism when they reduce the complicated flux of history to the machinations of one actor or conspirator. In the mind of the shah and other advocates of conspiracy theories, US or British attempts to deny their alleged omnipotence were in themselves "proof" of the veracity of the theory and the real power of these others. One of Iran's most notable novels in the twentieth century, called *My Uncle Napoleon*, is a brilliant satire of this proclivity.[49]

Moreover, as both British and US Embassy officials knew, the power they possessed in people's minds was "a two-edged weapon." It could give a "misleading impression" of these countries' ability to influence, and thus have responsibility for, events in Iran, but it also afforded them more of a chance to "offer advice and see them effectively implemented."[50]

By the time of the failed 1979 transition to democracy, no country was deemed as powerful in Iran as the United States—blamed by the royalists for the Revolution and for betraying the shah, and considered a foe by the new regime, accused of conspiring to bring back the monarchy or fomenting a civil war in Iran. As a US Embassy memorandum, written on the eve of the Revolution, made clear, "The 'secret hand' theory which is deep in the Iranian grain . . . blames the US (among others) for Iran's many problems."[51] In spite of this clearly exaggerated perception, the policies of the Eisenhower and Kennedy administrations helped expedite the evolution and growth of democratic forces in Iran, while the Nixon Doctrine aborted US pressure for democratization in Iran just when it was most needed. The controversial George Ball report, prepared in December 1978, captures these dynamics. Sent by President Carter to assess the situation in Iran, Ball wrote in his special report for the president, "All parties are looking to the United States for signals."[52] If the resolution of the crisis was, according to Ball, to no small measure now dependent on US policy, he was no less unequivocal about the role of the United States in creating the crisis. "We made the

Shah what he has become. We nurtured his love for grandiose geopolitical schemes and supplied him the hardware to indulge his fantasies." Ball goes on to say that once the Nixon Doctrine "anointed him as protector of our interests in the Persian Gulf," the United States became dependent on the shah. "Now that his regime is coming apart under the pressures of imported modernization," not only must the United States unambiguously end the Nixon Doctrine but pressure the shah to give up much of his power and "bring about a responsible government that not only meets the needs of the Iranian people but the requirement of our own policy."[53] Surely Nixon and his doctrine played a crucial role in the genesis of the crisis that led to the failed transition to democracy. What Ball failed to point out was the critical roles the Kennedy and Eisenhower administrations played in the evolution of democratic forces.

The Kennedy Push for Democracy and the Shah's Premature "China Model"

As early as 1958 the US Central Intelligence Agency and State Department were convinced that unless something drastic was done in the realms of politics and economics, Iran was heading toward a revolution. In September 1958, the National Security Council met to discuss a new "Special National Intelligent Estimate" claiming that the shah's regime "is not likely to last long." It was decided that the United States must work hard to "convince the Shah that the most immediate threat to his regime lays in internal instability rather than external aggression."[54] The shah must, in other words, reduce his "preoccupation with military matters" and focus more on social development. The shah was to be pressed for prompt, "meaningful, political, social, and economic reforms." The main opposition to the shah was decided to be "the growing educated middle class" discontent with "Iran's antiquated feudal structure and the privileges of the ruling classes."[55] These groups were portrayed as further angered by the corruption of the military, political, and civil service authorities, including members of the royal family and the shah himself. It was further decided that should the shah resist these proposed changes, the United States should take immediate steps toward "developing appropriate contacts with emerging non-communist groups."[56] Unless there was a controlled revolution toward democracy and a market economy from the top, the United States was convinced, a radical revolution from the bottom, one that might benefit the Soviet Union, would be inevitable. As early as 1966, the State Department's Bureau of Intelligence and Research "pointed to basic difficulties for the Shah. . . . The realities of the future will not include the indefinite polarization of one-man rule; in some fashion that cannot yet be discerned, it appears likely that the Shah will confront a choice between allowing greater participation in government or seriously risking a fall from power."[57] Much the same language could be and indeed was used in 1978 to describe US options on the eve of the Revolution.

The changes the United States was proposing between 1958 and 1963 altered the economic and political face of Iran and the foundations of the shah's basis of support. These pressures augmented domestic demands for democracy and the shah's own recognition that there something was rotten in the state of the Iranian society. A market economy was to replace the semifeudalism of the postwar years, and the authoritarianism of the period would also give way to a more democratic polity, with the shah assuming more and more the role of a symbolic figurehead, as stipulated in the Constitution. Though the shah had also long believed that, unless he led such a "controlled revolution," chaos and radicalism would be unavoidable, the CIA had for many years believed that "Mohammad Reza Pahlavi is incapable of taking necessary actions to implement"[58] the needed reforms. It was a measure of US anxieties about the future of Iran and of the US desire to convince the shah about the urgency of the situation that the US Embassy in Tehran chose to keep silent when it was contacted by General Valiollah Gharani[59] and informed about his intended coup attempt. Gharani was at the time the head of military intelligence, and along with a group of more than thirty officers and officials he was planning to seize power, force the shah to play a merely symbolic role, and appoint as prime minister an old nemesis of the shah, Ali Amini. The coup attempt failed—most probably because British intelligence informed the shah;[60] not only was Gharani given a surprisingly light sentence, but within two years, as a direct result of US pressures, Ali Amini was indeed appointed prime minister. Amini's mandate was to bring about reforms and a rapprochement with the shah's opponents.

When talking of middle-class and moderate opposition to the shah, more than any group the State Department meant the National Front, created by Mossadeq. Although the United States was involved in the overthrow of the Mossadeq government in August 1953—for many the "original sin" of US policy in Iran—from the late 1950s, the US policy changed; it began to see the National Front as the harbingers of democracy and political reform in Iran. From 1959 the shah was under pressure from the United States to reconcile with this group. In 1978, on the eve of the failed transition to democracy, these pressures reached fever pitch. The National Front leaders failed to capitalize on these pressures on both occasions, but more than anyone else, Ayatollah Khomeini used them to his own benefit. The fact that his appointed prime minister for the provisional revolutionary government in 1979 and nearly every one of the ministers in that cabinet had been at one time affiliated with the National Front indicates Ayatollah Khomeini's ability for tactical compromise. In the early 1960s, many of these religious figures had split from the National Front and created their own party: the Freedom Movement. Indeed, the Freedom Movement was picked by Ayatollah Khomeini to form the first postrevolution cabinet in Iran.

But the secular National Front leadership ultimately decided against making peace with the shah, first in 1962 and then again in 1978. In 1962 the memory of August 19, 1953, and the fall of Mossadeq was fresh on their minds. Mossadeq was still under virtual house arrest and barred from taking part in politics. Though they were ostensibly representatives of Iran's moderate middle class, the leaders of the National Front preferred the puritan politics of uncompromising opposition to the shah over the pragmatic realism of unity with a weakened shah as a possible first step toward establishing democracy. In the famous words of Khalil Maleki, himself a supporter of Mossadeq and a onetime leader of the National Front, "These [National Front] leaders are not even demagogues; they are merely followers of the demos."[61] Maleki was in those days the lone voice advocating a pragmatic reconciliation with the shah, particularly against what he considered the patently more reactionary clergy. But leaders of the National Front followed the same policies in 1962 as in 1978—on both occasions preferring an alliance with Ayatollah Khomeini, who opposed a coalition with a substantially weakened shah. The 1962 decision begat fifteen more years of the shah's authoritarianism; in 1978 the National Front leadership not only refused to form a national unity government but it blocked and succeeded in defeating efforts by two of their leaders—Gholam-Hussein Sadiqi and Shapour Bakhtiyar—to form a coalition government. In fact, in 1978 Karim Sanjabi, the presumptive leader of the National Front, traveled to Paris, on his way to a convention of socialist parties of the world. He met with Ayatollah Khomeini and abdicated all pretense of leading an independent secular movement. In a communiqué he issued after his meeting with Khomeini (a statement Khomeini refused to sign, lest the secular leader develop delusions that he was on par with the ayatollah), he accepted not only Khomeini's leadership but also the increasing role of Islam in shaping the ideology of the movement. No wonder that upon his return to Tehran, Sanjabi told the shah "that no solution would work without a green light from Khomeini," and he would accept nothing short of the shah's abdication.[62]

But the failure of this coalition was not entirely the fault of the National Front and its zeal for puritan politics. The shah, too, was against the idea of reconciliation. Even in 1978, faced with the end of his dynasty, he was less than enthusiastic about forming such a coalition. In June 1978, in a private meeting with British officials where he described his decision to liberalize, he went on "vitriolic denunciations of the old National Front" and made it clear that it is beyond "the lines of political acceptability."[63] Later on, when he had no choice but to seek—indeed beseech from a much-weakened position—a coalition with the same leaders, he refused to abide by Sadiqi's request that he stay in Iran but out of politics. The shah also declined the request by General Fereydoon Jam to turn over the operational command of the armed forces. For Sadiqi, no less than for Bakhtiyar, Jam was their top pick for the critical portfolio of War Ministry. But the shah "stubbornly insisted not only on retaining his role . . . of commander-in-chief . . . but also on controlling the military budget."[64] Jam was arguably the sole charismatic officer who could have potentially held the military together and under the command of a Sadiqi or Bakhtiyar government. Rebuffed by the shah, Jam left Iran in disgust. It took the military thirty-six days before it turned against Bakhtiyar and tried to make its peace with the mullahs.

In 1961, cognizant of the Kennedy administration's keen interest in introducing reforms in Iran, the shah told the US ambassador that if there is to be any meaningful reform in Iran, it has to come under the aegis of the shah and no one else. He also made it clear, on numerous occasions, that "he would abdicate rather than accept the position of a figurehead."[65] That was why, in 1961, appointing Amini was, for the shah, a lesser of two evils compared to sharing power with the National Front, and for the Kennedy administration was only a step in the direction of more stability and democracy in Iran. In 1978 the shah's options were far more limited.

Amini, supported by the Kennedy White House, insisted on having more power and independence than previous prime ministers, but he still did not have complete freedom to form his cabinet. Powerful ministries as well as the size of the military budget remained in the shah's hands. The most controversial member of the Amini cabinet was easily Hassan Arsanjani. Like Amini, Arsanjani was an old hand in Iranian politics, but unlike Amini he had been unabashed in his criticism of the shah. He was a charismatic orator, a muckraking journalist, a self-styled socialist by avocation, and a lawyer by vocation. In the Amini cabinet he was in charge of land reform and the Ministry of Agriculture.

The Arsanjani appointment became far more important when it became clear that implementing land reform would be the centerpiece of Amini's plans for the "controlled revolution" he had come to lead. Something of a consensus exists among scholars and politicians, landlords and peasants that Arsanjani's radicalism and charisma, his ambitions and his political acumen, made the Amini plan for land reform far more radical than initially intended.[66] When the US Embassy showed concern about Arsanjani's increasing radicalism, Amini reassured them by suggesting that such rhetoric was initially needed for "taking the wind out of the sails of the National Front."[67] At an appropriate time, Amini assured the US ambassador, "He would accept [Arsanjani's] offer to resign."[68]

While nearly all in the regime supported Amini's changes—eventually called the White Revolution or the Shah and People Revolution—there was considerable opposition to it from the landed gentry, who were losing their properties; from the clergy, who objected to any policy that questioned the sanctity of private property or allowed women the right to vote and enter the political domain; and finally from the military, which believed Amini would cut the military budget and pave the way for Soviet influence.[69] At least two generals—Hadj Ali Kia and Teymour Bakhtiyar—in fact contacted the White House and sought US support for a coup in favor of the shah, and against Amini. President John Kennedy personally instructed the US government to use all means necessary to discourage these two generals "from initiating any action against the Amini government."[70] Even moderate forces outside the National Front refused to support these reforms.

Many of Iran's moderates and supporters of democracy dismissed the changes as cosmetic. Radical forces believed the shah neither willing nor able to make any serious reforms. One man, however, questioned the wisdom of the land reform from the perspective of long-term economic and political development. He is known as a planning and economic prodigy, and thus his democratic vision has been eclipsed by the substance and often-stern style of his management of banks. His name was Abolhassan Ebtehaj, and ever since his appointment as the director of the Plan Organization in 1955, he had survived in power simply because of the shah's continued support. By 1961 Ebtehaj's luck ran out, and he ended up in prison.

But even in prison, Ebtehaj never shied away from expressing his often unique, sometimes contrarian views. When learning about the shah's plans for land reform and his upcoming trip to the United States, Ebtehaj decided to write a pithy "Personal and Confidential" letter from prison to his "friends in America," hoping to convince them to stop the Iranian government's plans. Ebtehaj was easily the most relentless advocate of an Iranian market economy, a viable middle class and a capitalist class sure of its investments, and democracy as a context wherein these forces could best interact and grow. His singularity as an advocate of political prudence, social development, and economic moderation has not received the attention they deserve.

In his letter from prison, Ebtehaj offered ten reasons why the land reform was detrimental to Iran's long-term capitalist and democratic developments. Under a "capitalist system of free enterprise," he wrote in his letter from prison, "it is not right and just that a person may own any number of factories . . . but denied the right to own more than a certain amount of farm land." He agreed that absentee landlordism was a curse and a problem for Iranian agriculture and the economy, but he suggested searching for ways to overcome "the drawbacks . . . without resorting to sequestration." Instead of confiscating property, he offered a "land reform brought about through a system of taxation, where farms" would be taxed based not on "actual but optimum yields." He proposed a simple but sophisticated system of taxation that would ultimately bring about the desired changes in the country's agricultural system without undermining the idea of private property.[71]

Ebtehaj's critique is particularly important in its contrast with the shah's willingness, indeed eagerness, to use the discourse of revolution and the practice of forced sequestration to promote his own political ends, and his vision of development. Before long, the shah would begin to talk incessantly of the White Revolution, and all manner of "sequestration" became part and parcel of the various principals of his revolution. The shah had a pseudosocialist, "statist" vision of the economy, in which the state could and should become an economic Leviathan. Commensurate with this economic model—even the foundation of the idea— was that only an authoritarian king can lead such profound transformations. As Ebtehaj had predicted, not long after the land reform the shah proved willing to forcefully expropriate the country's only private television station, the first private university, and the country's richest private mine. By the mid-1970s, industrialists were ordered, by royal fiat, to give at least 50 percent of their company's share of stocks to their workers. In the months before the Revolution, he deputized an army of university students to punish, even imprison, those who allegedly contributed to inflation. He threatened to use the military to bring down prices.

Not only members of the bazaar—the traditional heart of trade in Iran and a source of support for moderate change in modern Iran—but even members of the modern industrialist class were disgruntled with these economic policies. A speech to the senate by Gassem Lajevardi, a scion of one of the most important industrialist families in Iran at the time and himself a senator, embodied this disgruntlement. What Lajevardi discreetly demanded was more democracy and rule of law as a way to guarantee long-term investment.[72]

The speech was important from a different perspective. There was an unwritten contract between the shah and Iran's entrepreneurial class, particularly those in the modern sectors. They would not engage in politics and would accept the shah's absolute leadership, and in return they could count on the government's pro-business policies. For two decades, buoyed by rising oil prices, the covenant worked. Iran witnessed impressive socioeconomic growth. Iran was in fact among the fastest-growing developing economies in the world. But the covenant came back to haunt the regime and the entrepreneurial class when the system went into a crisis. The entrepreneurs were in 1978 either critical of the shah or politically inactive, impotent, and unable to successfully defend the regime or their own investments. To what extent did the shah's constant conjuring of revolutionary rhetoric make the idea and concept of revolution an accepted part of the Iranian political discourse? Did the shah's sequestrations undermine the ability or resolve of Iran's private sector to come to his defense when his regime went into a crisis in 1978? How much did these grandiose promises of rising standards of living, of surpassing Germany and Japan, fuel the population's rising expectations and contribute to the classical J-curve of expectations rising faster than the government's ability to satisfy them?[73] In other societies, the word "revolution" brings to mind cataclysmic changes. By 1978, the word had been a constant part of Iran's political vocabulary for almost two decades. By then, the idea of expropriating successful businessmen had also become "normal." When, in the months after the Revolution, the regime confiscated the properties of more than fifty of Iran's largest industrialist families, the decision was only a surprise because of the size of the confiscation, not for the fact of the confiscation itself.

As early as 1975 Richard Helms, onetime head of the CIA and then US ambassador to Iran, captured the essence of the shah's risky endeavors by writing in his end-of-tour report, "The conflict between rapid economic growth and modernization vis-à-vis a still autocratic rule . . . is the greatest uncertainty of Iranian politics." Helms went on to say, "Alas history provides discouraging precedents" for a peaceful resolution of this conflict. "I can recall no example of a ruler," he said, "willingly loosening the reins of power."[74] By the time the shah was willing to make some of those concessions, he was already deemed too vulnerable and weak by his opponents. They now wanted his throne, not an offer of a democratic opening.

During his more harshly authoritarian days, the shah had followed a political scorched-earth policy, eliminating or curtailing all moderate opposition. All genuine political parties were declared illegal, and in their place he willed into existence first a two-party system, and then something called the "Progressive Circle"; the group eventually became a political party called Iran Novin or New Iran Party, and its founding members, Hassanali Mansur and Amir-Abbas Hoveyda, were Iran's prime ministers from 1964 to 1976. CIA state chief in Tehran, Gratian Yatsevitch, played a crucial role in creating and strengthening the Progressive Circle, initially intended to "take the wind out of the sail" of the National Front and other moderate opposition forces that refused to make peace with the shah.[75]

Once in power, however, members of the new party, particularly Hoveyda—the prime minister for thirteen years—not only made no effort to promote democracy but also became a great facilitator of the shah's increasing authoritarianism. As the price of oil jumped and the social fabric of Iranian society changed with stunning rapidity, and as the need for a more democratic polity increased with the rise in the number of Iranians belonging to the technocratic and middle classes, the shah became more and more authoritarian. The rapidity of these changes fueled his grandiosity and his belief that he was "anointed" to defy the age-old dictum that modern middle classes want a share of power. The faux moderates of Iran Novin became his sycophantic servants, and the real moderates—whether inside the National Front or members of Iran's growing middle class—swelled the ranks of the opposition. These were, of course, conveniently the days of the Nixon administration and the Nixon Doctrine. The shah was, according to this doctrine, the designated guarantor of security in the Persian Gulf, and the US government was ordered to sell the shah as much arms as he desired and to stop pressuring him for more liberalization. Prudent moderates, advocating reform and democracy, as well as radical advocates of change from every political persuasion, were shunned or barred from politics. The shah believed that the clergy—with the exception of radicals like Ayatollah Khomeini and his supporters—were his reliable allies in the fight against communists or secular nationalists. In October 1969, when "moderate religious leaders" sent a message to the shah and to the US Embassy that they were worried "about the situation" in the country and "angry at Khomeini" for putting them in a difficult position of either choosing his radicalism or being branded as a "reactionary mullah of the court," the shah chose to ignore their warnings. More than once, similar warnings from the moderate clergy (about everything from the shah's sudden decision to change the calendar to new laws about women to family protection laws) were ignored. Open letters and declarations from secular moderate politicians were not just ignored, but the moderates were also often punished. Assadollah Alam, the powerful court minister for more than a decade, constantly reminded the shah that he had successfully "deracinated" radical clergy like Khomeini in 1963, when Alam was the prime minister. He convinced the shah that the clerics still left in Iran had no choice but to support the shah and are not "important enough" to deserve a royal response.[76] The more the moderate clergy was ignored by the shah, the easier it became for Ayatollah Khomeini and his radical allies to gain and consolidate hegemony over religious forces in Iran.[77] As a result, when the regime went into a crisis in 1977, the clerical network, led by Khomeini, turned out to be the only force capable of offering itself as a viable alternative to the shah. By promoting economic changes that created a new, more wealthy and educated middle class, the shah inadvertently created the forces necessary for a democratic transition. His scorched-earth political policy, however, denied these forces either a share of power or an opportunity to organize, even within the limits clearly set out by the Constitution. When George Ball concluded that the United States should urgently seek "to open a disavowable [*sic*] channel of communication" with the opposition, they had no choice but to negotiate with Ayatollah Khomeini and his entourage.[78] Iran's democratic opposition was in a similar bind. Their alliance with Khomeini was indeed a marriage of strange bedfellows, but in many ways the unavoidable consequence of the shah's contradictory policies.

By the early 1970s, as the shah learned of his cancer and as he grew disgruntled with, or even afraid of, the newfound arrogance in the New Iran Party[79]—with party congresses looking more like Communist Party rituals, and their requisite delegations from fraternal parties and party songs performed by comrades, arms locked in unity—he began to search for a remedy. He asked to meet with Mehdi Samii, one of Iran's most respected technocrats, with extensive connections among moderates and the leaders of the National Front. The shah told Samii of his worries about the future and the "problem of transition"—particularly after his death—asking Samii to form a new political party that would indeed succeed in soliciting the support of Iran's educated middle classes for a peaceful transition. For almost five months, Samii met regularly with the shah, discussing and setting out the parameters of what the new party would be allowed to do. It would have been a loyal opposition party, a centrist party with hints of social democratic ideas in its proposed platform. But then the price of oil suddenly quadrupled, and in Samii's words, "Suddenly His Majesty changed his mind, and pulled the plug on the party."[80] Instead of facilitating the creation of a genuine centrist democratic party, the shah instead opted for the disastrous idea of a one-party system. All other parties were dismantled in favor of the new Rastakhiz (Resurgence) Party. When fifteen years earlier, a grassroots loyal opposition movement called Rastakhiz was launched by a dependable ally of the shah, the movement was dismantled simply because party meetings were reported to sport no pictures of the shah.[81] The new resurgence was a stillborn monster, and an immediate source of discontent, even ridicule. The fact that key party ideologues were from the ranks of lapsed Stalinists made the organization behave more and more like a pseudo-Stalinist monstrosity of bad ideas and even worse politics.[82] Some think the idea came to the shah from Egypt's president Anwar Sadat; others point the finger to a group of five, mostly US-trained technocrats who suggested the one-party system based on Huntington's prescription for political development in developing countries.[83] Whatever the source, the idea was a political liability that added to the already brewing sense of social discontent.

Not long after the creation of the party, the Carter administration came to power, and the US president's advocacy of human rights ended the Nixon-era ban on pressuring the shah to democratize. Moreover, in the last years of the Nixon administration and for much of the Ford administration, Iran and the United States were fighting a quiet war of diplomacy on the price of oil. Eventually, the United States made a covert pact with Saudi Arabia to bring down the price of oil. Some scholars have even claimed that the drop in the price of oil precipitated the fall of the shah.[84] Just as Iran's oil revenues were no longer rising, the Carter administration resumed pressure on the shah to democratize and liberalize. The timing could not have been worse: the shah was sick and the economy was in a downturn. The normal instabilities that accompany any authoritarian regime's attempt to democratize only augmented the effects of the economic crisis. By 1978, Iran's GNP growth in real terms dropped to 2.8 percent. This recessionary slowdown was exacerbated by unusually high inflation rates. Like much of the West, Iran also faced the strange hybrid phenomenon of "stagflation." Some in the US Congress began to worry about Iran's budgetary priorities and the fact that, in line with the shah's views, precedence was given to military matters over social needs. These anxieties led to ideas to "link Iran's human rights performance with arms transfer."[85] It is hard not to be tempted to consider what might have happened in Iran if the US Congress had developed such a matrix a decade earlier, when Nixon had given the shah his now-famous carte blanche to buy any nonnuclear weapon system he desired. But in 1978, such a matrix was just one more indication to the Iranian opposition that the shah's position in the West was precarious and vulnerable. The shah's deteriorating emotional and physical condition combined with these other factors to create the perfect storm that was the Revolution.

Other than Britain and the United States, the Soviet Union was also imagined by both the shah and the democratic opposition to play a key role in determining developments in Iran. In the months leading to the failed 1978 transition to democracy, the shah's Cold War fears of Soviet machinations were augmented by a series of events that convinced him that the Soviet Union was out to overthrow him as well. In 1977 SAVAK arrested the KGB's top spy in Iran. He was a two-star general of the Iranian military and had been, for almost three decades, a paid agent of the KGB.[86] For much of his political life, the shah had an exaggerated view of the KGB's power in Iran.[87] As it happened, the general was in fact one of only two paid agents of the KGB.[88] In 1975, even rumors of the shah's philandering were, according to the shah, a "KGB operation." For its part, the KGB worked hard to fan the flames of these fears. They circulated the rumor that they had even "influenced the Shah's choice of his third wife."[89] Exaggerated as these claims were, Soviet moves in 1978 left little doubt about their intentions.

On November 19, 1978, Leonid Brezhnev threatened an invasion of Iran, if "anti-Soviet" elements were to gain the upper hand in the country. The statement was, in short order, followed by a confidential letter to President Carter, "suggesting that because the Soviets have a long border with Iran, they should enjoy a special position of influence."[90] Ever since 1917, Soviet leaders had tried to turn Iran into another Finland, where "anti-Soviet activities" could trigger a Russian invasion. They used Article 6 of a 1921 agreement with Iran—or more accurately their self-serving interpretation of that article—as a legal basis for their attempted "Finlandization." Iran had initially agreed to the article only in the context of the tumultuous situation in the years after the 1917 revolution. The article in fact allowed Soviet intervention only if White Russian forces used Iran as a base of attack against the newly established Bolshevik government. But in subsequent years, the Soviets had their own, "expanded" interpretation of the article and used it many times to threaten an attack on Iran. The 1978 Brezhnev letter was only the latest iteration of this attempt.

Moreover, leaders of the Soviet-backed Tudeh Party, who had been living in Eastern Europe or the Soviet Union for more than two decades, returned to Iran in 1978, revived the old party apparatus, and aggressively supported Ayatollah Khomeini and the most antidemocratic, anti-US wings within the clergy and the opposition. They even lent their support to the electoral campaign of Sadeq Khalkhali—the infamous "hanging judge" in charge of the Islamic Revolutionary courts in the months after the Revolution and responsible for hundreds of death. Tudeh Party members infiltrated the new Islamic bureaucracy, including the newly formed Revolutionary Committees that took over the security of neighborhoods and workplaces.[91] The party further tried to endear itself to the clergy by passing on intelligence about opposition activities. At one time, the commander of the Iranian navy was a party sympathizer. As Rafsanjani makes clear in his daily journals, top party leaders (including Noural-Din Kianouri, first secretary of the party central committee) met with him intermittently and passed on information that was sometimes new and important—such as the time the party informed the clergy of a pending coup originating in one of Iran's air force bases—and sometimes only as an excuse to keep their contacts with high-ranking officials of the regime.[92] The party used its extensive propaganda apparatus to promote anti-US and antidemocratic slogans.

Aside from these returning old Tudeh Party cadres, Jimmy Carter's advocacy of human rights convinced the shah to release nearly all of the almost four thousand Iranian political prisoners. Nearly every one of these newly released prisoners had long experience in underground organizational techniques. Dozens had been trained by radical Palestinian groups and knew the methods of terrorism—romanticized in those days of Franz Fanon and his apotheosis of violence, as the art of urban guerrilla warfare. Their release strengthened the opposition, weakening the resolve of the regime and SAVAK, but also weakened the prospects of democracy in Iran. Most of these recently released prisoners were schooled in Stalinist models of Marxism and dismissed liberal democracy as a "frivolous" and "fraudulent" bourgeois gimmick. Even forces loyal to the Mojahedin-e Khalq, though ostensibly following an Islamic ideology, were in fact supporting an eclectic mix of Leninism and their own version of Islamic "liberation theology."[93] The handful of clerics in prison at the time—from Ayatollah Montazeri and Mahmoud Taleghani to Rafsanjani and Ghollam Hossein Haggani—joined the ranks of Ayatollah Khomeini supporters, most of them becoming—soon after their release—members of the secret Revolutionary Committee that ran the day-to-day affairs of the movement, and after the fall of the shah, of the new regime. Before long, in Iranian political discourse even the word "liberal" became synonymous with decadence and servile subservience to "colonialism." The dominant discourse was one of radical revolution and the purgative power of violence, not democracy and the rule of law. The few brave voices of reason and moderation—like Mostafa Rahimi—were drowned out in the deluge of revolutionary romance. When the regime's "revolutionary courts" began to execute members of the ancient regime after summary trials, when grotesque pictures of their bullet-ridden bodies were published all over the front pages of the country's daily papers, it was these radical groups, many enjoying the political capital of having been in the forefront of the fight against the old regime, that not only applauded this violence but demanded even more. Their "revolutionary" blood lust ended only when the same courts began to execute hundreds of leftist opponents of the regime. Nothing united these disparate forces as well as their opposition to "imperialism," particularly that of the United States, and "decadent" liberal democracy.

Another factor adding to the rise of radical undemocratic discourse was the Confederation of Iranian Students. From the late 1950s, thousands of Iranian students had begun to converge on European and US universities. Until then, educational sojourns to the West had been a privilege limited to the children of the elite. Indispensable to the shah's modernization plans was a large, trained technocratic class. But Iran lacked the educational infrastructure to train such a class. Sociologists have called the late 1950s the age of the technocrats. US policy in Iran also advocated that new young technocrats must gradually take the place of traditional politicians. From the late 1950s, cheap bus and train service from Iran to Europe became available, and before long, students from all social classes began to arrive in the West. The more radical elements used their newfound freedom in Western democracies to create the Confederation of Iranian Students.[94]

Throughout the 1970s, the confederation became a powerful source of propaganda against the shah, in favor of either Khomeini or yet another "proletarian revolution." Dominated by the left and structured along the lines of a "United Front" suggested by Stalin in the 1930s—communists leading the largest number of democratic forces in a common battle—The Confederation of Iranian Students was instrumental in turning the students' democratic aspirations into a force for radicalism that was invariably critical of "bourgeois democracy." As the shah's regime showed signs of collapse, leaders of the confederation returned to Iran, joining forces advocating not a democratic transition but a radical revolution. Before long, at least one hundred of them were executed by the new regime's firing squads. The student movement's leftist tendencies and Khomeini's abilities to pitch his ideas in a language that made it part of the "anti-imperialist discourse" made it easier for this strange alliance of modernizing students and a demodernizing cleric such as Khomeini. Recent scholarship on the debt that radical anti-Western Islamic discourse owes to Western critics of modernity, democracy, and enlightenment shows why it was easy for Iranian intellectuals to mistakenly assume as similar the traditional antimodern ideas of Ayatollah Khomeini and those of modern radical critics of the West and of modernity.[95]

An unfortunate romance also developed—and even continues to this day—between leftist Western intellectuals and the clerical regime that came to power in Iran. Some of the most renowned Western intellectuals fell prey to this strange romance. The regime's egregious breaches of the democratic rights of the Iranian people were often overlooked by these Western leftists because of what they alleged was the regime's "struggle against imperialism." Michel Foucault's brief infatuation with Ayatollah Khomeini as the embodiment of a radically new "critique of modernity" is arguably the most risible and tragic example of this romantic folly.[96]

The shah refused to ever accept the significance of domestic dynamics in the events that led to his downfall. In his view, the whole revolution was a conspiracy of outside forces against him. He changed his mind about who masterminded the conspiracy but never wavered in the belief that the conspiracy was the causal root. Even in his last book, *Answer to History*, written in exile and long after he had been "unkinged," he argued with surprising certainty that it was a conspiracy of Western and Communist forces that overthrew him. He stated that to "understand the upheaval in Iran . . . one must understand the politics of oil." He goes on to claim that as soon as he began to insist on a fair share of oil wealth for Iran, "A systematic campaign of denigration was begun concerning my government and my person. . . . It was at this time that I became a despot, an oppressor, a tyrant. . . . This campaign began in

1958, reached its peak in 1961. Our White Revolution halted it temporarily. But it was begun with greater vigor in 1975 and increased until my departure."[97] What he failed to understand was that the democratic aspirations of the Iranian people begat that movement, and his own social and economic policies of the 1960s and 1970s, or in brief his authoritarian modernization, helped created the very social forces—particularly the middle class and the new technocratic class—that united to overthrow him. He dismisses nearly every opposition to his rule as a tool of Western governments.[98] In 1977, as the movement was picking up momentum, he ordered some of his top oil negotiators to meet with Western oil companies and "give them what they want."[99]

Even when the shah sought domestic sources of the Revolution, he had a myopic vision. He concluded that he should have exercised more authoritarianism and not less. "Today, I have come to realize that the events of 1978–9 are attributable in part to the fact that I moved too rapidly in opening the doors of the universities, without imposing more severe preliminary selection. The entrance exams were too easy."[100] He calls the students "spoiled children" who helped wreak havoc on Iran.

If miscalculations and misguided policies prepared the ground for Ayatollah Khomeini's rise to power, his charisma, his willingness to use brute force to eliminate his opponents and even his uncooperative allies, as well as the trauma of the eight-year war with Iraq and of the hostage crisis—where US diplomats were held hostage for 444 days—gradually enabled him to suppress his democratic allies. The first draft of the new constitution for the Islamic Republic—modeled on the liberal democratic structures of the Fifth French Republic—was tabled in favor of a different constitution that placed a disproportionate share of power in his—and eventually his successors' hands.

The policy to forcefully require Islamic cover (hijab) on every women in the public domain, and changes in the country's family laws—replacing them with Shiite sharia—gave rise to a women's movement that has remained a bulwark of Iran's democratic efforts. Moreover, the effort to enforce sharia on every facet of life—from women's dress to whether men wear a tie—helped politicize every element of quotidian affairs. Faced with the brute force of the regime and its new tools of containment—from the IRGC and the Ministry of Intelligence to Basij and committees in every neighborhood—democratic aspirations gradually but inexorably turned the arenas of civil society and everyday life into new venues for resistance. Instead of opting for a regime change, through a frontal assault on power, they set out to change the regime through a gradual change of society. Politics and power are, in a sense, ultimately about changing lives. Faced with overwhelming structures of power, the discontented population began to chip away at the cultural hegemony of the regime, changing everyday lives in ways directly opposite to the cultural engineering designs and desires of the clerical leadership—the dream of "soul-craft."

The end of the eight-year war with Iraq nearly coinciding with the death of Ayatollah Khomeini and the hurried anointment of Ali Khamenei as his successor—a process that required a change in the Constitution to allow a cleric of his low standing to assume the highest spiritual position in the country[101]—gave rise to a new pragmatism, embodied in the eight-year presidency of Rafsanjani. His immense institutionalized power, compared to Khamenei's new ascent to the role of the supreme leader, gave rise to what scholars call a period of "dual power." It also begat a new, albeit inadvertent, impetuousness to the democratic movement. Improved economic conditions increased the size of the middle class and haltingly helped revive elements of the private sector. Moreover, the decision to rapidly expand the number of university campuses around the country—partially to absorb the hundreds of thousands of veterans of the war with Iraq returning to a stagnant economy—changed the intellectual fabric of Iranian society. The regime's overall success in fighting illiteracy, and the continued migration of peasants to the cities, only increased the de facto power of the urban educated strata that are historically known as advocates of democracy. If today there are more than 4.5 million college students in Iran, it is to no small measure the result of the rapid expansion of the Free Islamic University in virtually every town and city in the country.

If "economic recovery and rebuilding" was a motto of the Rafsanjani postwar presidency, the gradual entry of the IRGC into the economic domain was another inadvertent consequence of this period. Rafsanjani, in his own words, wanted limited IRGC presence in the economy to help rebuild the country; Khamenei wanted their expansive presence not just in the economic domain but in politics as well. Bereft of charisma and clerical credentials for the role of supreme leader, Khamenei needed the political muscle and allegiance of the IRGC to maintain power. It was in two senses a Faustian wager: inexorably the commanders of the IRGC amassed more and more power, and relying on brute force to stay in power compromised Khamenei's legitimacy as a leader. Within a decade, the IRGC would have a dominating presence in both domains, and the Ahmadinejad presidency was both the crowning accomplishment of this presence and a golden opportunity to expand it. The Rafsanjani years were also marked by a spree of killing of opposition figures inside and outside Iran—and in spite of many shocking revelations about the extent of these murders, a full reckoning about them and about how many fell prey to them is yet to come.[102]

Rafsanjani's presidency ended with the convincing victory of Mohammad Khatami, a reformist cleric who had been forced to resign as minister of Islamic Guidance when radical conservative forces accused him of lax cultural attitudes.[103] In 1997 Khatami was elected president in a landslide as hitherto dormant forces of civil society, student groups, the women's movement, and democratic activists converged to give Khatami and his policies a convincing victory. Khatami's motto was "rule of law" at home and a "dialogue of civilizations" abroad. Hundreds of magazines, newspapers, groups, and civil society organizations began to develop a culture and discourse of democracy.

Yet radical conservatives led by Khamenei turned their hegemony of the judiciary and of the military-intelligence complex into a blunt instrument against Khatami's promised changes. They used the courts cynically to turn the idea of the rule of law into a mechanism for arbitrary arrests and intimidation. The more Khatami proved unwilling to use his electoral mandate to challenge the conservative camp, the bolder they became in subverting his policies. In this period, Saeed Hajjarian—part of the Khatami brain trust and a onetime leading official in the intelligence ministry—came up with the theory that the way toward democracy in Iran will go through a process of amassing power on the streets and negotiating for democratic concessions at the top. He barely escaped an assassin's bullet, and the inability of Khatami to deliver on his political promises, along with worsening economic conditions, led to disgruntlement with reformists. The result of the conservative push for consolidated power was the 2005 election of Ahmadinejad—leading to eight years of economic incompetence and corruption, and systematic efforts to stymie the democratic and reformist movements. A facile populism, with eerie resemblance and coordination with Chavez's style of authoritarianism in Venezuela, developed in Iran.[104] By the end of his disastrous first term, some in the conservative camp had concluded that Ahmadinejad's tenure had been disastrous. Khamenei, however, was still keen on keeping his "favorite" president in power—a man he called the most capable head of government in Iran's modern history—and thus the stage was set for a major political showdown in the 2009 election.

A new democratic opposition was born after the disputed June 12, 2009, presidential election that changed the face of Iranian politics—and Iran. A nation encumbered with the bombast and faux populism of Ahmadinejad—including his denial of the Holocaust and his dismissal

of UN resolutions against Iran by suggesting that the international community can "shove it"—and implicated in many alleged acts of support
for terrorism and cheating on its nuclear program suddenly became a
beacon of democratic hope. The movement generally known as the
Green Movement, for the color of banners and bandanas used by many
of its supporters, was widely praised as a new, nonviolent, nonutopian,
and popular paradigm of change, partially empowered by twenty-first-
century technology. If the democratic aspirations of the people in 1979
were deformed by a combination of naiveté and utopianism—the power
of the dream of soul-craft—in 2009 a prudent pragmatism, a desire for
gradual change, or in short, hopes for statecraft, shaped the contours of
the Green Movement. For the conservatives, the 2009 election turned
out to be critical for their attempt to consolidate power; the reformists
and the democratic opposition, on the other hand, suddenly lined up
behind the candidacy of Mir-Hossein Mousavi in the hope of chipping
away at the power of despotism. The Guardian Council, responsible for
vetting candidates, allowed him to run. Considering that he had been for
eight years a prime minister and a favorite of Ayatollah Khomeini—
indeed so much so that in Mousavi's political skirmish with Khamenei
in the early 1980s, Ayatollah Khomeini had clearly sided with the prime
minister, and even chastised Khamenei, who was then president—
rejecting his candidacy was hard to justify. Moreover, the conservatives
calculated that Mousavi's lack of charisma and his long absence from
politics limited his electability.[105] But as in the case of Khatami, Iran's
nascent civil society, the women's movement, student groups, and a
wide coalition of the electorate suddenly came to life. Vast networks of
supporters, often connected through mobile phones and the Internet,
grew around the country in support of the Green Movement. Artists and
scholars, no less than politicians and activists, helped create a movement that was mass-based and increasingly assertive and powerful. But
as recently leaked tapes of meetings of top IRGC commanders leave no
doubt, conservatives were committed to prevent at any cost a victory for
the reformists. It was, in the words of IRGC's top commander, a "red
line"—confirming the charge by democratic forces that they "engineered" the result and hurriedly announced Ahmadinejad a first-round
winner. There was, the commander confides to his comrades, no telling
what would happen if the election went to a second round.[106]

The day after the "engineered" results of the June 12 election were
announced, hundreds of thousands of people poured into the streets of
Tehran and other major cities. At their height, the demonstrators are said
to have gathered close to 3 million people—marching in peace and

demanding simply, "What happened to my vote?" In essence, in those few words, they captured the fundamental ideals of Iran's democratic movement—the right of the people, as sovereigns, to determine their own future.

As demonstrations continued and allegations of fraud were offered by at least two of the "losing" candidates—Mousavi and Karroubi—on June 18, Khamenei delivered a Friday prayer sermon wherein he dismissed the protestors' complaints, unambiguously sided with Ahmadinejad (praising his "revolutionary" credentials), and threatened the opposition with brute force. What he promised, he delivered. IRGC and Basiji units were unleashed on peaceful demonstrators. More than 4,000 activists were arrested, and at least seventy, and by some accounts up to 200, were killed. Eventually, many leaders of the Green Movement— erstwhile key members of the regime's intelligence and political elite— were arrested and put on trial in scenes eerily reminiscent of the Stalin show trials of the 1930s. When Karroubi, Mousavi, and Zahra Rahnavard, Mousavi's assertive wife—the first time a candidate's wife had taken an active role in her husband's campaign in the history of the Islamic Republic of Iran—refused to accept the results of an election they considered fraudulent, on the direct order of Khamenei they were put under house arrest. No indictments were ever issued, and even after four years of illegal incarceration, with the trio refusing to back down and Khamenei seeing no option but to keep them incarcerated, their imprisonment has been a lingering issue for both the democratic opposition and the regime.

By the end of Ahmadinejad's second and final term, the economy was in shambles.[107] Even conservatives realized the necessity of change. A whole array of candidates—from reformists like Khatami to pragmatists like Rafsanjani—announced their intention to run for president. While some like Khatami were threatened into withdrawing by a propaganda campaign, others, like Rafsanjani, were—in spite of his role as one of the chief architects of the regime—eliminated by the Guardian Council—in his case, his age was used as an excuse. Before long, Hassan Rouhani, a man of ferocious pragmatism and an unfailing ability to find and align himself with the center of power in Iran's labyrinthine political structure, emerged as the compromise candidate of reformists, democrats, women, and even many conservatives who were seriously concerned about the country's political isolation and economic crisis.

Rouhani cleverly aligned himself with many demands of Iran's democratic movement. He, like Khatami, promised a government based on rule of law at home—more precisely a government of prudence and optimism—and of reconciliation abroad. He suggested that the time had come to normalize relations with the United States and attempt to find a solution to the nuclear impasse. He won a first-round victory in 2013, making him the seventh president of the Islamic Republic of Iran. His ability to stay close to virtually all the competing, even conflicting, factions within the regime; his success in remaining a confidant of Supreme Leader Ali Khamenei while maintaining close ties to former president Rafsanjani (and these days Khamenei and Rafsanjani are again the two competing pillars of clerical power in the country[108]); his experience as Iran's onetime lead nuclear negotiator; and finally, his more recent affinities with Iran's democratic forces have all combined to give him a singular role in shaping the Islamic Republic of Iran at a critical moment.

Trained at both a traditional seminary in Qom and a modern Western university (Glasgow Caledonian University, where he received a doctoral degree in constitutional law), Rouhani is among a handful of clerics who have stayed at the pinnacle of power for the entire life of the regime, including key posts during the eight-year war with Iraq and five terms in Parliament. He is, in demeanor and discourse, polite but with a hint of haughtiness. Always fashionably dressed—yes, clerical robes vary widely in design and quality—he has a knack for finding the mot juste, some sufficiently ambiguous metaphor in which both his allies and critics hear their desired meanings. Standing a few feet away from Khamenei during his inauguration—wherein the vote of the people is "confirmed" by Khamenei and the elected president is "appointed" to his post by the leader—Rouhani declared, with no apparent irony, that the age of despotism had ended.

For Rouhani, discretion is the better side of valor. In the days before the election, he went out of his way to show his close ties to Khatami, Iran's reformist president from 1997 to 2005. But when conservative forces refused to allow Khatami to participate in the inaugural ceremonies in Parliament, Rouhani refused to put up a public fight. At the same time, in spite of dire warnings from websites close to Khamenei and the IRGC, Rouhani had included in his eighteen-man cabinet some key figures close to the reformists and to Rafsanjani. His nominee for the critical ministry of oil—the most important source of income for the regime—is Bijan Zangeneh, a man who, after Iran's 2009 contested presidential election, represented Mousavi in tense negotiations with Khamenei. His nominee for the foreign ministry, Javad Zarif, was easily his most important olive branch to the United States and the rest of the international community. The US-educated nominee was the country's onetime representative to the United Nations and has extensive ties to US political and financial leaders.

One of Rouhani's most contested appointments was his choice of Ali Janati as minister of Islamic Guidance—the son of an archconservative but himself an advocate of moderation and relative openness in matters of culture and social networks. He has been under constant attack from conservatives ever since he took office. Culture wars have become a focal point for conservative attacks on not just Janati but, through him, the entire Rouhani administration. Everything from his attempt to ease censorship and increase respect for Iranian people's private sphere—"you can't take people to paradise in chains," he famously declared—to his belief in allowing people access to Facebook—illegal in Iran yet with more than 5 million members—have subjected him to virulent attacks by radical conservatives. In the meantime, regardless of the tempest at the top, at the microsocial level, every facet of life, from aesthetics and ethics of sexual relations to the nature of political discourse, is witnessing a period of profound experimentation and defiant disregard for the shibboleths of the reigning dogma. While cynics believe the clerical despots' toleration of these "private heterotopias" make them merely a tool of repressive tolerance, a security valve to safely release enough pressure to preclude a direct political challenge to the status quo, the gradual grind of these changes is changing the nature of life in Iran—and changed lives is the ultimate measure and goal of politics.

Ironically, events since June 12, 2009, have shown that many of the top leaders in the Islamic regime, particularly Ayatollah Khamenei, seem to have drawn exactly the wrong conclusions about why the shah fell. Though they came to power as the result of the shah's inability to see the power of rising middle and technocratic classes and of his unwillingness to share power with these classes, like the shah, they blame "outside forces" for the continued perseverance of these democratic forces. Concessions by the shah, they believe, led to his demise, whereas every indication points to the axiom that his inability or unwillingness to make concessions in time begat his fall. The intransigence of despots has resulted in the fact that the same democratic coalition that in the 1905–1909 period demanded a constitution, and in 1979 overthrew the shah, continues to fight for democracy. And the only acceptable end to this long journey is democracy in Iran. The forces that attempted to create democracy in Iran more than a hundred years ago have only grown and become more experienced. Everything from the language and logic of democracy to institutions of civil society are today far more developed than they were in 1905 or 1979. Events after the 1979 Revolution have only delayed but not destroyed the Sisyphean quest for democracy.

Notes

1. For a discussion of the movement and its rise, see Amanat, *Resurrection and Renewal*.

2. For an erudite reading of the history of Shiism, see Daftary, *A History of Shi'i Islam*.

3. For an interesting discussion of these challenges in Egypt, see, for example, Toth, *Sayyid Qutb*. The case of Qutb is particularly relevant to Iran, as Khamenei has been influenced by him and has translated some of his books into Persian. Fuad Ajami does a masterful job of summarizing these challenges in the larger Arab context; see Ajami, *The Arab Predicament*

4. For a brief account of Nuri's ideas, see Nuri, "Refutation of the Idea of Constitutionalism," pp. 37–54.

5. PRO, "Iranian Internal Situation, 12 October 1978."

6. PRO, "Iranian Internal Situation, 16 September 1978."

7. Central Intelligence Agency (CIA), "Mohammad Reza Pahlavi, Shah of Iran," October 23, 1978. I obtained a copy through a Freedom of Information Act request.

8. Zonis, *Majestic Failure*. Zonis used psychological theories to argue that the men and women whom the shah relied on for his selfhood were all gone by the time of the Revolution.

9. PRO, "Letter by ACI Samuel to Foreign Office, July 18, 1955."

10. CIA, "Mohammad Reza Pahlavi."

11. Pahlavi, *Mission for My Country*. More than once he claims divine protection and revelation. In later years he repeated these claims, suggesting that many of his decisions are made after divine inspiration.

12. For a discussion of some of the theories developed in Europe to legitimize monarchy, see Kantrowicz, *The King's Two Bodies*.

13. PRO, "Iranian Internal Situation, 12 December 1978."

14. NSA, "Strength and Durability of the Shah's Regime."

15. Fardust was alleged to have been working with Khomeini for many years. The Islamic regime published two volumes of damaging material on the shah that it claimed to be the general's prison memoirs. For a brief account of his life, see the chapter on General Fardust in Milani, *Eminent Persians*.

16. As is evident even from the rather lengthy title of his book, there is a sharp difference between Huyser's perception of the purpose of his mission and that of the shah and the general. See Huyser, *Mission to Tehran*.

17. Parviz Sabeti, interview with author, September 3, 2005.

18. Documents of SAVAK published after the Revolution reveal the extent of this monitoring over the lives of artists, activists, and even moderate politicians such as Ali Amini. Their every move was monitored by SAVAK.

19. Mehdi Samii, a prominent technocrat, describes an angry shah telling him and a few others gathered in a meeting, "After all we have given them, why are they still opposing us?" Samii dared to declare that the problem is that they consider what the shah thinks he has given them as their rights. Mehdi Samii, interview with author, September 3, 2008.

20. PRO, "British Embassy to Foreign Office, 25 September 1978."

21. NSA–Bureau of Intelligence and Research, Department of State, "Studies in Political Dynamics in Iran."

22. Shawcross, *The Shah's Last Ride*, p. 99.

23. PRO, "30 October 1978, Prime Minister's Office to Foreign Ministry."

24. Kurzman, *The Unthinkable Revolution in Iran*.

25. Two different studies, one by Mohammad Mokhtari, and the second by Mehdi Bazorgan—the first a poet and the second the first IRGC prime minister—come up with slightly different percentages about the content of the slogans. For a discussion of the two studies, see Milani, *The Making of the Islamic Revolution*, p. 136.

26. NSA, "Ambassador Foroughi," September 17, 1979.

27. For Iran's encounter with modernity and the influence of its ideas on intellectual discourse, see Milani, *Lost Wisdom*. I have also written about these ideas in two books in Persian: *Tajadod va Tajadod Setizi dar Iran* [Modernity and Its Foes in Iran], published in Iran and now in its ninth printing, and *King of Shadows,* published in Los Angeles, and still, after seven years, waiting to clear the censors.

28. For a collection of Khomeini's books, see *Islam and Revolution*. For a brief biographical sketch of his life and intellectual development, see the chapter on Khomeini in Milani, *Eminent Persians*.

29. For a brilliant exposition of this history, see Hāeri-Yazdi, *Hekmat va Hokumat*.

30. For a brief overview of these two versions of Shiism, see Milani, "New Democrats," pp. 17–19.

31. Arash Naraghi's chapter in this collection is an informed exposition of this theory.

32. See the Quran, 2:256.

33. All quotes from Matini, "The Most Truthful Individual in Recent History."

34. All three were given prominent positions in the early days of the Revolution. All three were eventually swept away from power. Bani-Sadr was impeached after being elected the first president of the republic. Qotb-Zadeh was executed after he was alleged to have been involved in an attempted coup. Yazdi was dismissed as foreign minister and has been in and out of prison on various political charges.

35. Rafsanjani's daily journal (*Khaterat*) for the year 1982 shows that as plans for impeaching Bani-Sadr are made behind the scenes, there is also an attempt to convince Khomeini to change his mind and allow Khamenei to run (Rafsanjani, *Khaterat*, pp. 240–282). The book is available online at Rafsanjani's website, hashemirafsanjani.ir.

36. Ganji, *Bud-o Namud Khomeini*.

37. US Embassy, Tehran, "Moves Toward Government Unification, 8/3/79."

38. See Mousavi's fourteenth statement, available at www.kalame.com.

39. Schirazi, *The Constitution of Iran,* p. 293.

40. NSA, "Current Foreign Relations."

41. The first attempt to study conspiracy theories from a scholarly perspective was undertaken by Ashraf, "The Appeal of Conspiracy Theories to Persians," pp. 57–88.

42. Hofstadter's seminal "The Paranoid Style in American Politics" was later republished as a part of a book, in Hofstadter, *The Paranoid Style in American Politics and Other Essays*, pp. 77–86.

43. For conspiracy theories as a form of political participation, see Anderson, "Conspiracy Theories, Premature Entextualization, and Popular Political Analysis." For a brilliant depiction of what engagement in conspiracy theorizing, particularly about the British, does to the fabric of life and political thought in an average middle-class family in Iran, read the now classic novel *My Uncle Napoleon.* Written by Iraj Pezeshkzad, and translated into English by Dick Davis. First published by Mage, the book was also made into one of Iran's most acclaimed television series. There is now a small library of books and articles written about who and why the novel was written—many seeing a British hand in its publication.

44. For a thorough discussion of conspiracy theories in Iran, read Chehabi, "The Paranoid Style in Iranian Historiography," pp. 155–205; for a psychological approach to this proclivity, see Zonis and Craig, "Conspiracy Thinking in the Middle East."

45. For a description of the nativist tendency in Iran as well as the othering process, see Boroujerdi, *Iranian Intellectuals and the West*, pp. 1–76.

46. PRO, "British Embassy to Foreign Office, September 29, 1978."

47. Popper, *The Poverty of Historicism.*

48. Before Popper, theories were deemed scientific simply if they were verifiable. Popper added the qualification that they must also be falsifiable, or allow for new data to disprove the theory. See Popper, *Conjectures and Refutations.*

49. Pezeshkzad, *My Uncle Napoleon.*

50. PRO, "British Embassy to Foreign Office, September 29, 1978."

51. US Embassy, Tehran, "Alternative Views from the Province."

52. Ball, "Issues and Implication of the Iranian Crisis, December 1978," p. 16.

53. Ibid., p. 2.

54. US Department of State, "Statement of US Policy Toward Iran," p. 613.

55. Ibid., p. 606.

56. Ibid., p. 613.

57. NSA, "Political Internal Issues."

58. CIA, "Stability of the Present Regime in Iran." Much the same sentiment is reflected in another National Intelligence Estimate (NIE), see NSA, "The Outlook for Iran."

59. For the story of the General Gharani affair from the perspective of his life, see Milani, *Eminent Persians,* pp. 445–451.

60. See the chapter on General Gharani in Milani, *Eminent Persians.* I have also interviewed General Hassan Alavi-Kia, the deputy director of SAVAK at the time, who was involved in investigating the case (interview with author, San Diego, September 3, 2006).

61. Maleki, *Do Nameh*. Both letters are addressed to Dr. Mossadeq and in them Maleki describes the situation and offers biting criticism of the National Front leadership.

62. PRO, "Tehran to Foreign Office, 19 December 1978."

63. PRO, "Tehran to Foreign Office, 6 July 1978."

64. Ball, "Issues and Implication of the Iranian Crisis, December 1978," p. 3.

65. JFK Presidential Library, "Tehran to State Department, May 13, 1961."

66. Several scholarly reports about the land reform are more or less in consensus that Arsanjani had a radicalizing effect. See, for example, Najmabadi, *Land Reform and Social Change in Iran*, p. 83.

67. JFK Presidential Library, "Tehran to State, June 28, 1961."

68. Ibid.

69. For a detailed account of the landed gentry's attempt to fight the land reform, and their de facto alliance with the clergy, see Majd, *Resistance to the Shah*. For the role of the clergy, see S.H.R., *Baresi va Tahli Nehzat-e Imam Khomeini*. This book's author, S.H.R., is reported to be a chief of staff to Khomeini during his years of exile. While the latter book borders on hagiography, the former is sometimes overly personalized in its attack on the Pahlavi regime.

70. JFK Presidential Library, "25 May 1961 Memo for Philip Talbott."

71. Ebtehaj, *Memoirs*, pp. 853–857.

72. A copy of his speech was given to me, courtesy of Senator Lajevardi.

73. Davies, "The J-Curve of Rising and Declining Expectations as a Case of Some Great Revolutions and a Contained Rebellion." For a brief discussion of the curve in relations to Iran's revolution, see for example, Milani, *Iran's Islamic Revolution*, p. 16.

74. NSA–US Embassy, Tehran, "End of Tour Report, August 4, 1975."

75. For a detailed account of the US Embassy and the CIA's role in these developments, see Milani, *Persian Sphinx*, pp. 135–171. Of particular interest are the chapters on "Progressive Circle" and the "White Revolution."

76. Alam recounts other episodes in the fifth volume of his memoir. I have discussed the letters and the response, and how the government's decision to ignore them strengthened Khomeini. See Milani, "Alam and the Roots of the Iranian Revolution."

77. NSA, "Religious Leaders Fear Departure of the Shah."

78. Ball, "Issues and Implication of the Iranian Crisis, December 1978," p. 9.

79. Manuchehr Shahgoli, a close ally of Hoveyda, went to the US Embassy at the time and told diplomats that the shah dismantled the party and opted for the one-party system because he "realized how strong the party itself was getting. . . . The Shah decided it was time to crush yet another organization." NSA–US Embassy, Tehran, "Hoveyda Loyalist Lets Off Steam."

80. Mehdi Samii has kindly provided me with his notes, taken at the time of his meetings with the shah. They are a remarkable document in the honesty of their discussion.

81. See the chapter on Mesbah-Zadeh in Milani, *Eminent Persians*, pp. 399–406.

82. For a tragicomic narrative of these lapsed Stalinists fighting on behalf of their patrons—Hoveyda and Alam—in developing party structure and ideology, see Hamid Shokat's interview with Kourosh Lashai, in his series on the oral history of the Iranian new left; Shokat, *Jonbesh Daneshjouee*.

83. I have written at some length about the origins of the one-party idea in Milani, *Persian Sphinx,* pp. 275–287.

84. For a detailed, behind-the-scenes account, see Cooper, "Showdown in Doha."

85. NSA, "A Brief Overview of the US-Iran Relations," p. 27. The report was prepared in the early 1980s; it has no author or other indications about who commissioned it.

86. For an account of the agent's arrest and life, see Milani, *Eminent Persians,* pp. 462–468.

87. For an account of the KGB in Iran, see Andrew and Mitrokin, *The World Was Going Our Way,* pp. 165–176.

88. For another account of the KGB in Iran, see Kuzichkin, *Inside the KGB,* pp. 115–141.

89. Andrew and Mitrokin, *The World Was Going Our Way,* p. 175.

90. Ball, "Issues and Implication of the Iranian Crisis, December 1978."

91. For an account of how the Tudeh vision gradually dominated much of the left, see Behrooz, *Rebels with a Cause.* Many memoirs of members of the Tudeh Party and of the Fedaeeyane Khalg, a leftist guerrilla group that gradually gave up its radical ways and adopted the ideology of the Tudeh, have been since published. For an example, see Aslani, *The Crow and the Red Rose,* pp. 3–60.

92. Rafsanjani's daily journals include numerous reports about such meetings. For example, see *Khaterat,* volume 130, 1981–2, p. 276.

93. For a more or less impartial description of the group, see Abrahamian, *The Iranian Mojahedin.* The famous Murphy Report prepared for the US State Department describing the group as a terrorist organization is a critical account of their work. The group has taken the State Department to federal court four times to have its name removed from the list, all to no avail.

94. There are now two histories of the confederation, one in Persian and in two volumes, and the second a shorter, one-volume account in English. See Shokat, *Jonbesh Daneshjouee.*

95. For example, see Mirsepassi, *Political Islam, Iran, and the Enlightenment Philosophies of Hope and Despair.*

96. For a detailed account of this romance, see Afary and Anderson, *Foucault and the Iranian Revolution.*

97. Pahlavi, *Answer to History,* pp. 93–97.

98. Ibid., p. 146.

99. Mohammad Ali Movahhed, interview with author, London, September 17, 2009. He was one of the top negotiators for Iran. He has written a two-volume authoritative history of the oil movement, from the time of Mossadeq until the fall of the shah.

100. Pahlavi, *Answer to History,* p. 116.

101. Mohsen Kadivar has written about these machinations in some detail; see http://en.kadivar.com/the-trivialization-of-shii-marjaiyyat-impeaching-irans-supreme-leader-on-his-marjaiyyat/, accessed on July 15, 2014.

102. Many reports, articles, and court hearings have dealt with aspects of these crimes. For an account of one of the most controversial assassinations, for example, see Hakakian, *Assassins of the Turquoise Palace.*

103. In the eleventh volume of his daily journals, Rafsanjani has offered glimpses into these early signs of culture wars as waged by Khamenei and his conservative allies. See Rafsanjani, *Sazandeghi va Shokoufaee.*

104. I have written at some length about the Ahmadinejad presidency. See Milani, "The Pious Populist," pp. 7–14.

105. See my essays on Mousavi: Milani, "The Mousavi Mission," reprinted in Milani, *The Myth of Great Satan;* and for a synoptic account of the Green Movement, see http://iranprimer.usip.org/blog/all/Abbas%20Milani, accessed July 15, 2014.

106. For the transcript of the tape, and commentaries from a site that is close to Mousavi, see www.kalame/1393/11/hlm-186448, accessed July 15, 2014.

107. In the introduction to this collection, we offered an overview of the state of economy in 2013.

108. Once Khamenei was elected the new supreme leader, he and Rafsanjani shared power in what some scholars have called the period of dual power in Iran. Gradually Khamenei chipped away at his onetime friend and ally's power. For a discussion of the dual power theory, see Arjomand, *After Khomeini.*

Epilogue

A History of
Postrevolutionary Iran

A Prose Poem by
Simin Behbahani

February 1979:

With high expectations for the revolution, Iranians clenched their
fists and selflessly offered martyrs with the hope that freedom soon
shall blossom.

> This spring, we might see
> a garden adorned not with scattered petals,
> the smell of freedom is in the air
> so fragrant a breeze has never been.

March 1979:

On the first days after the revolution, on every street corner, we saw
in the hands of children images of bullet-riddled bodies; we saw
images of those executed without a trial and without due process, all
in the name of justice.

> I can't look: a corpse lies on the ground
> bullets punctuate its horrifying outline
> "the Book, the Scale, and the Iron"[1]
> are verses heaven has sent to guide us
> but this is "justice" with a dagger in its sleeves.

This chapter was translated from the Persian by Farzaneh and Abbas Milani.

. . . From "Justice" I flee, since it too represents oppression.
"Justice" is needed where oppression rules.[2]

May 1979:

It was the beginning of unrest in the city of Kurdistan. We opened
fire on ourselves. The earth turned crimson with the blood of our
brethren:

> The sky is crimson, the firmaments too
> the moon and Mars and the stars too
> red blushed, green became pallid. . . .

September 1979:

After speedy executions without trials and persistent arrests, after
confiscations and street riots, after the spread of false accusations
and vendettas and opportunism, terror crept in the air. Hope turned
into doubts. Many of Iran's artists, writers, and poets left the country,
Yadollah Ro'yai and Lo'bat Vala among them.

> Doubts, doubts, doubts at dusk,
> when you can't tell wolf and sheep apart,
> when a sickly, jaundiced, light
> has spread itself on the dirt of the threshold.
> The gray line on the horizon:
> what is it blowing our way?
> Is it the lead of the lies of the night?
> Or the silver of the dawn's truth?
> Uncertain, full of dread, the traveler ponders
> at the threshold of his journey,
> "Shall I wait or begin?"
> With doubts settled in the shelter of the eyes,
> faith will repudiate truth
> even if it shows its face.[3]

May 1980:

From the girls in my class, I heard whispers of warmongering. I was
baffled. The revolution was for the pursuit of peace, not war. In the

hearts of the youth, who had never experienced war, they began to plant the seeds of hatred.

> Oh Child of today, if you love war,
> I'm the child of yesterday,
> I loathe war.
> Since I found this world steeped in blood and madness
> I have made my principle to dispute war.
> . . . Purify it with water. Perfume it with the rose's essence
> you cannot wash out bloodstains with blood.[4]

August 1980:

Nader Naderpour, too, left the country. As fate would have it, he spent six years in Paris and fifteen in Los Angeles. As a farewell gift I offered him a poem.

> May your flight be joyous, as you leave
> may your voice be green, as you leave
> . . . The wings of your far-flung poetry
> have spread the world over.
> Maybe my running tears
> will bring you home again.

And yet Naderpour never returned, traveling to eternity and longing for his country. He composed *False Dawn* (1981), *Blood and Ashes* (1988), and *The Earth and Time* (1995) in exile.

October 1980:

And then the seeds of hatred produced their bitter fruits. The first bombs exploded over the Mehrabad Airport. The Iran-Iraq War had begun.

> We wished no war
> but here it is.
> War; this inferno, this ball of fire,
> "May there be no war," I had ventured,
> but war is upon us.
> Oh, my homeland, I vow to you
> I'll be yours for as long as I live.

My poetry and passion and joy are all here,
my coffin and my grave shall be here too.

November 1980:

The war dragged on, contrary to all expectations. Khoramshahr [the
City of Joy] became Khouninshahr [the City of Blood]. Iranian youth
showed great valor and offered many sacrifices, as did small children
and the elderly.

> Write, write, write this epic of resistance
> History! Write the tale of this season of blood
> write of the stone thrown by a playful child
> write of the pickax's gash, carried by a helpful elder
> write of those who cried out "Death or Honor"
> and embraced death with courage
> Write. Write.

Unbending and strident commands, constant arrests, an atmosphere
of fear and trembling, of terror and cold, shortages of fuel, repeated
blackouts, selfless martyrdoms, shortages of food, closure of all
universities, and the escape of fourteen-year-old boys from their
homes to the warfront in search of martyrdom all worked to create
an intolerable situation. Many Iranians had already chosen exile in
the early stages of the revolution; many more, fearing a twenty-year
prolongation of the war, endured many dangers and left the country.

> Go so that I can stay. Go so that I can stay
> For estrangement from my home, I cannot bear.
> Till my body's time has ended
> till my limb and veins have withered
> the same "tale of the reed"[5] you'll hear from me.
> . . . I and the children, the aged, and the grief of the valiant warriors
> go so that I can stay.

March 1981:

Sa'id Soltanpour, a member of the secretariat of the Writers'
Association of Iran, was arrested. With every passing day, the war
made the atmosphere of terror heavier.

Tick tock, Tick tock.
Oh, how the instant moves
humbly, by compulsion, on its path.
. . . It rises with the sun, in shimmering gold.
It sinks with the bleeding sunset in a well.
. . . Oh . . . oh . . . my life goes . . . instant by instant.[6]

May 1981:

All universities were shut down indefinitely. Demonstrations mired
in violence escalated. Prisons were filled. The Writers' Association
of Iran was under attack, its documents, lecture tapes, and other
materials were confiscated. The association was eventually shut
down. Some of the writers, including Dr. Mahyar Khalili and Ehsan
Naraghi, and a few lawyers were imprisoned. Shahrnoush Parsipour
was incarcerated for four years and seven months.

Dark, angry, Arabic, the script of your violence
soft and blue tile, the symbol of our compliance
the bruise of your lash, running with red blood
has painted amazing flowers in blue and golden yellow
monkeylike, you still bask in imitating Arabs
what uncouth manners you have
how fake is your mimicry.

July 1981:

A big explosion killed some 100 leaders of the government. The
cause remained shrouded in secrecy. Harassments increased. Sa'id
Soltanpour's execution marked the beginning of mass executions.
Girls and boys under the age of sixteen were among the victims.

The house was cloudy once, the house is bloody now
such was then, thus it is now.
. . . The old tiger drags the young gazelle in her blood
the law of the jungle shames religion now.
Youthful brides of crystal-like bodies and arms
have graves as nuptial chambers and earth as pillows now.
Cut the diamond, then crash it, what creed is this now?[7]

The security of writers was endangered. Many bore a thousand hardships and saved their lives by leaving the country: Mehdi Tehrani, Nasser Pakdaman, Ali Asghar Hajsedjavadi, Hassan Hessam, Mohsen Hessam, Nassim Khaksar, Esma'il Kho'i, Gholem Hossein Sa'edi, Reza Alamehzadeh, Eslam Kazemiyeh, Ahmad Karimi-Hakkak, Atefeh Gorgin, Ne'mat Mirzadeh, Homa Nateq, Mohsen Yalfani. Sa'edi became ill and died in exile. Kazemiyeh committed suicide. Others continue to be active and write. Long be their lives.

December 1982:

We stayed behind and witnessed accusations, condemnations, harassment, patience, blood, death, and martyrdom in order to stay.

> This is no dawn; this is no dawn
> blood has drained of its vein and the night has paled.
> This is no galaxy; it's the dead body of a youth facing Mecca
> this is no Karoun River
> it is the flowing tears of mothers
> nurturing every river, falling day and night
> may God be his enemy and may he be estranged from God
> He, who has sown hatred in the heart of the masses.

March 1982:

In the midst of destruction, on the threshold of the New Year, in our minds we harbored hopes of an improvement, though unattainable it seemed.

> My country, I will build you again,
> if need be, with bricks made from my life.
> I will build columns to support your roof with my bones,
> I will inhale again the perfume of flowers
> favored by your youth.
> I will wash again the blood off your body
> with torrents of my tears.[8]

April 1985:

Trees had blossomed, but no one could see the spring. The war would not end. Our days were drenched in tears and blood and a

downpour of missiles. Many newspapers and journals such as
Bustan, Nameyeh Kanoun-e Nevissandegan, Ketab Jom'eh, Borj,
Mess, Bamdad, Ayandegan, Ketab Cheragh, and every independent
publication were shut down. After a while *Adineh* began publication.
In "the dark night of desperation," it was a ray of sunshine.
Doniyah-ye Sokhan and *Mofid* and later *Gardoun, Farhang-e*
Tosee'eh, Karnameh, Nafeh, Negah-e Now, Kelk, and its reincarnation,
Bokhara, began publication and continue to do so this day.

August 1988:

The war finally ended, and this was the voice of our hearts.

> Our tears are sweet, our laughter venomous.
> We are pleased when sad, and sad when pleased.
> We wash one hand in blood, the other we wash the blood off.
> We cry as we laugh at the futility of both these acts.
> Eight years have passed; we haven't discovered their meaning.
> We have been like children, beyond any account or accounting.
> . . . We wished for a war, it brought us misery,
> now repellant we wish for peace.
> We pulled wings and heads from bodies,
> now seeking the cure we are busy grafting.
> Will it come to life, will it fly,
> the head we attach, the wing we stitch?[9]

Summer 1990:

At the invitation of Mahmoud Dow'latabadi some forty young and
old writers gathered at the house of Mansour Koushan to help the
victims of the earthquake. The meeting turned into the beginning of
a new phase of activity for the Writers' Association of Iran.
Government newspapers spared us no insult. Nevertheless the
Advisory Council of the Writers' Association of Iran was formed.

> I'm no twig to bend easily
> I am the tall unyielding pine
> in me is the essence of resilience
> even if I am cut into pieces.
> . . . Let the willow tremble
> let the wind billow

the shame of the wind and the willow is not for me
I am the tall unyielding pine.

June 1991:

I was invited to Azad University to read poetry, and I did. I was
repeatedly summoned to the revolutionary court, and the newspapers
had a field day attacking and insulting me. I wrote,

If the snake is domestic
I will give it shelter.
I will be fond of it still
even if it does cruel things.[10]

March 1993:

On March 13, 1993, Sa'idi Sirjani, the defiant poet and writer, was
detained on false charges of possessing opium in his pocket.

When they plant accusations in your innocent pocket
a flood of tears and disgust flows from your black eyes,
suppose, they plant in your cloth proof of your guilt,
have no fear
as the soul of the world is a witness to your innocence.
Bonded with your pen, why fear prison and chain
write, write freely,
such is your way and no other.

I sent the poem to *Arash* in Paris where it was published. In April the
Advisory Council of the Writers' Association of Iran wrote a letter to
the head of the judiciary and demanded justice and Sirjani's freedom.
In the autumn of 1994 under physical and mental torture, Sa'idi Sirjani
died in prison.

August 1994:

The text of the declaration of 134 members of the Writers'
Association of Iran, later to be known as "Text 134," was published.
It reaffirmed the rights of all writers and objected to censorship,
harassment, and detainment of writers. It attracted international
attention.

November 1995:

The body of Ahmad Mir'alai, a writer and translator, was found in the alleys of the city of Isfahan, a bottle of alcohol in his pocket, implying that he had died because of abuse. And of course, no one believed it. Oppression was such that open protest was not an option, only oblique suggestions such as this:

> Footsteps, footsteps, footsteps
> leave a trail of footprints
> voices, loud and muffled,
> travel with time, step by step.

May 1996:

The hung body of Gazaleh Alizadeh, a novelist, was brought down from a tree in the village of Javarherdeh in Ramsar, implying that she had committed suicide. Everyone believed it, but I . . .

September 1996:

Mohammad Ali Sepanlou, Faraj Sarkouhi, Houshang Golshiri, Rowshanak Dariush, Mehrangis Kar, and I were guests in the house of the cultural attaché of the German Embassy when we got arrested. Mahmoud Dow'latabadi and Reza Barahani had not joined us and were not present. We spent the night in prison and were set free the next day. Why? I have no idea.

During the same period a group of twenty-one writers were on their way to Armenia at the invitation of its Pen Association. On the way, the driver tried to send the bus off a cliff after he himself managed to escape with great agility. The trunk of a tree obstructed the bus and the passengers were saved. Houshang Golshiri, Reza Barahani, and I had declined the invitation. But why they wanted to kill twenty-one writers was never made clear.

November 1996:

I was in Germany on my way to America for a series of lectures and poetry readings. I heard that on his way to Germany from Iran, Faraj Sarkouhi had disappeared. In his book, *Yas va Das* (The Jasmine and

the Sickle) he has recorded the story of his
incarceration, torture, and other problems. For close to a year and a
half he suffered through many difficulties. He now lives in Germany.
Borrowing from the poet Ahmad Shamlu, he tells his oppressors,
"How can you enjoy the garden and the trees / you who address the
jasmine in the language of the sickle."

November 1997:

The Ministry of Guidance invited me to read poetry at a hall with the
capacity of 2000 people. I pulled out of my purse the written text of
a speech, which revolved around the harassment, censorship, and the
oppression that had been inflicted on the writers for eighteen years. I
began to read, but halfway through the microphone was cut off. I
continued at the top of my voice. The lights were shut off. I walked
further upstage in order to use the light streaming through from the
auditorium. The curtain was pulled down. I stepped in front of it.

It was the audience's exuberant show of support that saved me that
day. The next day, I read the entire speech for one of the [diaspora]
radios. It was broadcast on most stations. I was threatened with
death, and the vicious attacks of the media began yet again.

> Oh you enemies of mine
> what have I ever said other than the truth
> in response to your insults I refrain from cursing you

Summer 1998:

The body of Gafar Hosseini, writer and translator, was found in his
house two or three days after his death. Shortly thereafter, Hajizadeh,
the poet from Kirman, and his son were mutilated in the dark of the
night. Majid Sharifzadeh's body was found in the street. And Pirooz
Davani disappeared.

December 1998:

That valiant Iranian Dariush Foruhar and his poet wife, Parvaneh
Eskandari, were cut into pieces in their home. A few days later,
Mohammad Mokhtari and then Mohammad Ja'far Pouyandeh were
strangled to death. Their bodies were found in the alleys.

How crimson and fragrant is this flower severed from its root,
resting next to an axe.
. . . This violence, in different degrees,
has nestled in the hearts
like a dagger or like a needle.

And then:

The prisons are graced with the presence of writers, journalists,
students, intellectuals, and nationalists. Their total number my
memory cannot contain. Among the members of the Writers'
Association of Iran, Shahrnoush Parsipour has experienced prison two
more times. Mehrangis Kar was incarcerated for more than a month;
Shahla Lahiji, for more than a month; Shirin Ebadi, close to a month;
Mohammad Khalili, one month. Ali Reza Jabari is spending his
second year behind bars, and Dr. Nasser Zarafshan his third.

Let me ask you then, what is there to write about under the
circumstances I have described in summary fashion here? And how?

Nonetheless, we have written incessantly, and the younger generation
is writing even more than we have.

Notes

1. Verses on Laws, Judgments, and Punishments from chapter 42, verse 17
of the Quran.
2. Behbahani, *A Cup of Sin,* p. 89.
3. Ibid., p. 86.
4. Ibid., p. 42.
5. Opening lines of Rumi's *Mathnave,* well known as "Any Lines of Poetry
by Iranians": "Here the tales told by the reed / complaining of separation / from
the time I was cut from the reed bed / men and women have cried with me in
sympathy" (ibid., p. 80).
6. Ibid., p. 78.
7. The line refers to the fact that Islam prohibits the execution of virgin
girls, and it has been reported that when such girls were condemned to die, they
were first raped.
8. Behbahani, *A Cup of Sin,* p. 68.
9. Ibid., p. 28.
10. Ibid., p. 18.

Bibliography

Abedin, Mahan. "Iran After the Elections," *Middle East Intelligence Bulletin* 6, no. 2/3 (February–March 2004).

Abrahamian, Ervand. *The Iranian Mojahedin.* New Haven, CT: Yale University Press, 2009.

Adamic, Lada, and Natalie Glance. "The Political Blogosphere and the 2004 Election: Divided They Blog," Proceedings of the Third International Workshop on Link Discovery, March 1, 2005, www.blogpulse.com/papers /2005/AdamicGlanceblogwww.pdf, accessed July 7, 2009.

Afary, Janet, and Kevin Anderson. *Foucault and the Iranian Revolution: Gender and the Seductions of Islamism.* Chicago: University of Chicago Press, 2005.

Afshar, Ali Reza. "Ashena'i ba tashkilat va mamuriyatha-ye Basij" [A Guide to Basij Organization and Missions], *Journal of Basij Studies* 19 (Fall 1993): 17–32.

Afshar, Ali Reza. "Interview with General Ali Reza Afshar," *Javannewspaper,* no. 377, November 23, 2010.

Ajami, Fouad. *The Arab Predicament: The Arab Thought and Practice Since 1967.* Cambridge: Cambridge University Press, 1992.

Akhavi, Shahrokh. "Elite Factionalism in the Islamic Republic of Iran," *Middle East Journal* 41, no. 2 (Spring 1980): 181–201.

Alavi, Nasrin. *We Are Iran.* London: Portobello Books, 2005.

Alfoneh, Ali. "The Basij Resistance Force: A Weak Link in the Iranian Regime?" *Policy Watch* 1627, February 5, 2010, www.washingtoninstitute.org/policy -analysis/view/the-basij-resistance-force-a-weak-link-in-the-iranian-regime, accessed July 7, 2014.

Amanat, Abbas. *Resurrection and Renewal: The Makings of the Babi Movement in Iran, 1844–1850.* Ithaca, NY: Cornell University Press, 1989.

Amnesty International. "Annual Report 2012," https://www.amnesty.org/en /region/iran/report-2012, accessed March 10, 2014.

Anderson, Jon W. "Conspiracy Theories, Premature Entextualization, and Popular Political Analysis," *Arab Studies Journal* 4, no. 1 (Spring 1996): 96–102.

Andrew, Christopher, and Vasili Mitrokin. *The World Was Going Our Way: The KGB and the Battle for the Third World.* New York: Basic Books, 2005.

Arjomand, Saïd Amir. *After Khomeini*. Oxford: Oxford University Press, 2009.

Ashraf, Hamid. "The Appeal of Conspiracy Theories to Persians," *Princeton Papers*, no. 5 (Winter 1997).

Aslani, Mehdi. *The Crow and the Red Rose: Memoirs of Prison*. Koln: Arash Publishers, 2009.

Aslani, Minoo. "Empowering Female Managers Is the Core of the Women's Basij Organization's Activities," *Sepah* (IRGC news website), November 8, 2009, www.sepahnews.com/shownews.Aspx?ID=966435fe-fe2f-42df -b832-f4e27a1b8d97, accessed July 13, 2014.

Babakhanian, Karim. "Sisters Basij and Intelligent Defense with Soft Threats," *Javan* (newspaper), November 27, 2008, p. 11.

Baji, Yasaman. "Iran: Khamenei Likely to Hold Onto Weakened Ahmadinedjad," Inter Press Service, October 25, 2012, www.ipsnews.net/2012/10/iran -khamenei-likely-to-hold-onto-weakened-ahmadinejad/, accessed March 10, 2014.

Bakhtiari, Bahman. *Parliamentary Politics in Revolutionary Iran: The Institutionalization of Factional Politics*. Gainesville: University Press of Florida, 1996.

Ball, George. "Issues and Implication of the Iranian Crisis, December 1978," George Ball Papers, Princeton University Library, Steeley G. Mudd Manuscript Library, Box 30, Doc. no. MC031.

Bayat, Asef. *Life as Politics: How Ordinary People Change the Middle East*. Stanford, CA: Stanford University Press, 2010.

Behbahani, Simin. *A Cup of Sin: Selected Poems,* trans. Kaveh Safa and Farzaneh Milani. Syracuse, NY: Syracuse University Press, 1999.

Behrooz, Maziar. "Factionalism in Iran Under Khomeini," *Middle Eastern Studies* 27, no. 4 (October 1991): 597–614.

Behrooz, Maziar. *Rebels with a Cause: The Failure of the Left in Iran*. London: I. B. Tauris, 2000.

Benkler, Yochai. *The Wealth of Networks: How Social Production Transforms Markets and Freedom*. New Haven, CT: Yale University Press, 2006.

Bjorvatn, Kjetil, and Kjetil Selvik. "Destructive Competition: Factionalism and Rent-Seeking in Iran," *World Development* 36, no. 11 (2008): 2314–2324.

Boroujerdi, Mehrzad. *Iranian Intellectuals and the West*. Syracuse, NY: Syracuse University Press, 1996.

Burke, Jason, and Saeed Kamali Dehghan. "Mass Trial for Iran Protest Leaders," *The Observer*, August 2, 2009, www.theguardian.com/world/2009 /aug/02/mass-trial-iranian-opposition-politicians, accessed July 12, 2014.

Chaffee, Steven H., and Yuko Miyo. "Selective Exposure and the Reinforcement Hypothesis: An Intergenerational Panel Study of the 1980 Presidential Campaign," *Communication Research* 10, no. 1 (1983): 3–36.

Chehabi, Houchang E. "The Paranoid Style in Iranian Historiography." In *Iran in the 20th Century: Historiography and Political Culture*, ed. Touraj Atabki. London: I. B. Tauris, 2009.

CIA (Central Intelligence Agency). "Stability of the Present Regime in Iran: Secret Special National Intelligence Estimate," NSA, no. 362, August 25, 1958.

Cooper, Scott. "Showdown in Doha: The Secret Deal That Helped Sink the Shah of Iran," *Middle East Journal* 62, no. 4 (Autumn 2008): 567–591.

Daftary, Farhad. *A History of Shi'i Islam*. London: I. B. Tauris, 2014.

Davies, James. "The J-Curve of Rising and Declining Expectations as a Case of Some Great Revolutions and a Contained Rebellion." In *Violence in America*, ed. Hugh Davis Graham and Ted Robert Gurr. New York: Sage Publications, 1969.

Ebtehaj, Hushang. *The Seasoned Silk-Minded: Talk to Sayeh*. Tehran: Sokhan Publisher, 2003 [1391].

Ebtehaj, Khaterat-e Abolhassan. *Memoirs,* 2 vols. 2 printings. Tehran: Elmi Publishers, 1996 [1375].

Ehteshami, Anoushiravan. *After Khomeini: The Iranian Second Republic*. London: Routledge, 1995.

Ehteshami, Anoushiravan, and Reza Molavi. *Iran and the International System*. London: Routledge, 2012.

Eisenstadt, Michael. "The Security Forces of the Islamic Republic and the Fate of the Opposition," *Policy Watch* 1538, June 19, 2009, www.washington institute.org/templateC05.php?CID=3076, accessed, July 7, 2014.

Esfandiari, Golnaz. "Iran's Writers Association Criticizes State Pressure," RadioFreeEurope/RadioLiberty, January 24, 2014, www.rferl.org/content /iran-writers-association-criticizes-state-pressure/25241663.html, accessed March 10, 2014.

Eshkevari, Hasan Yousefi. Yousefieshkevari.com, blog, http://yousefieshkevari .com, accessed March 10, 2014.

Fars News. "Educating of 17,000 Sport Coaches at the Sport Basij Organization," *Fars News Agency*, February 11, 2014, www.farsnews.com/news text.php?nn=13921122000870, accessed July 12, 2014.

Fars News. "The Organized Basij Member Passed Twenty Millions," *Fars News Agency*, November 22, 2013, www.farsnews.com/newstext.php?nn =13920901000212, accessed July 13, 2014.

Faruru News Agency. "Khat faghr dar Iran" [Poverty Line in Iran], September 8, 2009, www.fararu.com/vdchzxnx.23nzvdftt2.html, accessed July 13, 2014.

Fassihi, Farnaz. "Inside the Iranian Crackdown," *Wall Street Journal,* July 11, 2009, http://online.wsj.com/article/SB124726981104525893.html#mod=todays _us_page_one, accessed July 13, 2014.

Fathalizadeh, Aidin. "Forces to Reckon With: The Basij," *Goftogoo: Dialogue on Iran and Iranians* 2 (2003): 8–9.

Fathi, Nazila. "Iran's Top Leader Dashes Hopes for a Compromise," *New York Times,* June 19, 2009, www.nytimes.com/2009/06/20/world/middleeast/20 iran.html, accessed July 12, 2014.

Floor, Willem. "*Luti*, a Persian Term with a Variety of Meanings, with Both Positive and Negative Connotations," *Encyclopaedia Iranica*, 2010, www.iranica.com/articles/luti, accessed July 7, 2014.

Frey, Dieter. "Recent Research on Selective Exposure to Information." In *Advances in Experimental Social Psychology,* vol. 19, ed. L. Berkowitz. New York: Academic Press, 1986.

Fukuyama, Francis. "Iran, Islam and the Rule of Law," *Wall Street Journal,* July 27, 2009, http://online.wsj.com, accessed March 10, 2014.

Ganji, Akbar. *Bud-o Namud Khomeini* [Essence and Appearance of Khomeini]. Berlin: Gardoon Publisher, 2013.

Ganji, Babak. *Iranian Strategy: Factionalism and Leadership Politics*. Wiltshire: Defence Academy of the United Kingdom, Research and Assessment Branch, 2007.

Geertz, Clifford. "Thick Description: Toward an Interpretive Theory of Culture." In *Readings in the Philosophy of Social Science,* ed. Michael Martin and Lee C. McIntyre. Cambridge, MA: MIT Press, 1994, pp. 213–233.

Ghasami, Mahdi. "The Study of Basij Sport and Cultural Clubs' Role in Keeping of Unity of Basijis," *Basij Studies Quarterly,* nos. 18–19 (Spring and Summer 2003): 185–196.

Ghasemiyan, Hassen. *Akhlaq va Adab-e Moashera-te Basij* [Basij Ethics and Etiquette]. Tehran: Publication of the Representative of the Supreme Leader, Basij Resistance Force, IRGC, 2000.

Gholami, Mehdi. "A Basiji's Opinion on the Pathology of the Basij," Hamian-e velayat, Website of the Supporters of the Supreme Leadership–Students' Basij Group, January 23, 2010, http://imamkhamenei.ning.com/group/Basij ?groupUrl=Basij&id=4822314:Group:1499&page=4#comments, accessed July 13, 2014.

Golkar, Saeid. "Cultural Engineering Under Authoritarian Regimes: Islamization of Universities in Postrevolutionary Iran," *Digest of Middle East Studies* 21, no. 1 (2012): 1–23.

Golkar, Saeid. "The Feminization of Control: Iran's Women Militia and Social Order in Iran," *Hawwa: Journal of Women of the Middle East and the Islamic World* 11, no. 1 (2013): 16–40.

Golkar, Saeid. "The Ideological-Political Training of Iran's Basij," *Middle East Brief,* Brandeis University, Crown Center for Middle East Studies (Fall 2010), www.brandeis.edu/crown/publications/meb/meb44.html, accessed July 7, 2014.

Golkar, Saeid. "Liberation or Suppression Technologies? The Internet, the Green Movement, and the Regime in Iran," *International Journal of Emerging Technologies and Society* 9, no. 1 (2011): 50–70.

Golkar, Saeid. "Organization of Oppressed or Organization for Oppressing: Analyzing the Role of the Basij Militia of Iran," *Journal of Politics, Religion and Ideology* 3, no. 4 (2002): 455–471.

Golkar, Saeid. "The Paramilitarization of the Economy: The Case of Iran's Basij," *Armed Forces and Society* 38, no. 4 (October 2012): 625–648.

Golkar, Saeid. "Politics of Piety, Moral Control of Iranian Society," *Journal of the Middle East and Africa* 2, no. 2 (2011): 207–219.

Golkar, Saeid. "The Reign of Hard-line Students in Iranian Universities," *Middle East Quarterly* 17, no. 3 (Summer 2010): 21–29.

Hadadian, Saeid. "Dialogue with Raja News," Raja, November 28, 2011, http://rajanews.com/detail.asp?id=108896, accessed July 13, 2014.

Hāeri-Yazdi, Mehdi. *Hamshahri Newspaper*, no. 724 (July 6, 1995).

Hāeri-Yazdi, Mehdi. *Hekmat va Hokumat* [Wisdom and Government], London: n.p., 1995.

Hāeri-Yazdi, Mehdi. *Kherad-nameh Sadra*, no. 2 (September 1995).

Hāeri-Yazdi, Mehdi. *Nameh-e Farhang*, no. 17 (Tehran, Spring 1995).

Hafezi, Parisa. "Iran Cleric Says Obeying Ahmadinejad Like Obeying God," Reuters, August 13, 2009, http://in.mobile.reuters.com/article/worldNews /idINIndia-41743720090813, accessed March 10, 2014.

Hajjarian, Saeed. *Az Shahed-e Qodsi ta Shahed-e Bazari* [From Sacred Beauty to the Market Beauty]. Tehran: Tarh-e No, 2001 [1380].

Hajjarian, Saeed. "Farayand-e Orfi shodan-e feqh-e Shi'i" [The Process of Secularization of Shi'ite Jurisprudence]. In *Az Shahed-e Qudsi ta Shahed Bazari* [From Sacred Beauty to Secular Beauty]. Tehran: Tarh-e No, 2001 [1380].

Hajjarian, Saeed. "Ja'meeh Shenasi-e Feqh" [Sociology of Islamic Jurisprudence], *Aaiyn Magazine*, no. 6 (n.d.).

Hajjarian, Saeed. "Nameh be yek rafiq" [A Letter to a Friend], http://ayande.ir, accessed July 12, 2014.

Hakakian, Roya. *Assassins of the Turquoise Palace*. New York: Grove Press, 2011.

Hashemi, Nader, and Danny Postel. *The People Reloaded: The Green Movement and the Struggle for Iran's Future*. Brooklyn, NY: Melville House, 2010.

Hashemi, Seyyed Muhammad. *Hoquq-e Asasi-e Jomhouri-e Islami-e Iran* [Constitutional Law of the Islamic Republic of Iran], vol. 2, ed. 20. Tehran: Mizan, 2008 [1387].

Hodgson, Marshall G. S. *The Venture of Islam*. Chicago: University of Chicago Press, 1974.

Hofstadter, Richard. *The Paranoid Style in American Politics and Other Essays*. Cambridge, MA: Harvard University Press, 1996.

Horowitz, Richard. "A Detailed Analysis of Iran's Constitution," *World Policy Institute*, October 12, 2012, www.worldpolicy.org/blog/2010/10/12/detailed -analysis-iran%E2%80%99s-constitution, accessed March 10, 2014.

Hosseini, Seyed Masih. "A Good Basiji Is Not Usually a Member of the Basij," *Hawazah*, March–April 2008, www.hawzah.net/fa/magazine/magart/6438 /7039/85387, accessed July 13, 2014.

Human Rights Watch. *Human Rights Watch World Report, 2010: Events of 2009*. New York: Seven Stories Press, 2010.

Huyser, Robert E. *Mission to Tehran: The Fall of the Shah and the Rise of Khomeini Recounted by the US General Who Was Secretly Sent at the Last Minute to Prevent It*. New York: Harper and Row, 1986.

IFES (International Foundation for Electoral Systems). "IFES Election Guide—Country Profile: Iran," n.d., www.electionguide.org/countries/id/103/, accessed July 12, 2014.

"Iran: Violent Crackdown on Protesters Widens." Human Rights Watch, June 24, 2009, www.hrw.org/news/2009/06/23/iran-violent-crackdown-protesters -widens, accessed July 12, 2014.

Iran Chamber Society. "Iran Chamber Society: The Constitution of Islamic Republic of Iran," www.iranchamber.com/government/laws/constitution _ch03.php, accessed July 12, 2014.

"Iran Pulse—Iranian Parliamentary Corruption Scandal Implicates Notorious Figure," *Al-Monitor,* January 3, 2014, www.al-monitor.com/pulse/originals /2014/01/iran-parliament-corruption-mortazavi.html, accessed March 10, 2014.

"Iran Pulse—Rouhani's Biopic Surprises Iranian Voters," *Al-Monitor,* June 5, 2013, www.al-monitor.com/pulse/originals/2013/06/hassan-rouhani-iran -elections-documentary-tv.html, accessed March 10, 2014.

"Iran's Closure of Reformist Newspaper Raises Concerns About Press Freedom," *The Guardian*, November 4, 2013, www.theguardian.com/world /2013/nov/04/irans-closure-of-reformist-newspaper-raises-concerns-about -press-freedom, accessed March 10, 2014.

"Iran's Show Trials: The Hard-Liners Build Their Case," *Time*, August 3, 2009, http://content.time.com/time/world/article/0%2C8599%2C1914294%2C00 .html, accessed July 12, 2014.

Javadi-Amoli, Abdollah. *Velayat-e Faqih: Velayat-e Feqh va Edalat* [Velayat-e Faqih: Guardianship of Jurisprudence and Justice]. Qom: Osara' Institute, 2000.

Jeffery, Simon. "Iran Election Protests: The Dead, Jailed and Missing," *The Guardian*, July 29, 2009, www.theguardian.com/world/blog/2009/jul/29 /iran-election-protest-dead-missing, accessed July 12, 2014.

JFK Presidential Library. "Tehran to State Department, May 13, 1961."

JFK Presidential Library. "Tehran to State, June 28, 1961."

JFK Presidential Library. "25 May 1961 Memo for Philip Talbott," Foreign Relations of the United States, vol. 18, Microfilm Supplements.

Kadivar, Mohsen. *Daghdagh-hai Hokumat-e Dini* [Some Concerns About Religious Government]. Tehran: Nashr-e Ney, 2001.

Kadivar, Mohsen. *Hokumat-e Velai'i* [Government Headed by a Vali]. Tehran: Nashr-e Ney, 2000.

Kadivar, Mohsen. *Nazari-ehai-e Dolat dar Fiqh-e Shi'i* [The Theories of Government in Shi'i Fiqh]. Tehran: Nashr-e Ney, 1997.

Kadivar, Mohsen. "Velayat-e Faqih and Democracy," www.kadivar.com, accessed July 12, 2014.

Kamali Dehghan, Saeed. "Mahmoud Ahmadinejad Faces Impeachment Threat," *The Guardian*, June 22, 2011, www.theguardian.com/world/2011/jun/21 /mahmoud-ahmadinejad-iran-president-impeachment, accessed March 10, 2014.

Kamrava, Mehran. "Military Professionalization and Civil-Military Relations in the Middle East," *Political Science Quarterly* 115, no. 1 (Spring 2000): 67–92.

Kantrowicz, Ernst H. *The King's Two Bodies: A Study in Mediaeval Political Theology*. Princeton, NJ: Princeton University Press, 1957.

Kelly, John, and Bruce Etling. "Mapping Iran's Online Public: Politics and Culture in the Persian Blogosphere," *Berkman Center Publication*, no. 2008-01, April 6, 2008, http://cyber.law.harvard.edu/publications/2008/Mapping _Irans_Online_Public, accessed July 8, 2014.

Khomeini, Ruhollah. *Islam and Revolution: Writings and Declarations of Imam Khomeini*, trans. Hamid Algar. Berkeley, CA: Mizan Press, 1981.

Khomeini, Ruhollah. *Islamic Government: Governance of the Jurist*. Tehran: Nashr-e Markaz Publishing, 1970 [1343].

Khomeini, Ruhollah. *Kashf-ol-Asrar*. Tehran: Nashr-e Markaz Publishing, 1944 [1323].

Khomeini, Ruhollah. *Sahifeh-ye Noor.* 21 volumes. Tehran: Nashr-e Markaz Publishing, 2004 [1383].

Khomeini, Ruhollah. *Velayat-e Faqih*. Tehran: Amir Kabir Publications, 1981 [1360].

Khosravi, Shahram. *Young and Defiant in Tehran*. Philadelphia: University of Pennsylvania Press, 2008.

Kile, Shannon N. *Europe and Iran: Perspectives on Nonproliferation*. Oxford: Oxford University Press, 2005.

Knutsen, Oddbjorn, and Elinor Scarbrough. "Cleavage Politics." In *The Impact of Values,* "Beliefs in Government," vol. 4, ed. Jan W. Van Deth and Elinor Scarbrough. Oxford: Oxford University Press, 1995.

Kumar, Ravi, Prabhakar Raghavan, Sridhar Rajagopalan, and Andrew Tomkins. "Trawling the Web for Emerging Cyber-Communities," *WWW8/Computer Networks* 31, no. 11–16 (1999): 1481–1493.

Kurzman, Charles. *The Unthinkable Revolution in Iran*. Cambridge, MA: Harvard University Press, 2004.

Kuzichkin, Vladmir. *Inside the KGB: My Life in Soviet Espionage,* trans. Thomas B. Beattie. New York: Pantheon, 1990.

"A Leap Forward for Iranian Journalism Nipped in the Bud," *The Guardian*, February 21, 2014, www.theguardian.com/world/iran-blog/2014/feb/21/a -leap-forward-for-iranian-journalism-nipped-in-the-bud, accessed March 10, 2014.

Lipset, S. M., and S. Rokkan, eds. *Party Systems and Voter Alignments: Cross-National Perspectives*. Toronto: Free Press, 1967.

Mahbobi, Reza. "Investigating of Factors Affecting the Decline or Increasing of Activities of Basij Resistance Bases," *Basij Studies Quarterly* 4, no. 11–12 (1996): 77–102.

Mahdavi, Mosa. "The Study of Governmental Employees About the Position of Basij in Offices," *Basij Study Journal* 6, no. 20–21 (2003): 117–120.

Mahdavi, Pardis. "The Sexual Revolution." Paper presented at the Hoover Institute's Iran Democracy Project conference Prospects for Democracy in Iran: Assessing the Regime and Opposition, Stanford University, November 2, 2007.

Majd, Mohammad Gholi. *Resistance to the Shah: Landowner and Ulama in Iran*. Gainesville: University Press of Florida, 2000.

Maleki, Khalil. *Do Nameh* [Two Letters]. Tehran: Ghatreh, 1958 [1357].

Martonosi, Péter. "The Basij: A Major Factor in Iranian Security," *Academic and Applied Research in Military Science (AARMS)* 11, no. 1 (2012): 27–38.

Matini, Jalal. "The Most Truthful Individual in Recent History," *Iranshenasi* 14, no. 4 (Winter 2003).

McElroy, Damien. "Ayatollah Ali Khamenei Backs Mahmoud Ahmadinejad in Address at Friday Prayers," *The Telegraph*, June 19, 2009, www.telegraph .co.uk/news/worldnews/middleeast/iran/5576925/Ayatollah-Ali-Khamenei -backs-Mahmoud-Ahmadinejad-in-address-at-Friday-prayers.html, accessed July 12, 2014.

McPherson, Miller, Lynn Smith-Lovin, and James M. Cook. "Birds of a Feather: Homophily in Social Networks," *Annual Review of Sociology* 27 (2001): 415–445.

McRae, Douglas W., and Michael Taylor. *The Analysis of Political Cleavages*. New Haven, CT: Yale University Press, 1970.

Mehrparvar, Hossein. *Didgah-hai Jadid dar Masael-e Hoquqi* [New Perspectives on Legal Issues]. Tehran: Etelaat, 1986.

Mesbah-Yazdi, Muhammad Taghi. *Porsesh-ha va pasokh-ha* [Questions and Answers], vol. 2. Qom: Entesharat-e Mo'assesseh-ye Amuzeshi va Pazhuheshi-ye Imam Khomeini [Imam Khomeini Institute Publications], 1988 [1377].

Mesbah-Yazdi, Muhammad Taghi. *Porsesh-ha va Pasokh-ha* [Questions and Answers]. Qom: Imam Khomeini Institute, 2001.

Milani, Abbas. "Alam and the Roots of the Iranian Revolution." In *King of Shadows*, ed. Abbas Milani. Los Angeles: Ketab Corp., 2005.

Milani, Abbas. *Eminent Persians: The Men and Women Who Made Modern Iran, 1941–1979*. Syracuse, NY: Syracuse University Press, 2008.

Milani, Abbas. "Iran's CyberJihad," *Foreign Policy,* July 7, 2010, www.foreign policy.com/articles/2010/06/07/irans_hidden_cyberjihad, accessed July 15, 2014.

Milani, Abbas. *King of Shadows: Essays on Iran's Encounter with Modernity*. Los Angeles: Sherkate Ketab Publishers, 2005.

Milani, Abbas. *Lost Wisdom: Rethinking Modernity in Iran*. Washington, DC: Mage, 2002.

Milani, Abbas. "The Mousavi Mission," *New Republic,* March 11, 2010.

Milani, Abbas. *The Myth of the Great Satan*. Stanford, CA: Hoover Institution Press, 2010.

Milani, Abbas. "New Democrats." *New Republic,* July 15, 2009.

Milani, Abbas. *Persian Sphinx: Amir Abbas Hoveyda and the Riddle of the Iranian Revolution*. Washington, DC: Mage, 1999.

Milani, Abbas. "The Pious Populist," *Boston Review* (November/December 2007): 7–14.

Milani, Abbas. *Tajadod va Tajadod Setizi dar Iran* [Modernity and Its Foes in Iran]. Tehran: Atiyeh Publishers, 2008 [1387].

Milani, Mohsen. *Iran's Islamic Revolution: From Monarchy to Islamic Republic*. Boulder, CO: Westview Press, 1988.

Milani, Mohsen. *The Making of the Islamic Revolution*, 2nd ed. Boulder, CO: Westview Press, 1999.

Mirsepassi, Ali. *Political Islam, Iran and the Enlightenment Philosophies of Hope and Despair*. Cambridge: Cambridge University Press, 2010.

Mobin, Seyed Ali. "The Study of Opinion of Sisters Basijis, Who Participated in Quranic Gathering at Azadi Stadium About the Basij Resistance Force" (report), Tehran, *Research and Study Center of IRIB* (March 1995).

Mokri, Akam. "Basij Was Not Intended to Be in Line with the Satan," Roozonline, December 1, 2009, www.roozonline.com/english/news3/newsitem/archive/2009/december/01/article/basij-was-not-intended-to-be-in-line-with-the-satan.html, accessed March 10, 2014.

Montazeri, Ayatollah. *Dirasah fi Wilayat al-Faqih wa Fiqh al-dawlat al-Islamiah* [Lectures on Guardianship of the Islamic Jurist and the Fiqh of Islamic State]. Translated from Arabic to Persian as *Mabani-e Feqhi Hokumat-e Eslami* [The Foundations of Islamic Government]. Tehran: Keyhan, 1988–1994.

Moqadam, Afsaneh. *Death to the Dictator! Witnessing Iran's Election and the Crippling of the Islamic Republic*. London: Bodley Head, 2010.

Moreno, Alejandro. *Political Cleavages: Issues, Parties, and the Consolidation of Democracy*. Boulder, CO: Westview Press, 1999.

Moslem, Mehdi. *Factional Politics in Post-Khomeini Iran*. Syracuse, NY: Syracuse University Press, 2002.

Muskus, Jeff. "Iran Bans Reform Party," *Huffington Post*, March 16, 2010, www.huffingtonpost.com/2010/03/16/iran-bans-reform-party_n_500 298.html, accessed July 12, 2014.

Najmabadi, Afsaneh. *Land Reform and Social Change in Iran*. Salt Lake City: University of Utah Press, 1987.

Naqdi, Mohammed Reza. "Lebas shakhsi" [Plain Clothes], Ansar News, December 3, 2009, www.ansarnews.com/news/3040/, accessed July 13, 2014.

Naraghi, Ahmad. *Awayd al-ayyaam* [The Benefits of Time]. Tehran: Sazman-e Tablighat-e Eslami, 1982.

Naraghi, Arash. "Abdulkarim Soroush va Kamal-e Proje Roshanfekri-e Dini" [Abdul Karim Soroush and the Completion of the Project of Islamist Intellectualism in Iran], www.arashnaraghi.org, accessed July 12, 2014.

Naraghi, Arash. "Lubb-e Lubab-e Qabz va Bast" [Condensed Essence of Contraction and Expansion of Shari'a]. In *Qabz va Bast-e Te'orik-e Shari'at*, 3rd ed., ed. Abdulkarim Soroush. Tehran: Serat, 1373 (1994).

"Nazaersanji az Danshe amouzan Piramzon Dars-e Amadeghi-e defai" [A Survey of Students About the Defense Readiness Course], *Basij Studies Quarterly*, no. 20–21 (Fall and Winter 2003): 113–116.

NSA (National Security Agency). "Ambassador Foroughi," September 17, 1979.

NSA. "Current Foreign Relations," no. 244, April 11, 1979.

NSA. "The Outlook for Iran: Secret National Intelligence Estimate NIE 36-40," no. 385.

NSA. "Political Internal Issues," no. 369, n.d.

NSA. "Religious Leaders Fear Departure of the Shah," no. 2048, January 9, 1969.

NSA. "Strength and Durability of the Shah's Regime," no. 486.

NSA–Bureau of Intelligence and Research, Department of State. "Studies in Political Dynamics in Iran," *Secret Intelligence Report* 13, no. 603.

NSA–US Embassy, Tehran. "End of Tour Report, August 4, 1975," no. 9799.

NSA–US Embassy, Tehran. "Hoveyda Loyalist Lets Off Steam," no. 2177, January 25, 1977.

Nuri, Shaykh Fazlallah. "Refutation of the Idea of Constitutionalism." In *Religion and Politics in Modern Iran*, ed. Lloyd Ridgeon. London: I. B. Tauris, 2005.

Ostovar, Afshon. "Iran's Basij: Membership in a Militant Islamist Organization," *Middle East Journal* 67, no. 3 (Summer 2013): 345–361.

Pahlavi, Mohammad Reza. *Answer to History*. New York: Stein and Day, 1980.

Pahlavi, Mohammad Reza. *Mission for My Country*. London: Hutchison Publishers, 1962.

Parchami, Davoud. "Measuring Public Attitudes Toward the Basij," *Basij Studies Quarterly*, no. 18–19 (Spring and Summer 2003): 45–90.

Parker, Tom. "Blogging Ahmadinejad in Tehran," *New York Times*, September 30, 2007, Opinion Section.

Pars Times. "Parties Law and Its Relevant Executive Regulations," www.pars times.com/law/parties_law.html, accessed March 10, 2014.

Pezeshkzad, Iraj. *My Uncle Napoleon*. Washington, DC: Mage, 1973.

Pitchford, Ruth. "Iran Parliament Passes 2011–12 Budget," Reuters, April 26, 2011, www.reuters.com/article/2011/04/26/iran-budget-approved-idUSPOM 65348720110426, accessed March 10, 2014.

Political Research Deputy of Islamic Republic of Iran. *Basiji Teenager: Strong Arm of the Future of the Country*. Tehran: Social Group–Political Research Deputy of Islamic Republic of Iran Broadcasting, 2007.

Popper, Karl. *Conjectures and Refutations*. London: Routledge, 2002.

Popper, Karl. *The Poverty of Historicism*. London: Routledge, 2002.

Press TV. "Basij, IRGC Support Iranian Government," Press TV, May 23, 2011, http://edition.presstv.ir/detail/181355.html, accessed July 12, 2014.

Princeton University. "1997 Presidential Election," June 20, 2013, www.princeton .edu/irandataportal/elections/pres/1997/, accessed July 12, 2014.

Princeton University. "Revolutionary Guards Employment Law," *Iran Social Science Data Portal*, October 13, 1992, https://www.princeton.edu/irandata portal/laws/revolutionary-guards-empl/, accessed July 13, 2014.

PRO (Public Record Office, England). "British Embassy to Foreign Office, 25 September 1978," PREM (Prime Minister's Office) 16/1719.

PRO. "British Embassy to Foreign Office, 29 September, 1978," PREM 16/1716.

PRO. "The British Hand," 25 September 1978, PREM 16/1719.

PRO. "Iranian Internal Situation, 16 September 1978," PREM 16/1719.

PRO. "Iranian Internal Situation, 12 October 1978," PREM 16/1719.

PRO. "Iranian Internal Situation, 12 December 1978," PREM/16/1719.

PRO. "Letter by ACI Samuel to Foreign Office, July 18, 1955," Foreign Office, 371/114810.

PRO. "Tehran to Foreign Office, 6 July 1978." FCO (Foreign and Commonwealth Office) 8/3184.

PRO. "Tehran to Foreign Office, 19 December 1978," PREM 16/1720.

PRO. "30 October 1978, Prime Minister's Office to Foreign Ministry," PREM 16/1719.

Radio Zamaneh. "Senior Conservative Cleric Renews Support for Ahmadinejad," Radio Zamaneh: Independent Media, Debate and E-learning for Iran, July 14, 2011, http://archive.radiozamaneh.com/english/content/senior -conservative-cleric-renews-support-ahmadinejad, accessed March 10, 2014.

Rafiehi, Ali. "Conversation with Director of the Deputy of Preparing the Textbooks of Islamic Research Institute of IRGC," *Morbiain Journal*, no. 2 (Spring and Summer 2001): 164–175.

Rafsanjani, Ali Akbar Hashemi. *Khaterat* [Daily Journal]. Tehran, 1981–1982 [1360]. www.hashemirafsanjani.ir.

Rafsanjani, Ali Akbar Hashemi. *Sazandeghi va Shokoufaee* [Development and Blossoming]. Tehran: Ma'aret Islami Publishers, 2014 [1393].

Ranani, Mohsen, "Egtesad Iran asir adam Etminan" [Iranian Economy in the Throes of Insecurity], www.iran-emrooz.net/index.php/politic/more/50238, accessed November 10, 2014.

Rubin, Michael. *Into the Shadows: Radical Vigilantes in Khatami's Iran*. Washington, DC: Institute for Near Eastern Policy, 2001.

Rumi. *Divan-e Shams*, ed. Forouzanfar. Tehran: Amir Kabir, 1966 [1345].

Sadeghi, Fatemeh. "Foot Soldiers of the Islamic Republic's 'Culture of Modesty,'" *Middle East Report* 250 (Spring 2009): 50–55.

Saeidzadeh, Seyed Mohsen. "About Seyed Mohsen Saeidzadeh," May 16, 2013, http://seyedmohsensaeidzadeh.wordpress.com/2013/05/16/about-seyed -mohsen-saeidzadeh/, accessed March 10, 2014.

Sāfi Golpāyegani, Lutfollah. "Majma-e Tashkhis-e Maslahat va Jaygah-e Qanooni An" [The Expediency Discernment Council and Its Legal Status]. In *Didgah-hai Jadid dar Masael-e Hoquqi* [New Perspectives on Legal Issues], ed. Hossein Mehrparvar. Tehran: Ettel'at Publishers, 1986.

Sahliyeh, Emile. "The Reforming Elections in Iran: 2000–2001," May 2002, www.sciencedirect.com, accessed November 10, 2014.

Salehi, Ayatollah. *Velayat-e Faqhi Hokumat-e Salehan* [Guardianship of the Islamic Jurist as the Governance of the Virtuous]. Tehran: Rassa, 1984.

Samii, Abbas William. "The Changing Landscape of Party Politics in Iran: A Case Study," April 3, 2006, www.payvand.com/news/06/apr/1014.html, accessed July 12, 2014.

Schahgaldian, Nikola B., and Gina Barkhordarian. *The Iranian Military Under the Islamic Republic.* Santa Monica, CA: RAND Corporation, 1987.

Schirazi, Asghar. *The Constitution of Iran: Politics and State in the Islamic Republic of Iran,* trans. Jon O'Kane. London: I. B. Tauris, 1997.

Sears, David O., and Jonathan L. Freedman. "Selective Exposure to Information," *Public Opinion Quarterly* 31 (1967): 194–213.

Shabistari, Muhammad Mujtahid. *Naqdī Bar Qirā'at-i Rasmī Az Dīn: Buhrānhā, Chālish'hā, Rāh-i hal'hā.* Tehran: Tarh-i Naw, 2002.

Shawcross, William. *The Shah's Last Ride.* London: Pan Books, 1989.

Shirazi, Robab. "The Study of Recalling and Usage Methods of Sisters Basijis," *Basij Studies Quarterly,* no. 23 (Summer 2004): 61–84.

Shokat, Hamid. *Jonbesh Daneshjouee: Confedarasion Mohaselin va Daneshjooyan Irani* [Student Movement: The Confederation of Iranian Students]. Tehran: Namek Publisher, 2013 [1392].

S. H. R. *Baresi va Tahli Nehzat-e Imam Khomeini* [Analysis of the Khomeini Movement]. Tehran, n.p., n.d.

Smith, Gordon. *Politics in Western Europe: A Comparative Analysis.* London: Heinemann Educational, 1972.

Soroush, Abdulkarim. *The Expansion of Prophetic Experience: Essays in Historicity, Contingency and Plurality in Religion,* ed. Forough Jahanbakhsh, trans. Nilou Mobasser. Leiden: Brill, 2009.

Soroush, Abdulkarim. "The Idea of Democratic Religious Government." In *Reason, Freedom, and Democracy in Islam: Essential Writings of Abdolkarim Soroush,* ed. and trans. Mahmoud Sadri and Ahmad Sadri. Oxford: Oxford University Press, 2000.

Soroush, Abdulkarim. "The Idea of Democratic Religious Government." In *Reason, Freedom, and Democracy in Islam,* ed. Abdulkarim Soroush. Oxford: Oxford University Press, 2002.

Soroush, Abdulkarim. "Maximalist Religion, Minimalist Religion." In *The Expansion of Prophetic Experience: Essays in Historicity, Contingency and Plurality in Religion,* ed. Abdulkarim Soroush, trans. Nilou Mobasser. Leiden: Brill, 2009.

Soroush, Abdulkarim. *Qabz va Bast-e Te'orik-e Shari'at* [The Theoretical Contraction and Expansion of Shari'a], 3rd ed. Tehran: Serat, 1994 [1373].

Taeb, Hossein. "ISNA Interview with Commander of Basij," ISNA news agency, November 30, 2008, http://Basij.imo.org.ir/DesktopModules/News /NewsView.aspx?TabID=0&Site=Basij.imo.org&Lang=fa-IR&Item ID=3732&mid=13695&wVersion=Staging, accessed July 13, 2014.

Tehrani, Hamid. "Iranian Muslim Bloggers," *History News Network*, http://hnn .us/articles/44774.html, accessed July 8, 2014.

Tila, Parvaneh, and Mohsen Ranjbar. "A Study of the Function of the Basij in the Province of Sistan and Baluchestan and Suggestions for Its Development," *Basij Study Quarterly,* no. 38 (Spring 2008): 131–146.

Torabi, Seyed Mostafa, and Nabiyollah Roohi. *Basij dar Partow-e Qanun* [Basij in the Ray of Law]. Tehran: Ayeh Cultural Publication, 2000.

Torbati, Yeganeh. "Ahmadinejad Accuses Iran Speaker's Family of Corruption," Reuters, February 3, 2013, www.reuters.com/article/2013/02/03/us -iran-politics-idUSBRE9120DG20130203, accessed March 10, 2014.

Torbi, Mostafi. *Influential Factors on Recruiting the Basijis*. Tehran: Basij Study and Research Institute, 2006.

Toth, James. *Sayyid Qutb: The Life and Legacy of a Radical Islamic Intellectual*. Oxford: Oxford University Press, 2013.

Tran, Mark. "Protesters Raped in Tehran Jail, Politician Claims," *The Guardian,* August 15, 2009, www.theguardian.com/world/2009/aug/14/protesters -raped-iran-jail, accessed July 12, 2014.

Trevor-Roper, Hugh. "The Phenomenon of Fascism." In *Fascism in Europe,* ed. S. J. Woolf. London: Routledge, 1981.

United Nations. "United Nations Treaty Collection," https://treaties.un.org /pages/viewdetails.aspx?src=treaty&mtdsg_no=iv-4&chapter=4&lang=en, accessed March 10, 2014.

US Department of State. "Statement of US Policy Toward Iran." In *Foreign Relations of the US, 1958–1960,* ed. Edward C. Keefer. Washington, DC: Publishing Services Division, 1993.

US Embassy, Tehran. "Alternative Views from the Province." In *Asnad-e Laneye Jasusi* [Documents from the Den of Spies], no. 16. Tehran, n.p., n.d.

US Embassy, Tehran. "Moves Toward Government Unification, 8/3/79." In *Asnad-e Laneye Jasusi* [Documents from the Den of Spies], vol. 16. Tehran, n.p., n.d.

Varzi, Roxanne. *Warring Souls: Youth, Media, and Martyrdom in Post-Revolution Iran*. Durham, NC: Duke University Press, 2006.

"Victory for a Religious Hardliner in Iran," *The Economist,* 27 June 2005, www.economist.com/node/4123204, accessed July 13, 2014.

Wehrey, Frederic, Jerrold D. Green, Brian Nichiporuk, Alireza Nader, Lydia Hansell, Rasool Nafisi, and S. R. Bohandy. *The Rise of the Pasdaran: Assessing the Domestic Roles of Iran's Islamic Revolutionary Guard Corps*. Santa Monica, CA: RAND Corporation, 2009.

Wolin, Sheldon S. *Politics and Vision: Continuity and Innovation in Western Political Thought*. Princeton, NJ: Princeton University Press, 2004.

Worth, Robert F. "Iran Denies Allegations That Protesters Were Raped in Prison," *New York Times,* August 12, 2009, www.nytimes.com/2009/08/13 /world/middleeast/13iran.html?_r=0, accessed July 12, 2014.

Yadoallahi, Nasroallah. *Barsi ellal va anghizehah jameh shankhti ozyat dokhtern dansh amoz dar Basij dansh amoozi* [Sociological Study of Moti-

vation of Female Students' Membership in Pupil Basij Organization].
Tehran: Management and Social Science, Islamic Azad University, Tehran
North Branch, 2007.

Young Journalists Club. "A Comprehensive Information System Should Establish for Identifying Veteran Students," October 28, 2012, http://goo.gl
/NgJVUg, accessed July 13, 2014.

Zianali, Alireza. "Sanjesh-e Angizeh-e Ghaleb Aghshar-e basij" [The Assessment of Dominate Motivation of Basij Strata], *Basij Studies Quarterly,* no.
16 (Fall 2002): 147–156.

Zimmt, Raz. "Elections Results for the Assembly of Experts and Local Councils: Preliminary Appraisal," *Iran Pulse,* no. 7 (December 2006).

Zimmt, Raz. "Iran's 2008 Parliamentary Elections," *Middle East Review of
International Affairs–Meria* 12, no. 2 (June 2008).

Zolqadr, Mohammed Baqer, "News and Analysis" (Akhbar va Tahlilha), *The
Internal Publication for Deputies of the Ideological and Political Unit in
IRGC* 8, no. 1730 (2005).

Zonis, Marvin. *Majestic Failure: The Fall of the Shah.* Chicago: University of
Chicago Press, 1991.

Zonis, Marvin, and Joseph Craig. "Conspiracy Thinking in the Middle East,"
Political Psychology 15, no. 3 (1994): 443–459.

The Contributors

Hossein Bashiriyeh has taught political sociology and Middle Eastern politics at the University of Tehran and at Syracuse University.

Simin Behbahani (1927–2014) began writing poetry when she was only twelve. For her resolute defense of the integrity of art, and her aversion to despotism of all forms, she has been rightly called the lioness of Iran. A collection of her poetry has been published in English as *A Cup of Sin* (translated by Farzaneh Milani and Kaveh Safa).

Larry Diamond is senior fellow at both the Hoover Institution and the Freeman Spogli Institute for International Studies at Stanford University.

Bruce Etling is a fellow at the Berkman Center for Internet and Society at Harvard University. Prior to joining the Berkman Center, he was a foreign service officer with the US Agency for International Development.

Saeid Golkar is lecturer in Middle East and North Africa studies at Northwestern University and senior fellow for Iran policy at the Chicago Council on Global Affairs.

Fatemeh Haghighatjoo, director of the Nonviolent Initiative for Democracy (NID), is an expert on Iran's internal affairs and a leading advocate of human rights and democracy in Iran. She was a member of Iran's reformist parliament in 2000–2004.

Mehrangiz Kar is a prominent lawyer, human rights activist, and author and one of the most celebrated activists in the history of the women's movement in Iran. Detained for her efforts to promote rule of law and human rights in Iran, she was forced to choose exile in the early 2000s. She is the recipient of numerous international awards, including the National Endowment for Democracy's democracy award, the Ludovic Trarieux International Human Rights Prize, the PEN/NOVIB Award, and the Donna Dell'anno Award of the Conseil De Lavallee Consiglio Regionale Della Valle d'Aosta in Italy, and in 2004 she was honored by Human Rights First.

John Kelly is founder and CEO of Graphika (formerly Morningside Analytics), a social media intelligence firm founded on technology that he developed to blend social network analysis, content analysis, and statistics to make complex online networks understandable. He is also an affiliate at the Berkman Center for Internet and Society at Harvard University.

Abbas Milani is Moghadam Director of Iranian Studies at Stanford University and codirector, with Larry Diamond, of the Iran Democracy Project at Stanford University's Hoover Institution.

Mohsen Namjoo is an Iranian artist, songwriter, singer, music scholar, and *setar* (traditional Persian lute) player based in New York. His unique musical style resembles a patchwork of the classical Persian poetry of Hafez, Rumi, and Saadi with Western rock, blues, and jazz. Hailed as the "Bob Dylan of Iran" by the *New York Times,* Namjoo is a visionary artist who speaks for and touches the souls of today's youth.

Arash Naraghi is assistant professor of philosophy and religion at Moravian College. His field of expertise consists of modernism in Islam, contemporary Shiism in Iran, ethical theories in Islam, and contemporary analytic ethics and philosophy of religion.

Mehdi Yahyanejad is a research scientist at the University of Southern California, where he is developing tools and resources that will facilitate the exchange of digital content among people with limited or no Internet access. Yahyanejad is also the founder of the website Balatarin.com, a popular user-generated news website in Persian.

Index

287

About the Book

Despite the relative calm apparent in Iran today, there is unmistakable evidence of political, social, and cultural ferment stirring beneath the surface. The authors of *Politics and Culture in Contemporary Iran*—a unique group of scholars, activists, and artists—explore that unrest and its challenge to the legitimacy and stability of the present authoritarian regime. Ranging from political theory to music, from human rights law to social media, their contributions reveal the tenacious and continually evolving forces that are at work resisting the status quo.

Abbas Milani is Moghadam Director of Iranian Studies at Stanford University and codirector, with Larry Diamond, of the Iran Democracy Project at Stanford's Hoover Institution. **Larry Diamond** is senior fellow at both the Hoover Institution and the Freeman Spogli Institute for International Studies at Stanford.